Gourmet's America

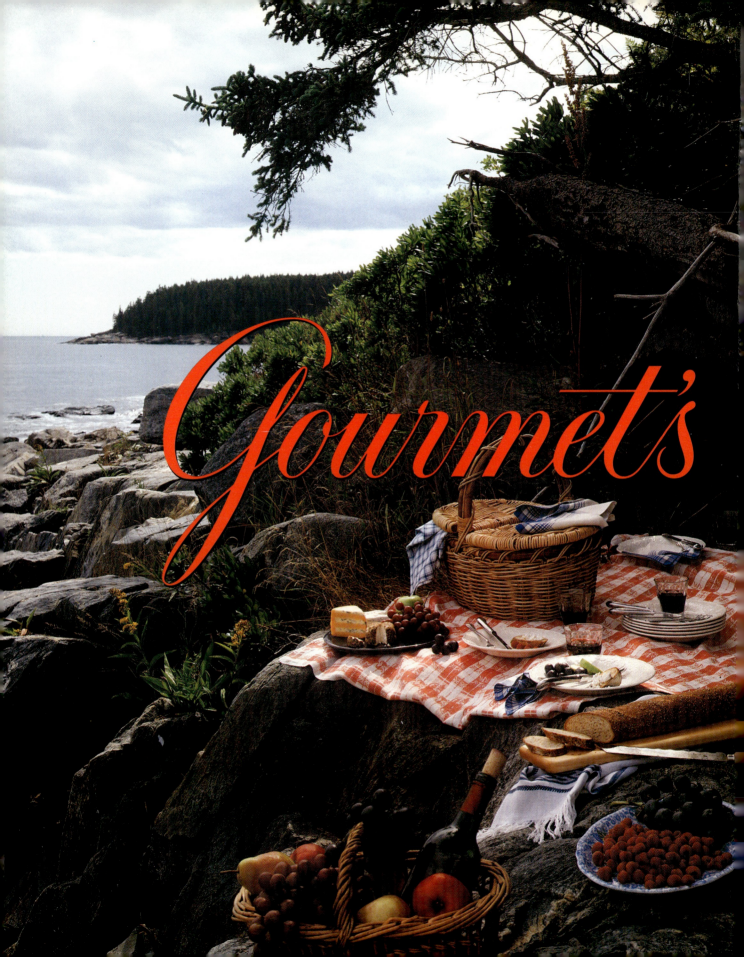

America

FROM THE EDITORS OF GOURMET

Food Photographs by Romulo A. Yanes

Condé Nast Books   Random House

New York

Copyright © 1994
The Condé Nast Publications Inc.
All rights reserved under International and
Pan-American Copyright Conventions.
Published in the United States by
Random House, Inc., New York, and
simultaneously in Canada by Random
House of Canada Limited, Toronto.

LIBRARY OF CONGRESS
CATALOGING-IN-PUBLICATION DATA

Gourmet's America / from the editors
of Gourmet.
    p. cm
  ISBN 0-679-43563-8
  1. Cookery, American. I. Gourmet.
TX715.G7145 1994
641.5973–dc20 94-1811

Some of the recipes in this work were
published previously in *Gourmet* Magazine.
Manufactured in the United States of America

98765432 24689753 23456789
First Edition

- indicates that a recipe can be made in 45 minutes or less.

- + indicates that a recipe can be made in 45 minutes or less, but requires additional unattended time.

All the informative text in this book was
written by Diane Keitt and Judith Tropea.

Front jacket recipes: Clockwise from top left:
"Fettuccine with Pine Nuts, Prosciutto,
and Brown Butter" (page 153); "Baked
Pears" (page 197); "Blood Orange Sorbet"
(page 167).

Back jacket recipes: Clockwise from top left:
"Pea and Goat Cheese Tart" (page 47);
"Butternut Squash Tartlets with Cheese
Lattice and Sunflower Seed Crust"
(page 95); "Papaya Salad" (page 181);
"Sopa de Lima" (page 141).

For Condé Nast Books
Jill Cohen, *President*
Ellen Maria Bruzelius, *Direct Marketing Director*
Kristine Smith-Cunningham,
    Advertising Promotion Manager
Lisa Faith Phillips, *Fulfillment Manager*
Tina Kessler, *Direct Marketing Administrator*
Jennifer Metz, *Direct Marketing Associate*
Diane Pesce, *Composition Production Manager*
Serafino J. Cambareri, *Quality Control Manager*

For *Gourmet* Books
Diane Keitt, *Editor*
Judith Tropea, *Associate Editor*

For *Gourmet* Magazine
Gail Zweigenthal, *Editor-in-Chief*

Zanne Early Zakroff, *Executive Food Editor*
Kemp Miles Minifie, *Senior Food Editor*
Alexis M. Touchet, *Associate Food Editor*
Leslie Glover Pendleton, *Food Editor*
Amy Mastrangelo, *Food Editor*
Lori Longbotham, *Food Editor*
Lori Walther, *Food Editor*
Jennifer G. Wehrle, *Assistant Food Editor*

Romulo A. Yanes, *Photographer*
Marjorie H. Webb, *Stylist*
Nancy Purdum, *Stylist*

Produced in association with
Media Projects Incorporated
Carter Smith, *Executive Editor*
Anne Wright, *Project Director*
Shelley Latham, *Project Editor*
Vivian Slee, *Project Editor*
Marilyn Flaig, *Indexer*

Salsgiver Coveney Associates Inc., *Design*

The text of this book was set in Garamond 3 and
Frutiger by Salsgiver Coveney Associates Inc.
The four-color separations were done by
The Color Company, Seiple Lithographers, and
Applied Graphic Technologies. The book was
printed and bound at R. R. Donnelley and Sons.
The paper is Citation Web Gloss, Westvaco.

acknowledgments

The editors of *Gourmet* Books would like to give special thanks to Irwin Glusker, *Gourmet's* art director, for suggesting that we put together a cookbook on America. His enthusiasm for the project was contagious, and we are indebted to him.

Many *Gourmet* colleagues worked on the book, and we would especially like to thank Zanne Early Zakroff, consultant for the project, who also developed the eight regional menus. Also, thank you to Leslie Glover Pendleton, who developed all the other new recipes, and to Alexis M. Touchet, Amy Mastrangelo, Lori Longbotham, Lori Walther, Jennifer Wehrle, and Kemp Minifie who answered our many questions and tested the recipes.

Throughout the book you will find exquisite food photographs by Romulo A. Yanes, styled by Marjorie Webb and Nancy Purdum, as well as photographs that capture the spirit of America, from Cotten Alston, Ken Bates, Richard Bowditch, Sonja Bullaty, Kay Chernush, Lans Christensen, Mark Ferri, Steve Firebaugh, Karen Halverson, Ronny Jaques, Mathias Oppersdorff, Nik Wheeler, and Romulo A. Yanes. We are grateful to these talented artists for sharing their work with us.

Thanks also to *Gourmet* editors Elaine Richard and Hobby McKenney, Anne Wright, John Kern, Shelley Latham, and Vivian Slee from Media Projects, and Toni Rachiele, for their meticulous editorial help with the manuscript.

And, finally, warm thanks to Karen Salsgiver, our designer, who, together with Laura Howell, has given us a little book that is very big on style.

table of contents

Introduction 9

10
new england
A Harvest Luncheon 13
Regional Recipes 18

34
the mid-atlantic
A Dessert Party 37
Regional Recipes 42

60
the south
A Southern Country Supper 63
Regional Recipes 68

86
the heartland
A Farmhouse Supper 89
Regional Recipes 94

112
the mountain states
A Roundup Lunch 115

Regional Recipes 120

136
the southwest
A Southwestern Sunset Dinner 139

Regional Recipes 144

162
california and hawaii
A Seaside Brunch 165

Regional Recipes 168

190
the northwest and alaska
An Elegant Dinner Party 193

Regional Recipes 198

Index 217

Table Setting Acknowledgments 233

The vegetable garden at Mount Vernon, Virginia

introduction

When you think of American food, what immediately comes to mind? A thick, juicy steak? Buttery corn on the cob? Or perhaps a slice of warm apple pie? These are certainly a few of our favorites, but in recent years new ingredients and condiments have expanded our palette of flavors as well as our pantries. After all, we have become a land of immigrants – 258 million strong and growing – and just as various nationalities assimilate into our society, so do the foods they introduce. Alongside fields of iceberg lettuce, for example, you will find crops of radicchio, endive, and arugula; and a dazzling array of specialty foods such as oils, vinegars, and cheeses and a fine selection of wines are all now produced domestically. Most of these items, impossible to find a mere ten years ago, are readily available for today's gourmet.

Gourmet's America is a celebration of our great land and all the foods it has to offer, both traditional and newly found, from sea to shining sea. America's bounty is truly awesome – vast, fertile lands yield myriad crops and sustain hearty game, livestock, and poultry, while streams, lakes, and bordering oceans teem with fish and shellfish. And our pages are filled with these riches! Our food editors studied the harvests, the populations, and the favorite dishes of all fifty states and then divided the country gastronomically into eight regions, each with its own distinctive characteristics: New England, the Mid-Atlantic, the South, the Heartland, the Mountain States, the Southwest, the Northwest and Alaska, and California and Hawaii. You will find an entire chapter dedicated to the culinary delights of each area, with a special menu and additional recipes for starters, entrées, side dishes, and desserts. Beautiful food photographs by Romulo A. Yanes bring many of these dishes into crisp focus, and other spectacular scenic photographs capture the unique spirit of each region.

Most American cookbooks are tomes of traditional old-fashioned dishes. *Gourmet's America* is different. Here you will find over 250 recipes: our own classics with exciting variations and over 100 brand-new ones that showcase America's ever-expanding pantry. The result is a contemporary collection that offers a fresh way of cooking. Almost every required ingredient can be conveniently purchased throughout the country. For the few delicacies that are difficult to find we offer reliable mail order sources. And when you are in a hurry, look for the ☺ or ☺+ symbol; these indicate a dish that can be made in 45 minutes, or 45 minutes plus additional unattended time. The index can also be used to find these quick recipes.

Gourmet's America will expand your thinking about American food and tempt you to cook with all the wonderful ingredients now at your fingertips. Perhaps, too, our collection will encourage you to see a bit more of America and to discover firsthand its remarkable regional flavors and extraordinary beauty.

Gail Zweigenthal
Editor-in-Chief

On this page, First Congregational Church, Williamstown, Massachusetts and right, autumn in the White Mountains, New Hampshire

Maine, New Hampshire,

new england

Vermont, Massachusetts, Rhode Island, Connecticut

new england

New England offers year-round beauty: sugar maples stand against blue skies, farm stands beckon with crates of strawberries and bushels of corn, white church spires poke through colorful foliage, and winding country roads are blanketed with newly fallen snow. Rocky beaches and boat-filled harbors line the rugged coast, while inland, quaint villages appear among dairy farms, apple orchards, and hiking and ski trails.

The Pilgrims landed at Plymouth, Massachusetts in 1620, fleeing from England in search of religious freedom. There they encountered Wampanoag natives, who introduced them to corn, beans, and squash and taught them how to farm, fish, and hunt; one year later they celebrated their survival with a Thanksgiving dinner of venison, turkey, oysters, eels, nuts, fruits, and vegetables.

In the late 1620s these first settlers were joined by their fellow Englishmen, the Puritans, and together they domesticated wild turkey and caught cod, mackerel, lobster, and crabs. They imported both dairy and beef cattle from Europe, and although known for their simple fare, they built trading ships that made it possible to acquire exotic ingredients: tea and spices from China; wines, brandy, and raisins from the Mediterranean; and molasses from the West Indies.

Eventually other Europeans arrived in the region, with their own culinary favorites: the Scottish and Welsh brought their recipes for scones, oatmeal breads, and leeks; the Germans offered sausage and sauerkraut dishes; the Portuguese demonstrated new ways to prepare fish; and the Italians introduced pasta and broccoli. The French from Canada contributed their own version of *cassoulet*, split pea soup, and various pork pies.

Squash, Apple, and Onion Tart with Sage

A HARVEST LUNCHEON

CRANBERRY BEET
SOUP WITH ORANGE

★

SQUASH, APPLE,
AND ONION TART
WITH SAGE

★

WILTED ESCAROLE
SALAD WITH BACON

★

MOLASSES CAKE WITH
MAPLE FROSTING

★

GLENORA FINGER
LAKES JOHANNISBERG
RIESLING 1992

Serves 6

new england menu

Our vegetarian Harvest Luncheon is as colorful as New England's autumn palette. The soup combines local cranberries with beets and oranges for a marvelous sweet but tangy taste. (Since cranberries can be frozen easily, and this soup is delicious hot or cold, you can serve it throughout the year. When shopping for fresh cranberries drop one . . . if it bounces, it is at its peak of freshness.) Then, regional butternut squash and apples are paired with lots of onions, garlic, thyme, and sage in a savory tart that is bursting with flavor. Although we serve the dish as an entrée, it also makes a wonderful starter. And, finally, molasses, maple extract, and strongly brewed tea appear with a host of spices in a simple cake for a quintessential New England dessert.

CRANBERRY BEET SOUP WITH ORANGE

- 2 pounds beets, scrubbed and trimmed, leaving 2 inches of stems intact
- 1 large onion, chopped (about 1 1/4 cups)
- 2 tablespoons unsalted butter
- 2 cups chicken broth
- 2 cups cranberries, picked over
- 2 large carrots, shredded coarse (about 1 1/2 cups)
- 1 teaspoon freshly grated orange zest
- 1/2 cup fresh orange juice, or to taste
- 2 tablespoons sugar, or to taste
- 6 thin orange slices for garnish

Preheat the oven to 400° F.

In a casserole with a tight-fitting lid roast the beets in the oven, covered, for 1 hour to 1½ hours, or until they are very tender. *The beets may be roasted 2 days in advance and kept covered and chilled.* Let the beets cool, uncovered, until they can be handled, peel them, discarding the stems, and cut them into 1-inch pieces.

In a 3-quart saucepan cook the onion in the butter over moderate heat, stirring, until it is golden. Add 3 cups water, the broth, the cranberries, the carrots, and the zest and simmer the mixture, uncovered, for 15 minutes, or until the cranberries are tender.

In a blender purée the cranberry mixture in batches until it is smooth and return it to the pan. Stir in the orange juice, the sugar, and salt and pepper to taste and heat the soup over moderate heat, stirring, until it is heated through. *The soup may be made 3 days in advance and kept covered and chilled.* Serve the soup hot or cold and garnish each serving with an orange slice. **Makes about 7 1/2 cups, serving 6.**

SQUASH, APPLE, AND ONION TART WITH SAGE

For the shell
pastry dough (recipe follows)
raw rice for weighting the shell

For the filling
- 2 tablespoons vegetable oil
- 1 1/2 pounds onions, halved lengthwise and sliced thin
- 2 garlic cloves, minced
- 2 teaspoons minced fresh sage leaves or 3/4 teaspoon dried, crumbled, plus sage sprigs for garnish
- 1/4 teaspoon dried thyme, crumbled
- 1/4 cup heavy cream
- 1 large Golden Delicious apple
- 1/2 pound butternut squash, peeled, halved lengthwise, seeded, and sliced thin crosswise
- 1/2 stick (1/4 cup) cold unsalted butter, sliced very thin

Preheat the oven to 425° F.

Make the shell: Roll out the dough 1/8 inch thick on a lightly floured surface and fit it into a 9 1/2-inch-square flan form set on a baking sheet, leaving a 1/2-inch overhang. Fold the overhang inward onto the sides of the shell and press it firmly against the flan form. Prick the shell lightly with a fork and chill it for 30 minutes or freeze it for 15 minutes. Line the shell with foil, fill the foil with the rice, and bake the shell in the lower third of the oven for 15 minutes. Remove the rice and foil carefully, bake the shell for 5 to 8 minutes more, or until it is golden, and let it cool in the flan form on the baking sheet.

Reduce the oven temperature to 375° F.

Make the filling: In a large heavy skillet heat the oil over moderately high heat until it is hot but not smoking, stir in the onions and the garlic with salt and pepper to taste, and cook the mixture, covered, over low heat, stirring occasionally, for 20 to 25 minutes, or until the onions are softened. Add the minced sage, the thyme, and the cream, bring the liquid to a boil, and simmer the mixture, stirring occasionally, for 3 to 5 minutes, or until it is thickened. Let the onion mixture cool. *The onion mixture may be prepared 1 day in advance and kept covered and chilled.* Spread the onion mixture evenly in the shell. Peel and halve the apple lengthwise, core it with a melon-ball cutter, and slice it very thin crosswise. Arrange the apple and the squash slices decoratively over the onion mixture, overlapping them, season them with salt, and top them with the butter.

Bake the tart in the upper third of the 375° F. oven for 15 minutes, cover the tart with foil, and bake it for 30 minutes more, or until the squash is tender. Let the tart cool in the flan form on the baking sheet set on a rack and transfer it to a platter, removing the flan form. Serve the tart warm or at room temperature garnished with the sage sprigs if desired. **Serves 6**.

Photo on page 13

⊙+ PASTRY DOUGH

- 1 1/4 cups all-purpose flour
- 3/4 stick (6 tablespoons) cold unsalted butter, cut into bits
- 2 tablespoons cold vegetable shortening
- 1/4 teaspoon salt

In a large bowl blend the flour, the butter, the vegetable shortening, and the salt until the mixture resembles meal. Add 2 tablespoons ice water, toss the mixture until the water is incorporated, adding additional ice water if necessary to form a dough, and form the dough into a ball. Dust the dough with flour and chill it, wrapped in wax paper, for 1 hour.

Lobster buoys on Cape Cod, Massachusetts

WILTED ESCAROLE SALAD WITH BACON

- 1 1/2 heads escarole, rinsed, spun dry, and torn into bite-size pieces (about 20 cups)
- 6 slices of bacon
- vegetable oil if necessary
- 2 large shallots, minced (about 1/2 cup)
- 1/3 cup cider vinegar
- 1 teaspoon sugar, or to taste

Put the escarole in a heatproof large salad bowl. In a skillet cook the bacon over moderate heat, turning it, until it is crisp, transfer it to paper towels to drain, and crumble it onto the escarole. Measure the fat in the skillet and add enough of the oil to total 4 tablespoons fat. In the fat cook the shallots over moderate heat until they are softened, add the vinegar and the sugar carefully, and boil the mixture, stirring, until the sugar is dissolved. Pour the hot dressing over the escarole mixture, add salt and pepper to taste, and toss the salad well. **Serves 6.**

MOLASSES CAKE WITH MAPLE FROSTING

For the cake
- 2 1/2 cups all-purpose flour
- 1 teaspoon baking soda
- 1 teaspoon baking powder
- 1 teaspoon cinnamon
- 3/4 teaspoon ground allspice
- 1/2 teaspoon ground ginger
- 1/4 teaspoon freshly grated nutmeg
- 1/2 teaspoon salt
- 1 1/2 cups chopped walnuts
- 1 cup strongly brewed tea
- 3/4 cup unsulfured molasses
- 4 large eggs
- 1/3 cup firmly packed dark brown sugar
- 3/4 cup vegetable oil

For the frosting
- 1 cup confectioners' sugar
- 1 stick (1/2 cup) unsalted butter, softened
- 1 teaspoon maple extract (available at specialty foods stores and some supermarkets)

Preheat the oven to 350° F. Butter a baking pan, 13 by 9 by 2 inches, and line the pan with well-buttered parchment.

Make the cake: In a large bowl sift together the flour, the baking soda, the baking powder, the cinnamon, the allspice, the ginger, the nutmeg, and the salt and stir in the walnuts. In a small bowl stir together the tea and the molasses. In another large bowl with an electric mixer beat the eggs until they are light and fluffy, beat in the brown sugar, and beat in the oil until it is just combined. Add the flour mixture in 3 batches alternately with the molasses mixture until the batter is smooth and pour the batter into the prepared pan. Bake the cake in the middle of the oven for 30 to 35 minutes, or until a tester comes out clean. Cool the cake in the pan and leave the cake in the pan.

Make the frosting: In a bowl with an electric mixer beat together the confectioners' sugar, the butter, and the maple extract until the frosting is smooth.

Spread the cake in the pan with the frosting.

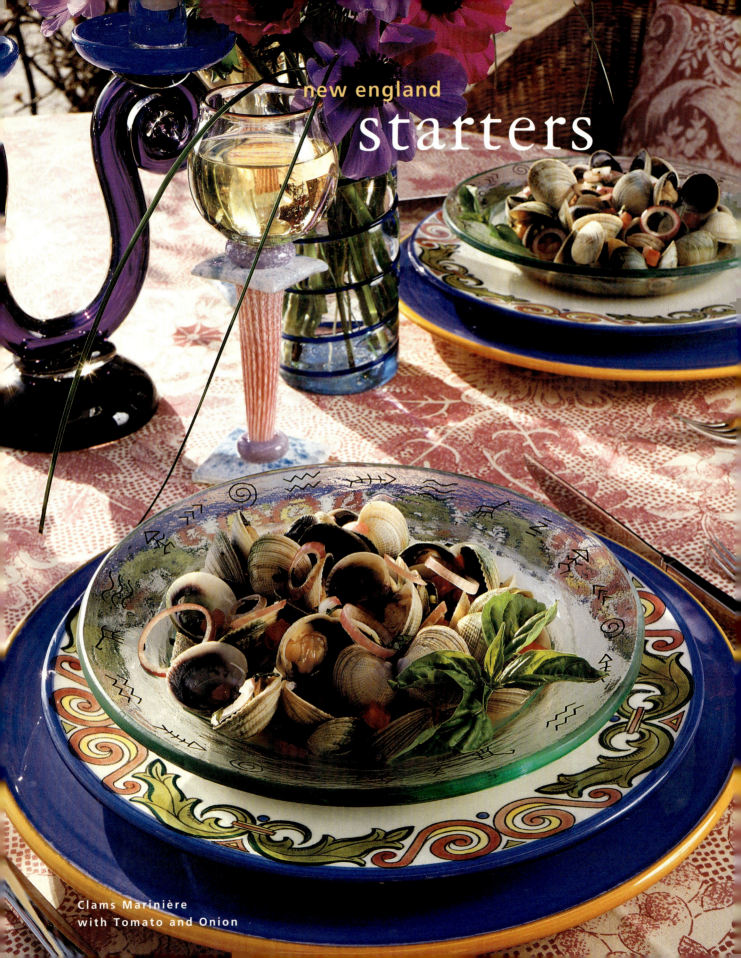

new england
starters

Clams Marinière
with Tomato and Onion

CLAMS MARINIÈRE WITH TOMATO AND ONION

- 1 cup dry white wine or dry vermouth
- 2 garlic cloves, minced
- 2 pounds 1-inch hard-shelled clams or thirty-six 2-inch hard-shelled clams, scrubbed well
- 3 plum tomatoes, seeded and chopped
- 1/2 small red onion, sliced thin
- 2 tablespoons minced fresh basil leaves, plus 4 sprigs for garnish
- 2 tablespoons unsalted butter, cut into bits
- 2 teaspoons fresh lemon juice

In a large saucepan combine the wine or the vermouth and the garlic, bring the mixture to a boil, and simmer it for 2 minutes. Add the clams, steam them, covered, for 3 to 5 minutes, or until they have opened, and discard any unopened ones. Transfer the clams with a slotted spoon to a large bowl and keep them warm, covered. Strain the cooking liquid through a fine sieve lined with rinsed and squeezed cheesecloth into a bowl and return it to the pan, cleaned. Add the tomatoes, the onion, and the minced basil and bring the liquid to a boil. Swirl in the butter and add the lemon juice. Divide the clams among 4 bowls, pour the sauce over them, and garnish each serving with a basil sprig. **Serves 4**.

MUSSELS AND NEW POTATOES IN DILLED CUCUMBER SAUCE

- 5 pounds mussels (preferably cultivated) scrubbed well in several changes of water and the beards scraped off if necessary
- 2 pounds small red (new) potatoes, scrubbed
- 1/2 cup peeled, seeded, and chopped cucumber, squeezed lightly in a kitchen towel, plus cucumber slices for garnish
- 1/4 cup sour cream
- 1/4 cup plain yogurt
- 3 tablespoons chopped fresh dill, plus sprigs for garnish
- 1 tablespoon plus 1 teaspoon fresh lemon juice
- 1 tablespoon plus 1 teaspoon Dijon-style mustard
- 1/2 teaspoon Tabasco
- soft-leafed lettuce leaves for lining the plates

Put the mussels in a kettle, set the kettle over high heat, and steam the mussels, covered, shaking the kettle once or twice, for 5 to 6 minutes, or until the shells have opened. Discard any unopened mussels. Remove the mussels, discarding the shells, and reserve them in a bowl, covered.

Cut the potatoes into ¾-inch pieces and in a steamer set over boiling water steam them, covered, for 8 to 10 minutes, or until they are just tender.

In a bowl combine the chopped cucumber, the sour cream, the yogurt, the chopped dill, the lemon juice, the mustard, the Tabasco, and salt and pepper to taste, add the mussels and the potatoes, and toss the mixture. Serve the salad on chilled plates lined with the lettuce and garnish it with the cucumber slices and the dill sprigs. **Serves 6**.

TOASTED SPICED SQUASH SEEDS

- 1 1/2 cups seeds and pulp freshly scraped from acorn squash, butternut squash, or pumpkin
- 2 teaspoons vegetable oil
- 1/2 teaspoon chili powder
- 1/4 teaspoon ground cumin
- 1 pinch of ground cloves
- 1/2 teaspoon salt
- 1/4 teaspoon black pepper

Preheat the oven to 375° F. Oil lightly a jelly-roll pan. Spread the squash seeds and pulp on the prepared pan and bake them for 10 to 15 minutes, or until the pulp separates from the seeds and the seeds are golden. Remove the pulp from the seeds, discarding the pulp.

In a bowl combine the oil, the chili powder, the cumin, the cloves, the salt, and the black pepper. Toss the seeds in the spice mixture, coating them evenly, and return them to the pan. Toast the coated seeds for 5 minutes, or until they are golden brown and crisp, and let them cool. *The seeds keep in an airtight container for 2 weeks.* **Makes 1 cup.**

CRISP-FRIED SCALLOPS WITH SPINACH DIP

For the dip
- 3/4 pound spinach (about 1 bunch), coarse stems discarded and the leaves washed well and drained
- 1 cup plain yogurt
- 1/4 cup mayonnaise
- 1/3 cup scallion, chopped
- 1 garlic clove, chopped
- 2 teaspoons minced fresh tarragon leaves or 1/4 teaspoon dried, crumbled
- 1 teaspoon white-wine vinegar, or to taste

- 1/2 cup all-purpose flour for dredging the scallops
- 2 large eggs
- 1/2 teaspoon salt
- 1/4 teaspoon cayenne
- 2 cups fine dry bread crumbs
- 1 pound bay scallops
  vegetable oil for deep-frying the scallops
  lemon wedges as an accompaniment

Make the dip: In a large heavy saucepan cook the spinach in the water clinging to the leaves, covered, over moderate heat, stirring once or twice, for 3 to 4 minutes, or until it is wilted, refresh it under cold water, and in a colander drain it well. Squeeze the spinach dry by handfuls and in a blender purée it with the yogurt, the mayonnaise, the scallion, the garlic, the tarragon, the vinegar, and salt and pepper to taste.

In three separate bowls have ready the flour, the eggs beaten with the salt and the cayenne, and the bread crumbs. Toss the scallops in the flour, coating them thoroughly, and in a colander shake off the excess flour. Add the scallops to the egg mixture, coating them, and transfer them to the bread crumbs, letting the excess egg drip off. Toss the scallops with the crumbs, transferring them as they are coated to a sheet of wax paper.

In a kettle heat 1 inch of the oil until it registers 375° F. on a deep-fat thermometer, in it fry the scallops by handfuls for 1 minute, or until they are crisp, and transfer them with a slotted spoon to paper towels to drain. Serve the scallops with wooden picks, the spinach dip, and the lemon wedges. **Serves 6**.

DEVILED EGGS WITH ANCHOVIES AND OLIVES

- 6 hard-boiled large eggs
- 3 flat anchovy fillets
- 1/4 cup mayonnaise
- 2 teaspoons Dijon-style mustard
- 2 tablespoons finely chopped pimiento-stuffed green olives
- 2 tablespoons minced fresh parsley leaves, or to taste

Halve the eggs lengthwise, in a food processor purée the egg yolks with the anchovies, the mayonnaise, and the mustard until the mixture is smooth, and transfer the mixture to a bowl. Stir in the olives, the parsley, and salt and pepper to taste, spoon the yolk mixture into the egg white halves, and chill the deviled eggs on a platter, covered, for 1 hour. **Makes 12 deviled eggs.**

HAM, CELERY, AND CHEDDAR SALAD

For the dressing
- 1/4 cup mayonnaise
- 2 teaspoons Dijon-style mustard
- 2 tablespoons apple cider
- 2 teaspoons minced fresh sage leaves, or 1/2 teaspoon dried, crumbled
- 2 tablespoons plain yogurt

- 3/4 pound cooked ham, diced (about 2 cups)
- 4 ribs of celery, diced (about 2 cups)
- 2 ounces extra-sharp Cheddar (preferably white), cut into small dice (about 3/4 cup)
- 1/4 cup diced sweet gherkin
  escarole leaves for lining the bowl

Make the dressing: In a small bowl stir together the mayonnaise, the mustard, the cider, the sage, the yogurt, and pepper to taste.

In a large bowl combine the ham, the celery, the Cheddar, and the gherkin, add the dressing, and toss the salad well. Line a salad bowl with the escarole leaves and mound the salad in the center. Serve the salad chilled slightly or at room temperature. **Serves 6.**

new england starters

new england entrées

Scrod with Broccoli Cream Sauce

SCROD WITH BROCCOLI CREAM SAUCE

- 1 1/2 cups trimmed, peeled, and chopped broccoli plus 1/4 cup small broccoli flowerets
- 1 red bell pepper, minced
- 2 tablespoons unsalted butter
- 4 6-ounce pieces scrod fillet
- 1/2 cup minced onion
- 1 cup dry white wine or dry vermouth
- 1/4 cup heavy cream

In a saucepan of boiling salted water cook the chopped broccoli until it is tender and drain it, reserving 3 cups of the cooking liquid. Refresh the cooked broccoli in a bowl of ice and cold water and drain it.

In a saucepan cook the bell pepper in 1 tablespoon of the butter, covered, over moderately low heat, stirring occasionally, until it is softened and keep it warm, covered. In a skillet large enough to hold the scrod in one layer combine the onion, the wine or the vermouth, and the reserved cooking liquid, bring the liquid to a boil, and simmer the mixture for 10 minutes. Add the scrod and poach it, covered, at a bare simmer, turning it once, for 8 to 10 minutes, or until it just flakes. Transfer the scrod with a slotted spatula to a plate and keep it warm, covered. Strain 1/2 cup of the cooking liquid into a blender and purée it with the cooked broccoli, the cream, and salt and pepper to taste. Transfer the sauce to a saucepan and cook it over moderately low heat, stirring, until it is heated through.

In a small saucepan of boiling salted water blanch the broccoli flowerets for 1 minute, drain them, and in a small bowl toss them with the remaining 1 tablespoon butter and salt and pepper to taste. Cover the bottom of a heated platter with a layer of the sauce, arrange the scrod on top, and garnish the platter with the broccoli flowerets and 2 tablespoons of the bell pepper. Add the remaining bell pepper to the remaining sauce and serve it with the scrod. **Serves 4.**

MEAT LOAF

- 2 large eggs
- 1/2 cup finely chopped onion
- 1/2 cup finely chopped green bell pepper
- 6 tablespoons ketchup
- 10 saltines, crushed fine (about 1/4 cup)
- 3 teaspoons Worcestershire sauce
- 1 1/2 teaspoons salt
- 2 pounds ground chuck (preferably not lean)
- 4 slices of bacon, halved crosswise

Preheat the oven to 400° F.

In a bowl whisk together the eggs, the onion, the bell pepper, 4 tablespoons of the ketchup, the saltines, the Worcestershire sauce, the salt, and pepper to taste, add the chuck, and blend the mixture with your hands until it is just combined (do not overmix). Form the mixture into two 8- by 4-inch loaves in a shallow baking pan, spread the remaining 2 tablespoons ketchup over the loaves, and drape half the bacon across each loaf. Bake the loaves in the middle of the oven for 30 minutes. **Serves 4.**

Clambake in a Pot

CLAMBAKE IN A POT

Lobsters and Steamers with Sage, Lemon, and Garlic Butter; White Onions and Red Potatoes; Corn on the Cob with Tomato Butter

- 12 ears of corn in their husks
- 12 1 1/4-pound live lobsters
- 4 pounds small white onions, outer skins discarded
- 4 pounds small red (new) potatoes, scrubbed
- 6 pounds steamers (soft-shelled clams), scrubbed
- sage, lemon, and garlic butter (recipe follows)
- tomato butter (recipe follows)

Remove the outer husks of each ear of corn until the innermost layer is reached. Peel back the pale green layers without breaking them off, discard the silk, and fold the husks back into place. In a very large (30- to 40-quart) stockpot containing 1 inch water layer in order the lobsters, the onions, the corn, the potatoes, and the steamers. Cover the stockpot and put it on a rack set 2 inches over glowing and lightly flaming coals (procedure follows). Steam the mixture for 30 minutes from the time the water boils, or until the steamers are cooked through (then the rest of the "clambake" will also be done). Transfer the steamers, the potatoes, the corn, the onions, and the lobsters with tongs to bowls or platters and serve the seafood with the sage, lemon, and garlic butter and the corn with the tomato butter. **Serves 12.**

to make a fire for Clambake in a Pot

In a pit dug in sand or dirt or in a large grill ignite enough charcoal to measure 6 to 8 inches deep. Let the charcoal burn for 30 minutes, or until the coals are glowing (white and still flaming lightly), and set a rack no more than 2 inches from the coals. (The stockpot can be put directly on the coals if desired.)

SAGE, LEMON, AND GARLIC BUTTER

- 4 sticks (2 cups) unsalted butter
- 4 large garlic cloves, halved
- 1/4 cup finely chopped fresh sage leaves
- 1/4 cup fresh lemon juice

In a saucepan melt the butter with the garlic, the sage, the lemon juice, and salt and pepper to taste, stirring occasionally. **Makes about 2 1/4 cups.**

TOMATO BUTTER

- 1 stick (1/2 cup) unsalted butter, softened
- 1 tablespoon tomato paste
- 1/4 teaspoon salt
- 1/2 teaspoon black pepper

In a small bowl combine well the butter, the tomato paste, the salt, and the pepper. **Makes about 1/2 cup.**

new england entrées

RINKTUM DITTY

Tomato Cheddar Sauce on Toast

2	tablespoons unsalted butter
2	tablespoons all-purpose flour
1 1/3	cups tomato juice
2	tablespoons medium-dry Sherry, or to taste
2	teaspoons sugar
2	teaspoons English-style dry mustard
2 1/2	cups grated sharp Cheddar (about 6 ounces)
4	slices of buttered toast, quartered
2	hard-boiled large eggs, chopped fine

In a heavy saucepan melt the butter over moderately low heat, add the flour, and cook the *roux,* whisking, for 2 minutes. Whisk in the tomato juice, the Sherry, the sugar, and the mustard, bring the mixture to a boil, whisking, and simmer it for 1 minute. Remove the pan from the heat, add the Cheddar gradually, whisking, and heat the mixture over low heat, whisking, until the cheese is melted. Divide the toast among 4 plates, spoon the sauce over it, and sprinkle each serving with some of the egg. **Serves 4 as a brunch or lunch entrée.**

TWO-GRAIN PANCAKES

1/3	cup cornmeal (preferably stone-ground)
1/4	cup whole-wheat flour
1/4	cup all-purpose flour
1	teaspoon baking powder
1	teaspoon sugar
1/2	teaspoon salt
1	large egg, beaten lightly
3/4	cup milk
1	tablespoon unsalted butter, melted vegetable oil for brushing the griddle pure maple syrup, heated, as an accompaniment

In a bowl whisk together the cornmeal, the flours, the baking powder, the sugar, and the salt, add the egg, the milk, and the butter, and whisk the batter until it is blended well. Heat a griddle over moderately high heat until it is hot enough to make drops of water scatter over its surface and brush it with the oil. Working in batches, drop the batter by large spoonfuls onto the griddle, cook the pancakes for 30 seconds to 1 minutes on each side, or until they are golden, and transfer them as they are cooked to a platter. Serve the pancakes with the syrup. **Makes about sixteen 2 1/2-inch pancakes.**

ASPARAGUS IN AMBUSH

- 4 crusty rectangular dinner rolls, each about 5 inches long
- 3/4 stick (6 tablespoons) unsalted butter
- 6 tablespoons minced onion
- 2 tablespoons all-purpose flour
- 2 cups milk
  freshly grated nutmeg to taste
- 3 teaspoons freshly grated lemon zest
- 1 1/2 pounds asparagus, trimmed and peeled
- 4 tablespoons minced fresh parsley leaves

Preheat the oven to 350° F.

With a serrated knife cut off the top fourth of each roll to form a lid and with a fork remove and discard the soft inner portion of the bottom sections, leaving four ¼- to ½-inch-thick shells. In a heavy saucepan melt the butter over moderately low heat, brush the insides of the bread shells and the lids lightly with about half the butter, and bake the shells and the lids on a baking sheet in the oven for 8 to 10 minutes, or until they are pale golden and crisp.

While the shells are baking, cook the onion in the remaining melted butter over moderately low heat, stirring, until it is softened. Add the flour and cook the *roux*, stirring, for 2 minutes. Add the milk in a stream, whisking, and bring the mixture to a boil, whisking. Add the nutmeg, the zest, and salt and pepper to taste and simmer the sauce, stirring occasionally, for 3 minutes.

While the sauce is simmering, steam the asparagus in a steamer set over boiling water, covered, for 3 to 4 minutes, or until it is crisp-tender. Divide the asparagus between the bread shells, stir the parsley into the sauce, and spoon the sauce over the asparagus. Top the asparagus with the lids. Serves 4 as a brunch or lunch entrée.

BROILED CORNISH HENS WITH MOLASSES AND ALLSPICE

- 1 tablespoon molasses
- 2 teaspoons fresh lemon juice
- 1 teaspoon ground allspice
- 2 Cornish hens, backbones removed and the hens flattened and patted dry

In a small bowl stir together the molasses, the lemon juice, the allspice, and salt and pepper to taste. Arrange the hens skin sides down on a lightly oiled rack of a broiler pan and brush them with some of the molasses mixture. Broil the hens about 4 inches from the heat, brushing them once with some of the remaining molasses mixture, for 10 minutes, turn them, and broil them for 4 minutes more. Brush the hens with the remaining molasses mixture and broil them for 4 to 5 minutes more, or until they are golden brown and cooked through. Serves 2.

new england side dishes

Honey Baked Beans

HONEY BAKED BEANS

- 4 cups dried navy beans, picked over, soaked in cold water to cover overnight, and drained
- 1 ham hock
- 1/4 pound salt pork, cut into 1/4-inch pieces
- 2 onions, chopped fine
- 1/2 cup dark honey (preferably buckwheat, available at natural foods stores, specialty foods shops, and some supermarkets)
- 1 cup ketchup
- 1/4 cup Dijon-style mustard
- 2 teaspoons black pepper, or to taste
- 2 tablespoons Worcestershire sauce, or to taste

In a kettle combine the beans and the ham hock with 8 cups water, bring the water to a boil, and simmer the mixture, covered partially, for 1 hour, or until the beans are just tender. While the beans are cooking, in a skillet cook the salt pork over moderately low heat, stirring occasionally, until it is golden, add the onions, and cook the mixture, stirring, until the onions are softened. Remove the skillet from the heat and stir in the honey, the ketchup, the mustard, the pepper, and the Worcestershire sauce.

Preheat the oven to 325° F.

Drain the beans, reserving the cooking liquid and the ham hock, remove the meat from the ham hock, and chop it fine. Return the beans to the kettle, stir in the honey mixture, the ham, and salt to taste, and pour the reserved cooking liquid over the bean mixture. Bake the beans, uncovered, in the middle of the oven for 45 minutes to 1 hour, or until most of the liquid is absorbed and a crust forms on top. **Serves 8 to 10.**

BAKED CANDIED ACORN SQUASH

- 4 1 1/4-pound acorn squash, halved lengthwise, seeded, and the stringy centers removed
- 1 stick (1/2 cup) unsalted butter
- 1/2 cup honey
- 1/2 cup firmly packed light brown sugar
- 1/2 teaspoon cinnamon
- 1/4 teaspoon ground ginger
- 1/4 teaspoon ground mace
- 2 tablespoons fresh lemon juice
- 1 tablespoon chopped pecans

Preheat the oven to 350° F.

Arrange the squash cut sides up in a shallow baking pan. In a stainless-steel or enameled saucepan combine the butter, the honey, the sugar, the cinnamon, the ginger, and the mace and cook the mixture over moderate heat, stirring, until the sugar is melted. Add the lemon juice and divide the mixture among the squash halves. Add enough hot water to the baking pan to reach ¼ inch up the sides of the squash and bake the squash in the oven, basting them occasionally with the sugar mixture, for 1 hour.

Remove the squash from the oven and increase the oven temperature to 375° F. Drain off all but 2 tablespoons water from the pan, sprinkle the pecans into each squash, and bake the squash, basting them occasionally, in the oven for 15 minutes more, or until they are glazed well and golden. Transfer the squash to a heated platter. **Serves 8.**

HARVARD BEETS

- 1 1/2 pounds small beets, without the stems (about 3 pounds with the stems), peeled and sliced 1/4 inch thick
- 1/2 stick (1/4 cup) unsalted butter
- 1/4 cup cider vinegar
- 3 tablespoons sugar
- 1 1/2 teaspoons cornstarch

In a large skillet combine the beets with the butter, 1 cup water, and salt to taste, bring the liquid to a boil, and simmer the beets, covered, for 12 minutes. Add the vinegar and the sugar and simmer the beets, uncovered, for 25 to 30 minutes more, stirring occasionally, or until they are tender and the liquid is almost evaporated. In a small bowl dissolve the cornstarch in ¼ cup water, stir the mixture into the beets, and simmer the beet mixture for 1 minute, or until the sauce is thickened. **Serves 4.**

GREEN BEANS WITH LEMON GARLIC BUTTER

- 2 pounds green beans, trimmed
- 1/4 cup minced shallot
- 1 garlic clove, minced (about 1 teaspoon)
- 3 tablespoons unsalted butter
- 1/2 teaspoon freshly grated lemon zest

In a large saucepan of boiling salted water cook the beans for 8 minutes, or until they are crisp-tender, and in a colander refresh them briefly under cold water. In a large skillet cook the shallot and the garlic in the butter over moderately low heat, stirring, until the shallot is softened. Add the beans, the zest, and salt and pepper to taste and cook the beans until they are heated through. **Serves 6 to 8.**

⊕ CABBAGE, CORN, AND PEPPER SLAW

- 3 cups finely shredded red cabbage (about 1/4 head)
- 3 cups finely shredded white cabbage (about 1/4 head)
- 1 cup cooked corn kernels (cut from about 2 ears) or frozen, thawed
- 1/2 cup sliced scallion
- 1 red bell pepper, cut into thin strips (about 1 1/2 cups)
- 1/4 cup minced fresh parsley leaves

For the dressing
- 3 tablespoons wine vinegar or fresh lemon juice
- 2 teaspoons Dijon-style mustard
- 1/3 cup olive oil, or to taste

In a large salad bowl combine the cabbages, the corn, the scallion, the bell pepper, and the parsley.

Make the dressing: In a bowl combine the vinegar or the lemon juice, the mustard, and salt and pepper to taste, add the oil in a stream, whisking, and whisk the dressing until it is emulsified.

Toss the slaw with the dressing and chill it, covered, for 30 minutes. **Serves 6.**

BOSTON BROWN BREAD

- 2 cups whole-wheat flour
- 1/2 cup cornmeal
- 1/2 teaspoon salt
- 3/4 cup dark honey (preferably buckwheat, available at natural foods stores, specialty foods shops, and some supermarkets)
- 2 teaspoons baking soda dissolved in 1 tablespoon hot water
- 2 cups buttermilk
- 1 cup raisins

Grease well two 1-pound coffee cans, line the bottom of each can with a round of wax paper, and grease the paper.

Into a bowl sift together the flour, the cornmeal, and the salt. In a small saucepan heat the honey to lukewarm, stir in the baking soda mixture and the buttermilk, and add the honey mixture to the flour mixture. Stir the batter until it is just combined, stir in the raisins, and divide the batter between the prepared cans. Cover each can with a double thickness of foil, tie the foil securely onto each can with kitchen string, and put the cans on a rack in a kettle. Add enough boiling water to the kettle to reach halfway up the sides of the cans and steam the breads, covered, for 1 hour to 1 hour and 10 minutes, or until a tester comes out clean. Transfer the cans to a rack, let the breads cool for 1 minute, and run a thin knife around the edge of each bread. Slide the breads out of the cans carefully and let them cool, upright, on the rack. **Makes 2 loaves.**

Boston Brown Bread

new england desserts

● WELLESLEY FUDGE CUPCAKES

For the cupcakes

- 2 ounces unsweetened chocolate, chopped fine
- 3/4 stick (6 tablespoons) unsalted butter, softened
- 1 cup firmly packed light brown sugar
- 2 large egg yolks
- 1 cup all-purpose flour
- 1 teaspoon baking powder
- 1/4 teaspoon salt
- 1/4 cup milk
- 1 teaspoon vanilla

For the frosting

- 2 ounces unsweetened chocolate, chopped fine
- 1 tablespoon unsalted butter
- 1 cup confectioners' sugar
- 4 teaspoons milk, plus additional to thin the frosting
- 1 teaspoon vanilla

Preheat the oven to 375° F. Line twelve 1/3-cup muffin tins with paper.

Make the cupcakes: In a metal bowl set over a pan of barely simmering water melt the chocolate with 6 tablespoons hot water, stirring, until the mixture is smooth and remove the bowl from the heat. In a large bowl whisk the butter with the brown sugar until the mixture is blended well and whisk in the egg yolks and the chocolate mixture. Onto a sheet of wax paper sift together the flour, the baking powder, and the salt and add the flour mixture to the chocolate mixture in batches alternately with the milk, stirring well after each addition. Stir in the vanilla, divide the batter among the prepared muffin tins, and bake the cupcakes in the middle of the oven for 18 to 20 minutes, or until a tester comes out clean. Transfer the cupcakes to a rack and let them cool.

Make the frosting while the cupcakes are baking: In a metal bowl set over a pan of barely simmering water melt the chocolate with the butter, stirring, until the mixture is smooth and remove the bowl from the heat. Stir in the confectioners' sugar, 4 teaspoons of the milk, and the vanilla and blend the frosting well (the frosting will thicken as it stands). When the cupcakes are cool, thin the frosting to the desired consistency with the additional milk, stirring in the milk drop by drop.

Spread each cupcake with some of the frosting. **Makes 12 cupcakes.**

APPLE BROWN BETTY

- 4 large McIntosh apples (about 1 1/2 pounds), peeled, cored, and sliced thin
- 1/4 cup firmly packed dark brown sugar
- 1/4 cup granulated sugar
- 1 tablespoon fresh lemon juice
- 1 teaspoon vanilla
- 1/4 teaspoon freshly grated nutmeg
- 2 cups stale white bread crumbs
- 1 stick (1/2 cup) unsalted butter, melted

Preheat the oven to 375° F. Butter a shallow 1-quart baking dish.

In a large ceramic or glass bowl combine well the apples, the sugars, the lemon juice, the vanilla, and the nutmeg. In another bowl combine the bread crumbs and the butter. Sprinkle half the crumb mixture in the prepared baking dish, top it with the apple mixture, and sprinkle the mixture with the remaining crumb mixture. Bake the dish, covered, in the oven for 45 minutes and bake it, uncovered, for 20 minutes more, or until it is golden brown and crisp. Serve the dessert warm. **Serves 4 to 6.**

RHUBARB BREAD PUDDING

- 1 pound rhubarb, trimmed and cut into 1-inch pieces (about 4 cups)
- 2/3 cup granulated sugar
- 1 1/2-pound loaf of stale French or Italian bread, cut into 1-inch cubes
- 2 cups half-and-half
- 1 cup milk
- 3 large eggs
- freshly grated nutmeg to taste
- 1 tablespoon firmly packed dark brown sugar
- 1/2 teaspoon cinnamon
- 3 tablespoons unsalted butter, cut into bits

In a ceramic or glass bowl combine the rhubarb with the granulated sugar and let it macerate for 1 hour.

Preheat the oven to 300° F. Butter a shallow 1 ½-quart baking dish.

In the prepared baking dish combine the rhubarb mixture and the bread. In a saucepan bring the half-and-half and the milk just to the boiling point. In a bowl beat the eggs, add the half-and-half mixture in a stream, beating, and stir in the nutmeg. Pour the custard over the rhubarb mixture, sprinkle the brown sugar and the cinnamon over the top, and dot the bread pudding with the butter. Put the dish in a baking pan and add enough hot water to the pan to reach halfway up the sides of the dish. Bake the bread pudding, covered with foil, in the middle of the oven for 30 minutes and bake it, uncovered, for 30 minutes more, or until a tester inserted in the center comes out clean. **Serves 4 to 6.**

MAPLE PUMPKIN PIE WITH WALNUT CRUST

For the crust
- 1 cup walnuts, toasted lightly and cooled
- 2 tablespoons firmly packed dark brown sugar
- 1 cup all-purpose flour
- 3/4 stick (6 tablespoons) cold unsalted butter, cut into bits
- 1/2 teaspoon salt
- raw rice for weighting the shell

For the filling
- 2 1/2 cups canned pumpkin purée
- 1 cup half-and-half
- 4 large eggs, beaten lightly
- 1/2 cup firmly packed dark brown sugar
- 3/4 cup pure maple syrup (preferably dark)
- 1 1/2 teaspoons maple extract (available at specialty foods shops and some supermarkets)
- 1 1/2 teaspoons cinnamon
- 1 1/2 teaspoons ground ginger
- 1/4 teaspoon ground allspice
- 1/2 teaspoon salt

whipped cream and pure maple syrup as accompaniments

Make the crust: In a food processor grind coarse the walnuts with the sugar and transfer the mixture to a bowl. In the food processor blend together the flour, the butter, and the salt until the mixture resembles meal and add it to the walnut mixture. Add 3 tablespoons ice water, toss the mixture until the water is incorporated, and press the dough onto the bottom and up the side of a 10-inch pie plate, crimping the edge decoratively. Prick the crust with a fork and chill it for 30 minutes. *The crust may be made 2 weeks in advance and kept wrapped well and frozen.*

Preheat the oven to 425° F.

Line the crust with foil, fill the foil with the rice, and bake the crust in the middle of the oven for 7 minutes. Remove the rice and foil carefully, bake the crust for 5 minutes more, and let it cool.

Reduce the oven temperature to 350° F.

Make the filling: In a large bowl whisk together the pumpkin purée, the half-and-half, the eggs, the sugar, the maple syrup, the maple extract, the cinnamon, the ginger, the allspice, and the salt until the filling is smooth.

Pour the filling into the crust, bake the pie in the middle of the oven for 55 minutes to 1 hour, or until it is just set in the middle, and let it cool on a rack. Serve the pie topped with the whipped cream and drizzled with the maple syrup.

CRANBERRY WALNUT CRUMB CAKE

- 1 3/4 cups all-purpose flour
- 1 teaspoon baking powder
- 1 teaspoon baking soda
- 1/2 teaspoon salt
- 1/2 stick (1/4 cup) unsalted butter, softened
- 1/4 cup vegetable shortening at room temperature
- 1 cup granulated sugar
- 3 large eggs
- 1 cup sour cream
- 2 teaspoons freshly grated orange zest
- 2 cups cranberries, picked over

For the topping
- 1 cup firmly packed light brown sugar
- 1/4 cup all-purpose flour
- 1/2 cup finely chopped walnuts
- 1/2 stick (1/4 cup) cold unsalted butter, cut into bits

Preheat the oven to 350° F. Butter and lightly flour a 13- by 9-inch baking pan.

In a bowl combine the flour, the baking powder, the baking soda, and the salt. In a large bowl cream the butter and the shortening, add the granulated sugar, a little at a time, beating, and beat the mixture until it is light and fluffy. Beat in the eggs, 1 at a time, beating well after each addition, and add the sour cream alternately in batches with the flour mixture, stirring until the batter is just combined. Fold in the orange zest and the cranberries and spread the mixture in the prepared pan.

Make the topping: In a small bowl combine the brown sugar, the flour, and the walnuts and blend in the butter until the mixture resembles coarse meal.

Sprinkle the topping evenly over the batter and bake the cake in the oven for 50 minutes, or until a tester inserted in the center comes out clean. Let the cake cool in the pan on a rack for 10 minutes, cut it into squares, and transfer it to a platter.

On this page, The Farmers' Museum and Village Crossroads in Cooperstown and right, a flock of Adirondack chairs patiently lines Blue Mountain Lake in the Adirondacks, both in New York

the

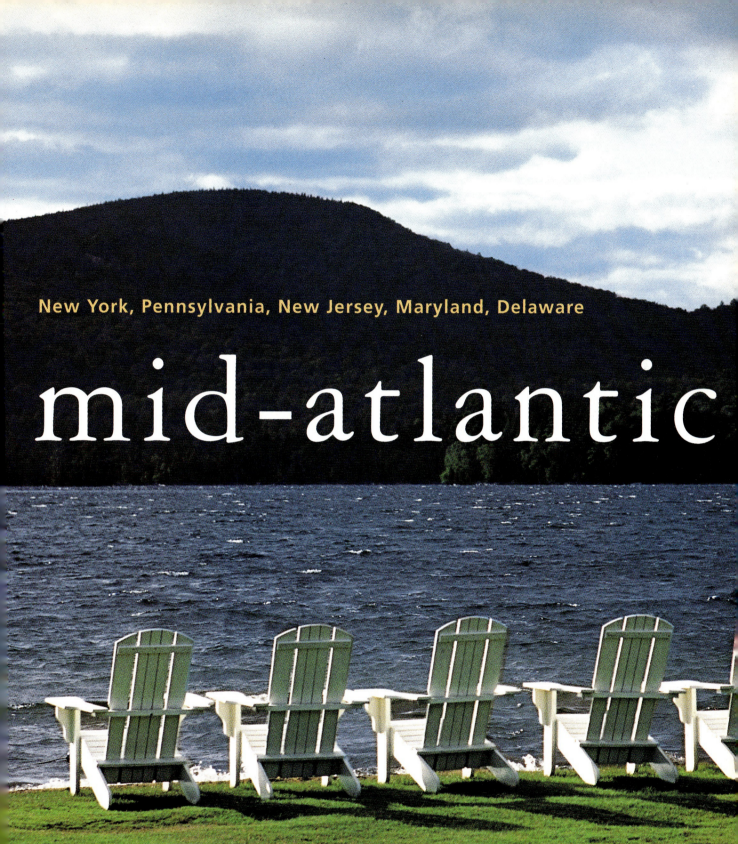

New York, Pennsylvania, New Jersey, Maryland, Delaware

mid-atlantic

the mid-atlantic

From the apple orchards dotting the Hudson Valley to the crab-, oyster-, and clam-filled Chesapeake Bay, the Mid-Atlantic region is blessed with bountiful harvests and culinary influences from around the world. With its natural harbors, the territory was one of the first to be settled by the English, Dutch, and Germans in the 1600s. As the home of Ellis Island in the late nineteenth century, it continued to welcome immigrants by the millions. Today, with 170 ethnic communities living side by side in New York City, this region is still the heart of America's melting pot.

Authentic regional dishes in the area come from the Pennsylvania Dutch (Mennonites, Amish, and Moravians), actually of German (Deutsche) and Swiss descent; these groups sought religious freedom in America in the eighteenth century. Over the years their old German recipes have been modified with local ingredients to produce comforting chicken and oyster casseroles, tasty preserves and jams, such as corn relish and crab-apple jelly, and delicious sweet pies filled with molasses, brown sugar, and spices.

While most of the states in the Mid-Atlantic region lie above the Mason-Dixon Line (the boundary between Pennsylvania and Maryland that has come to demark North and South), there is a strong influence of Southern cooking in Maryland and Delaware. Here spicy African-American seasonings and the lavish spreads of historic plantations in nearby Virginia characterize the cuisine.

Lady Baltimore Cake;
Lemon Buttermilk
Chess Tartlets

A DESSERT PARTY

LADY BALTIMORE CAKE
★
LEMON BUTTERMILK CHESS TARTLETS
★
FROZEN CRANBERRY MOUSSE WITH CRANBERRY CARAMEL SAUCE
★
BROWN SUGAR WALNUT FUDGE
★
PINEAPPLE UPSIDE-DOWN CAKE
★
OLD-FASHIONED SUGAR COOKIES
★
LIME CURD
★
AMBROSIA PUNCH
★

MARTIN BROTHERS
PASO ROBLES
MOSCATO ALLEGRO 1993
OR
FONTANAFREDDA
ASTI SPUMANTE

Serves 8

the mid-atlantic menu

Our Dessert Party menu celebrates America's love for sweets with a variety of delights that includes both Mid-Atlantic and Southern influences. The New York and New Jersey Dutch had a fondness for treats, and their *koekje* (small cakes) were the forerunners of our cookies. Here you will find our classic Old-Fashioned Sugar Cookies recipe that no one should be without. Use lard for a crisp and sandy cookie, or vegetable shortening for a crisp and chewy one. And, although it is a Southern creation, we've chosen to include the grand Lady Baltimore Cake here. An impressive dessert first made by Mrs. Alicia Rhett Mayberry from Charleston, South Carolina, this festive cake, along with our Ambrosia Punch, bows to the South.

LADY BALTIMORE CAKE

For the cake layers
- 2 sticks (1 cup) unsalted butter, softened
- 2 cups sugar
- 1 teaspoon vanilla
- 1/2 teaspoon almond extract
- 3 cups all-purpose flour
- 1 tablespoon baking powder
- 1/2 teaspoon salt
- 1 cup milk
- 7 large egg whites
- 1/4 teaspoon cream of tartar

- 2 cups sugar
- 6 large egg whites
- 2 teaspoons vanilla
- 1/2 cup finely chopped dried figs, plus sliced dried figs for garnish
- 1 cup pecans, toasted lightly and chopped fine, plus pecan halves for garnish
- 1/2 cup raisins, chopped

Preheat the oven to 325° F. Line 3 buttered 9-inch round cake pans with rounds of wax paper, butter the paper, and dust the pans with flour, knocking out the excess.

Make the cake layers: In a large bowl with an electric mixer cream the butter with the sugar until the mixture is light and fluffy and beat in the vanilla and the almond extract. In a bowl stir together the flour, the baking powder, and the salt, add the flour mixture to the butter mixture in batches alternately with the milk, and stir the batter until it is just combined. In another large bowl beat the egg whites with the cream of tartar and a pinch of salt until they just hold stiff peaks, stir one third of them into the batter, and fold in the remaining whites gently but thoroughly. Divide the batter among the prepared pans, smoothing the tops, and bake the cake layers, in batches if necessary, in the middle of the oven for 25 to 35 minutes, or until a tester comes out clean.

Let the cake layers cool in the pans on racks for 5 minutes, turn them out onto the racks, and let them cool completely. *The cake layers may be made 1 week in advance and kept wrapped well in plastic wrap and frozen. Let the layers thaw before proceeding.*

In a small saucepan combine the sugar and ¾ cup water, bring the mixture to a boil, stirring until the sugar is dissolved, and boil the syrup until it registers 248° F. on a candy thermometer. While the syrup is boiling, in a large bowl with an electric mixer beat the egg whites with a pinch of salt until they hold soft peaks. With the mixer running add the hot syrup in a stream, beat in the vanilla, and beat the icing until it is cool. Transfer 2 cups of the icing to a bowl, reserving the remaining icing, and fold in the chopped figs, the chopped pecans, and the raisins.

Arrange 1 of the cake layers, flat side up, on a serving plate, spread it with half the dried-fruit icing, and top the filling with another cake layer, flat side down. Spread the top with the remaining dried-fruit icing and top the filling with the remaining cake layer. Spread the top and side of the cake with the reserved plain icing and garnish the cake with the sliced figs and the pecan halves.

Photo on page 37

AMBROSIA PUNCH

- 2 4-pound pineapples, peeled and cut into pieces
- 4 cups fresh orange juice
- 2 15-ounce cans cream of coconut
- 3 cups chilled seltzer or club soda
- 1 cup light rum

In a food processor purée the pineapple in batches and strain the purée through a fine sieve into a bowl, pressing hard on the solids. Stir in the orange juice and the cream of coconut and stir the mixture until the cream of coconut is incorporated well. Chill the mixture, covered, until it is cold and stir in the seltzer or club soda and the rum. **Makes about 14 cups.**

LEMON BUTTERMILK CHESS TARTLETS

- pastry dough (page 15)
- 1/2 stick (1/4 cup) unsalted butter, softened
- 1 cup granulated sugar
- 3 large eggs
- 1/4 cup buttermilk
- 2 tablespoons cornmeal
- 1 teaspoon freshly grated lemon zest, plus thin strips of lemon zest tied into knots for garnish
- 3 tablespoons fresh lemon juice
- 1/4 teaspoon salt
- confectioners' sugar for dusting the tartlets

Roll out the dough ⅛ inch thick on a floured surface, fit it into 8 tartlet tins, each 3¾ inches across the top and ¾ inch deep, and roll a rolling pin over the edges of the tins to trim the excess dough. Chill the shells for 30 minutes.

Preheat the oven to 425° F.

In a bowl with an electric mixer cream the butter with the granulated sugar until the mixture is light and fluffy, beat in the eggs, 1 at a time, beating well after each addition, and beat in the buttermilk, the cornmeal, the grated zest, the lemon juice, and the salt. Divide the mixture among the tartlet shells and bake the tartlets on a baking sheet in the lower third of the oven for 15 minutes. Reduce the oven temperature to 350° F. and bake the tartlets for 10 to 15 minutes more, or until they are golden and set. Let the tartlets cool in the tins on racks until they can be handled, remove them from the tins, and let them cool completely on the racks. *The tartlets may be made 1 day in advance and kept covered loosely in a cool place.* Dust the tartlets lightly with the confectioners' sugar and garnish them with the lemon zest knots. **Makes 8 tartlets.**

Photo on page 37

FROZEN CRANBERRY MOUSSE WITH CRANBERRY CARAMEL SAUCE

For the mousse
- 1 cup dried cranberries (available at specialty foods shops), chopped
- 1/2 cup dark rum
- 4 large egg whites
- 1/2 cup sugar
- 1 cup well-chilled heavy cream
- 1 1/2 cups walnuts, toasted lightly, cooled, and chopped coarse

For the sauce
- 3/4 cup cranberry juice concentrate
- 1/4 cup heavy cream
- 2 cups sugar

Line an oiled metal loaf pan, 9 by 5 by 3 inches, with plastic wrap.

Make the mousse: In a small saucepan combine the cranberries and the rum, bring the mixture to a simmer, and remove the pan from the heat. Let the mixture cool. In a large metal bowl set over a saucepan of simmering water stir together the egg whites and the sugar until the mixture registers 160° F. on a candy thermometer, remove the bowl from the pan, and with an electric mixer beat the whites until they just hold stiff peaks. In a bowl with cleaned beaters beat the cream until it just holds stiff peaks. Drain the cranberries and add them to the whipped cream. Add the walnuts and the cream mixture to the whites, fold the mixture together gently but thoroughly, and spread it in the prepared pan. Freeze the mousse, covered with plastic wrap, for at least 6 hours. *The mousse may be made 5 days in advance and kept covered and frozen.*

Make the sauce: In a saucepan bring the cranberry juice concentrate, ½ cup water, and the cream to a boil and keep the mixture warm. In a dry large heavy skillet cook the sugar over moderate heat until it is a deep caramel color. Remove the skillet from the heat and carefully whisk in the warm cranberry mixture. Return the skillet to the heat and cook the sauce, whisking, until it is smooth.

Serve the sauce slightly warm over slices of the mousse. **Serves 8.**

BROWN SUGAR WALNUT FUDGE

- 2 cups firmly packed dark brown sugar
- 1 cup milk
- 3 tablespoons light corn syrup
- 2 ounces unsweetened chocolate, chopped
- 1/4 teaspoon salt
- 3 tablespoons unsalted butter, cut into bits
- 1 1/2 teaspoons vanilla
- 2 cups chopped walnuts

Butter an 8-inch square baking pan.

In a 4-quart heavy saucepan combine the sugar, the milk, the corn syrup, the chocolate, and the salt, cook the mixture over moderate heat, stirring, until the sugar is dissolved and the chocolate is melted, and cook it, undisturbed, until it registers 238° F. on a candy thermometer. Remove the pan from the heat, add the butter (do not stir it into the mixture), and let the mixture cool until it registers 140° F. Stir in the vanilla and the walnuts, beat the mixture with a wooden spoon for 30 seconds to 1 minute, or until it just begins to lose its gloss, and pour it immediately into the prepared pan, spreading it evenly. Let the fudge cool until it begins to harden, cut it into squares, and let it cool completely. *The fudge may be made 2 weeks in advance and kept in an airtight container lined with wax paper, separating the layers with wax paper, in a cool place.* **Makes about 2 pounds.**

PINEAPPLE UPSIDE-DOWN CAKE

- 1 1/2 sticks (3/4 cup) unsalted butter
- 2/3 cup firmly packed light brown sugar
- 3 cups 1-inch chunks fresh pineapple (about 1 pineapple)
- 1 1/2 cups all-purpose flour
- 1 1/2 teaspoons baking powder
- 1/2 teaspoon salt
- 1/2 teaspoon cinnamon
- 2/3 cup granulated sugar
- 2 large eggs
- 1 teaspoon vanilla
- 3/4 cup milk
- whipped cream or vanilla ice cream as an accompaniment

Preheat the oven to 350° F. Butter generously a 9- by 2-inch round cake pan.

In a small bowl stir together well ½ stick of the butter, melted, and the brown sugar and spread the mixture evenly in the prepared pan. Pat the pineapple very dry between several thicknesses of paper towel and arrange it evenly on the brown sugar mixture.

Into a bowl sift together the flour, the baking powder, the salt, and the cinnamon. In another bowl with an electric mixer cream the remaining 1 stick butter, softened, with the sugar until the mixture is light and fluffy, add the eggs, 1 at a time, beating well after each addition, and beat in the vanilla. Add the flour mixture in batches alternately with the milk, beginning and ending with the flour mixture and beating well after each addition.

Pour the batter into the pan, spreading it evenly, and bake the cake in the middle of the oven for 45 to 55 minutes, or until a tester comes out clean. Let the cake cool in the pan on a rack for 15 minutes, run a thin knife around the edge, and invert the cake onto a plate.

Serve the cake warm or at room temperature with the whipped cream or the ice cream.

OLD-FASHIONED SUGAR COOKIES

- 1/2 cup lard or vegetable shortening, melted and cooled
- 1/2 stick (1/4 cup) unsalted butter, melted and cooled
- 1 cup sugar, plus additional for coating
- 1 large egg
- 1 teaspoon vanilla
- 2 cups all-purpose flour
- 2 teaspoons baking soda
- 3/4 teaspoon salt

In a large bowl stir together the lard or shortening, the butter, 1 cup of the sugar, the egg, and the vanilla. Into the bowl sift together the flour, the baking soda, and the salt and stir the mixture until it forms a dough. Chill the dough, covered, for at least 2 hours or overnight.

Preheat the oven to 375° F. Lightly grease baking sheets.

Roll rounded tablespoons of the dough into balls, roll the balls in the additional sugar, coating them completely, and arrange them 3 inches apart on the prepared baking sheets. Flatten the balls with the bottom of a glass dipped in the sugar (the edges will crack slightly) and bake the cookies in batches in the middle of the oven for 8 to 12 minutes, or until they are pale golden. Transfer the cookies to racks and let them cool. *The cookies keep in an airtight container for 1 week.* Makes about 32 cookies.

LIME CURD

- 2 large eggs, beaten lightly
- 1 stick (1/2 cup) unsalted butter, cut into bits
- 1/2 cup sugar
- 2 tablespoons freshly grated lime zest
- 3 tablespoons fresh lemon juice
- 1 tablespoon fresh lime juice

In a saucepan combine the eggs, the butter, the sugar, the zest, the juices, and a pinch of salt and cook the mixture over moderately low heat, whisking constantly, for 10 to 12 minutes, or until the curd is thick enough to hold the mark of the whisk and the first bubble appears on the surface. Transfer the curd to a small bowl, cover its surface with plastic wrap, and let the curd cool. Chill the curd, covered with the plastic wrap, for 1 hour and serve it with the sugar cookies. Makes about 1 1/4 cups.

⊕ CHILLED TOMATO BASIL SOUP

- 2 1/2 pounds (about 6) tomatoes, cored and cut into chunks
- 1 tablespoon cornstarch
- 1/2 cup beef broth
- 1 tablespoon fresh lemon juice
- 1/2 teaspoon sugar
- 10 whole fresh basil leaves, plus 1/3 cup chopped basil for garnish
- sour cream for garnish
- extra-virgin olive oil for drizzling the soup
- garlic *baguette* toasts (recipe follows) as an accompaniment

In a food processor purée the tomatoes and force the purée through a fine sieve into a saucepan, pressing hard on the solids. In a small bowl stir together the cornstarch and the broth and stir the mixture into the tomato purée. Bring the mixture to a boil, stirring, remove the pan from the heat, and stir in the lemon juice, the sugar, the whole basil leaves, and salt and pepper to taste. Let the soup cool and chill it, covered, for at least 8 hours. *The soup may be made 2 days in advance and kept covered and chilled.*

Discard the whole basil leaves, ladle the soup into 6 bowls, and garnish each serving with a dollop of the sour cream and some of the chopped basil. Drizzle the soup with the oil and serve it with the toasts. **Makes about 6 cups, serving 6.**

◯ GARLIC BAGUETTE TOASTS

- 1 large garlic clove, minced or forced through a garlic press
- 1/4 cup olive oil
- a French *baguette,* cut lengthwise into 6 long wedges
- coarse salt to taste

Preheat the oven to 375° F.

In a small skillet cook the garlic in the oil over moderate heat, stirring, until it begins to turn golden, brush the bread wedges with the oil, and on a baking sheet bake them in the middle of the oven for 10 minutes, or until they are golden. Sprinkle the toasts with the salt and break them in half. **Makes 12 toasts, serving 6.**

the mid-atlantic starters

CUCUMBER CUPS WITH HORSERADISH YOGURT

- 1 cup plain yogurt
- 1 14- to 16-inch seedless cucumber
- 3 scallions, minced
- 1 tablespoon drained bottled horseradish, or to taste, squeezed dry
- 1 tablespoon minced fresh parsley leaves, plus whole leaves for garnish

Drain the yogurt in a fine sieve set over a bowl and chill it, its surface covered with plastic wrap, overnight. Cut the cucumber crosswise into sixteen ¾-inch pieces and with a melon-ball cutter scoop out part of the centers, forming ¼-inch-thick cups. Sprinkle the cucumber cups with salt and let them drain, inverted, on paper towels for 10 minutes. In a bowl combine well the yogurt, the scallions, the horseradish, the minced parsley, and salt and pepper to taste. Pat the cucumber cups dry gently, divide the yogurt mixture among them, and arrange the whole parsley leaves decoratively on the top. *The filled cucumber cups may be made 1 hour in advance and kept covered and chilled.* **Makes 16 hors d'oeuvres.**

MANHATTAN-STYLE CLAM CHOWDER

- 2 dozen cherrystone or other hard-shelled clams
- 3 ounces salt pork, rind discarded, or bacon, cut into 1/4-inch pieces
- 1 1/2 cups chopped onion
- 1 cup chopped celery
- 1 bay leaf
- 1 pound boiling potatoes
- 1 28-ounce can plum tomatoes, drained and chopped, reserving the juice
- Tabasco to taste

Scrub the clams well. In a kettle steam the clams with 1 cup water, covered, over high heat, shaking the kettle, for 8 to 10 minutes, or until they are opened. Transfer the clams with a slotted spoon to a bowl, discard any unopened clams, and remove the clams from the shells. Strain the cooking liquid through a very fine sieve set over a large measuring cup and add enough water to measure 4 cups liquid. Chop the clams fine.

In the kettle, cleaned, cook the salt pork or bacon over moderately low heat, stirring, until it is crisp and golden, add the onion, the celery, and the bay leaf, and cook the mixture, stirring, until the celery is softened. Add the potatoes, peeled and cut into ¼-inch pieces, the tomatoes with the juice, the clam cooking liquid, the clams, and salt and pepper to taste and bring the mixture to a boil. Simmer the chowder, covered, stirring occasionally, for 20 to 25 minutes, or until the potatoes are tender, discard the bay leaf, and season the chowder with the Tabasco. **Makes about 12 cups, serving 6 to 8.**

HERBED HAM, CHEDDAR, AND MUSHROOM PHYLLO TRIANGLES

- 1 onion, chopped fine
- 10 ounces mushrooms, chopped fine and squeezed dry in a kitchen towel
- 2 tablespoons vegetable oil
- 1/2 pound cooked ham, chopped fine
- 1/2 pound Cheddar, chopped
- 1/8 teaspoon ground cloves
- 1/2 teaspoon dried sage, crumbled
- 1 1/3 cups fine fresh bread crumbs
- 1/3 cup minced fresh parsley leaves
- 3 large eggs, beaten lightly
- 20 *phyllo* sheets, cut lengthwise into 3-inch-wide strips, the strips stacked between 2 sheets of wax paper and covered with a dampened kitchen towel
- 2 sticks (1 cup) unsalted butter, melted

In a large heavy skillet cook the onion and the mushrooms in the oil over moderate heat, stirring occasionally, until the onion is softened. Add the ham and cook the mixture, stirring, for 5 minutes. Transfer the mixture to a bowl and stir in the Cheddar, the cloves, the sage, the bread crumbs, the parsley, the eggs, and salt and pepper to taste.

Preheat the oven to 350° F.

On a work surface arrange 1 strip of the *phyllo* with a short side facing you, brush it lightly with some of the butter, and put 1 heaping teaspoon of the filling about 1 inch from the bottom end of the strip. Fold the lower right corner of the strip up over the filling, forming a triangle of the folded *phyllo*, continue to fold the filled triangle up the entire length of the strip, and brush the triangle lightly with some of the butter. Form more triangles in the same manner with the remaining *phyllo*, filling, and butter, transferring them to baking sheets as they are formed. *The triangles may be made 1 week in advance and kept frozen in airtight containers. Do not thaw the triangles before baking.* Bake the triangles in the middle of the oven for 20 to 25 minutes, or until they are golden. **Makes about 80 triangles.**

FETTUCCINE WITH LEEK AND SOUR CREAM SAUCE

- the white and pale green part of 4 large leeks, split lengthwise, washed well, and sliced thin (about 3 cups)
- 1/4 cup olive oil
- 3 tablespoons dry white wine or dry vermouth
- 1/4 cup chopped fresh parsley leaves
- 1/2 cup sour cream
- 12 ounces dried fettuccine
- 3 hard-boiled large eggs, chopped

In a large heavy skillet cook the leeks in the oil over moderately low heat, stirring, until they are softened, add the wine or the vermouth, and simmer the mixture until the liquid is almost evaporated. Remove the skillet from the heat and stir in the parsley, the sour cream, and salt and pepper to taste. In a kettle of boiling salted water boil the fettuccine until it is *al dente*, reserve 1 cup of the cooking liquid, and drain the fettuccine. Add the fettuccine to the sauce and toss the mixture well, adding as much of the reserved cooking liquid as necessary to thin the sauce to the desired consistency. Sprinkle the dish with the eggs. **Serves 6 to 8.**

the mid-atlantic starters

the mid-atlantic

entrées

Pea and Goat Cheese Tart

PEA AND GOAT CHEESE TART

For the shell
- pastry dough (page 15)
- 3 cups raw rice or beans for weighting the shell

For the custard
- 1/4 pound mild goat cheese, such as Montrachet
- 1/2 cup ricotta
- 1 large egg
- 2 tablespoons milk
- 1/3 cup firmly packed fresh mint leaves

For the topping
- 2 cups shelled fresh peas (about 2 pounds unshelled), cooked (procedure follows), or a 10-ounce package frozen peas, thawed
- 1/4 cup minced radish
- 1/4 cup minced scallion
- 1 tablespoon fresh lemon juice
- 1 teaspoon Dijon-style mustard
- 3 tablespoons olive oil

about 4 radishes, sliced very thin, plus 1 small radish, sliced very thin, leaving the stem end intact, and fanned, for garnish

Preheat the oven to 425° F.

Make the shell: Roll out the dough into an 1/8-inch-thick round on a lightly floured surface, fit the round into a 9-inch tart pan with a removable fluted rim, and crimp the edge decoratively. Prick the bottom of the shell lightly with a fork and chill the shell for 30 minutes. Line the shell with foil, fill the foil with the rice, and bake the shell in the lower third of the oven for 15 minutes. Remove the rice and foil carefully, bake the shell for 8 to 10 minutes more, or until it is golden, and let it cool in the pan on a rack.

Reduce the oven temperature to 375° F.

Make the custard: In a food processor or blender purée the goat cheese with the ricotta, the egg, the milk, and the mint and season the custard with salt and pepper.

Pour the custard into the shell and bake the tart in the middle of the oven for 25 minutes, or until the filling is set and pale golden. Let the tart cool on a rack for 15 minutes and remove the rim.

Make the topping while the tart is cooling: In a bowl toss together the peas, the radish, and the scallion. In a small bowl whisk together the lemon juice, the mustard, and salt and pepper to taste, add the oil in a stream, whisking, and whisk the dressing until it is emulsified. Pour the dressing over the pea mixture and toss the topping well.

Spoon the topping onto the tart and arrange the radish slices and the fanned radish decoratively on the top. **Serves 4 as a luncheon entrée.**

to cook fresh peas

To simmer shelled fresh peas: For each cup of shelled fresh peas bring to a boil 1 cup water with 4 empty pea pods, add 1/2 teaspoon sugar, 1/4 teaspoon salt, and the 1 cup peas, and simmer the peas for 3 to 8 minutes, or until they are tender. Drain the peas in a colander and discard the pods. Refresh the peas under cold water and drain them well.

To steam fresh shelled peas: In a steamer set over boiling water steam the peas, covered partially, for 5 to 12 minutes, or until they are tender. Transfer the peas to a colander, refresh them under cold water, and drain them well.

GRILLED MARINATED BLUEFISH

- 1 cup white-wine vinegar
- 1 cup dry white wine or dry vermouth
- 4 garlic cloves, minced
- 1 small onion, minced
- 1 teaspoon ground cumin
- 1 teaspoon salt
- 1/4 teaspoon cayenne
- 4 1/2-pound bluefish fillets, skin side scored in several places

In a stainless-steel or enameled saucepan combine the vinegar, the wine or the vermouth, the garlic, the onion, the cumin, the salt, and the cayenne, bring the liquid to a boil, and simmer the mixture for 15 minutes. Let the marinade cool. Arrange the fillets in a shallow ceramic or glass dish just large enough to hold them in one layer, pour the marinade over them, and let the fillets marinate, covered and chilled, turning them frequently, for at least 3 hours or overnight. Drain the fillets over a saucepan and boil the marinade for 3 minutes.

    Grill the fillets, skin sides down, over glowing coals about 6 inches from the heat, basting them with the reserved marinade, for 4 to 6 minutes, or until they just flake when tested with a fork. (Alternatively, the fillets can be grilled in a ridged grill pan over moderately high heat in the same manner.) Transfer the fillets with a large spatula to heated plates. **Serves 4.**

BRAISED PORK CHOPS WITH CRACKED RYE

- 3 tablespoons vegetable oil
- 1 cup cracked rye (available at natural foods stores)
- 4 3/4-inch-thick shoulder pork chops (about 2 pounds), patted dry and seasoned with salt and pepper
- 1 large onion, chopped
- 1 teaspoon caraway seeds
- 1/4 teaspoon dried thyme, crumbled
- 1 cup apple cider
- 1 cup chicken broth

Preheat the oven to 325° F.
    In a heavy skillet heat 2 tablespoons of the oil over moderately high heat until it is hot, in it sauté the rye, stirring, for 3 to 5 minutes, or until it is golden and toasted, and transfer the rye to a bowl. In a wide flameproof casserole just large enough to hold the pork chops in one layer heat the remaining 1 tablespoon oil over moderately high heat until it is hot and in it brown the pork chops, patted dry. Transfer the chops with tongs to a plate, add to the casserole the onion, the caraway seeds, and the thyme, and cook the mixture over moderate heat, stirring, until the onion is softened. Add the rye and combine the mixture well. Arrange the pork chops over the onion mixture and add the cider, the broth, and salt and pepper to taste. Bring the liquid to a boil and braise the mixture, covered tightly, in the oven for 45 minutes, or until the pork is tender and the rye has absorbed the liquid. **Serves 4.**

SPICED BEEF STEW WITH TURNIPS

1/4	cup vegetable oil
1 1/2	pounds boneless lean chuck, cut into 1 1/2-inch pieces
1	cup beef broth
1	cup dry red wine
1	tablespoon tomato paste
1	teaspoon cinnamon
1/4	teaspoon ground allspice
1 1/2	pounds turnips, peeled and cut into 1-inch wedges
1	tablespoon cornstarch dissolved in 2 tablespoons water

In a stainless-steel or enameled kettle combine the oil and the chuck and stir the chuck to coat it with the oil. Add the broth, the wine, the tomato paste, the cinnamon, and the allspice, bring the liquid to a boil, stirring, and cook the mixture at a bare simmer for 1½ hours. Stir in the turnips and cook the stew at a bare simmer for 1 hour, or until the turnips are tender. Stir the cornstarch mixture, stir it into the stew with salt and pepper to taste, and simmer the stew, stirring, until the liquid is thickened. **Serves 6**.

RISOTTO WITH ZUCCHINI AND SCALLOPS

7 1/2	cups chicken broth
2/3	cup finely chopped onion
3	tablespoons unsalted butter
3	tablespoons olive oil
2	cups Arborio rice
2/3	cup dry white wine or dry vermouth
1 1/2	pounds zucchini, scrubbed, trimmed, and cut into 3/4-inch pieces
1/2	pound sea scallops, rinsed and cut into 3/4-inch pieces
2/3	cup freshly grated Parmesan

In a large saucepan bring the broth and 1½ cups water to a boil and keep it at a bare simmer. In a large heavy saucepan cook the onion in the butter and the oil over moderately low heat, stirring, until it is soft, add the rice, and cook the mixture over moderate heat, stirring with a wooden spatula, for 2 minutes, or until the rice is well coated with the fat. Add the wine or the vermouth and cook the mixture at a vigorous simmer, stirring, for 1 to 3 minutes, or until the wine is absorbed. Add ⅔ cup of the broth and cook the mixture at a vigorous simmer, stirring, for 3 to 5 minutes, or until the broth is absorbed. Add more of the broth, ⅔ cup at a time, stirring and simmering the mixture after each addition for 3 to 5 minutes, or until the broth is absorbed and the rice begins to soften. (About 5 cups of the broth will have been absorbed.) Add the zucchini and ½ cup more broth and simmer the mixture, stirring, for 3 to 5 minutes, or until the broth is absorbed. Add more of the broth, 1/2 cup at a time, stirring and simmering the mixture after each addition for 3 to 5 minutes, or until the broth is absorbed and the rice is barely *al dente*. (About 6½ cups of the broth will have been absorbed.) Add the scallops and ½ cup more broth and simmer the mixture, stirring, for 3 to 5 minutes, or until the broth is absorbed. (The mixture should be creamy, but the rice should be *al dente*. If necessary, add more broth and cook the mixture in the same manner until the rice is *al dente*.) Remove the pan from the heat, stir in the Parmesan and pepper to taste, and transfer the risotto to a heated serving bowl. **Serves 6**.

Crab Salad

CRAB SALAD

- 2 tablespoons mayonnaise
- 2 tablespoons *crème fraîche*
- 1 tablespoon fresh lemon juice
- 1 tablespoon chopped fresh chives
- 2/3 cup chopped seeded tomato, plus 2 large whole tomatoes
- 2/3 cup seedless cucumber, cut into 1/4-inch dice
- 2 cups picked-over lump crab meat, thawed and drained if frozen
- soft-leafed lettuce, rinsed and dried, for lining the plates

In a bowl whisk together the mayonnaise, the *crème fraîche*, the lemon juice, and the chives. In another bowl combine gently the chopped tomato, the cucumber, the crab meat, half the mayonnaise sauce, and salt and pepper to taste. Without cutting all the way through the bottoms, core the whole tomatoes and cut them into sixths, forming tulip shapes. Line 2 plates with the lettuce, center the tomatoes on the lettuce, and mound the crab salad on top. Serve the salad with the remaining sauce. Serves 2.

PENNSYLVANIA DUTCH-STYLE CHICKEN POTPIE

- 1 3 1/2-pound chicken
- 2 cups all-purpose flour
- 1 tablespoon cold vegetable shortening
- 1 teaspoon salt
- 1 large egg, beaten lightly
- 2 carrots, sliced thin
- 1 rib of celery, sliced thin
- 1 onion, minced
- 1 pound boiling potatoes (about 4)
- 1/3 cup finely chopped fresh parsley leaves

Season the cavity of the chicken with salt and pepper, put the chicken in a kettle just large enough to hold it, and add 14 cups water. Bring the water to a boil, simmer the chicken, covered, skimming the froth, for 45 minutes, or until it is tender, and transfer it to a large bowl. When the chicken is cool enough to handle, discard the skin and bones, cut the meat into bite-size pieces, and chill it, covered. Measure the stock remaining in the kettle and boil it until it is reduced to about 10 cups. Strain the stock through a sieve into a bowl, let it cool, uncovered, and chill it, covered, overnight.

In a bowl blend together the flour, the shortening, and the salt. In a small bowl whisk together the egg and 2/3 cup cold water, add the egg mixture to the flour mixture, and stir the mixture until it forms a soft but not sticky dough. Halve the dough, keeping half of it under an inverted bowl, roll out the other half on a heavily floured surface into a 12- by 10- inch rectangle, and cut it with a pastry wheel into 2-inch squares. Transfer the squares to a lightly floured baking sheet and roll out and cut the remaining dough in the same manner.

Discard the fat from the stock, return the stock to the kettle, cleaned, and bring it to a boil with the chicken, the carrots, the celery, the onion, the potatoes, peeled and sliced thin, and salt and pepper to taste. Add the noodle squares, a few at a time, stirring gently, simmer the mixture, covered, for 20 to 30 minutes, or until the vegetables and noodles are tender, and stir in the parsley. Serves 6 to 8.

the mid-atlantic entrées

the mid-atlantic side dishes

APPLE AND SPINACH SALAD

- 1 pound spinach, trimmed, washed well, and patted dry
- 2 large crisp red apples (about 1 pound), cored and diced
- 1/2 cup thinly sliced red onion
- 1/2 cup toasted chopped walnuts
- 2 tablespoons fresh lemon juice
- 1 tablespoon Dijon-style mustard
- 1/2 teaspoon sugar
- 2/3 cup olive oil

In a large salad bowl combine the spinach, the apples, the onion, and the walnuts. In a small bowl combine the lemon juice, the mustard, and the sugar, add the oil in a stream, whisking, and whisk the dressing until it is combined well. Whisk in salt and pepper to taste and toss the salad with the dressing. **Serves 6.**

SHREDDED BRUSSELS SPROUTS WITH CHESTNUTS AND BROWN BUTTER

- 1 tablespoon vegetable oil
- 1/2 stick (1/4 cup) unsalted butter
- 2 pints Brussels sprouts, trimmed, halved lengthwise, and sliced thin crosswise
- 1/2 cup (about 5) vacuum-packed whole chestnuts (available at specialty foods shops), chopped
- fresh lemon juice to taste if desired

In a large heavy skillet heat the oil and 1 tablespoon of the butter over moderately high heat until the foam subsides and in the fat sauté the Brussels sprouts with salt and pepper to taste, stirring occasionally, for 1 to 2 minutes, or until they are crisp-tender and golden. Transfer the Brussels sprouts to a shallow dish and sprinkle them with the chestnuts. In the skillet heat the remaining 3 tablespoons butter over moderately high heat, swirling the skillet occasionally, until the foam subsides and the butter is nut-brown and pour it and the lemon juice over the vegetables. **Serves 4 to 6.**

BREAD-AND-BUTTER PICKLES

- 6 Kirby cucumbers, sliced thin
- 2 onions, sliced thin
- 1 small red bell pepper, grated
- 2 tablespoons salt
- 1 1/4 cups cider vinegar
- 1/2 cup granulated sugar
- 1/2 cup firmly packed light brown sugar
- 2 teaspoons mustard seeds
- 1/2 teaspoon celery seeds
- 1/2 teaspoon ground turmeric
- 1/4 teaspoon ground cloves

In a large bowl combine the cucumbers, the onions, the bell pepper, and the salt and let the mixture stand, covered, for 3 hours.

In a stainless-steel or enameled saucepan combine the vinegar, the sugars, the mustard seeds, the celery seeds, the turmeric, and the cloves, bring the liquid to a boil, and cook the mixture over moderate heat for 5 minutes. Add the cucumber mixture, drained, rinsed, and patted dry, bring the mixture to a boil, and transfer it to a sterilized 1-pint Mason-type jar (procedure follows), filling the jar to within ½ inch of the top. Seal the jar with the lid. **Makes about 1 pint.**

to sterilize jars for pickling and preserving

Wash the jars in hot suds and rinse them in scalding water. Put the jars in a kettle and cover them with hot water. Bring the water to a boil, covered, and boil the jars for 15 minutes from the time that steam emerges from the kettle. Turn off the heat and let the jars stand in the hot water. Just before they are to be filled invert the jars onto a kitchen towel to dry. The jars should be filled while they are still hot. Sterilize the jar lids for 5 minutes, or according to the manufacturer's instructions, and keep them in the hot water until sealing the jars.

KAILKENNY
Kale and Mashed Potatoes

- 1 pound kale, stemmed and washed well
- 1 1/2 cups minced onion
- 1/2 stick (1/4 cup) unsalted butter
- 2 pounds russet (baking) potatoes
- 1/4 cup scalded milk if desired

In a kettle of boiling salted water cook the kale over moderately high heat for 5 minutes, or until it is tender. Reserve 1/2 cup of the cooking liquid, drain the kale in a colander, squeezing out the excess liquid, and chop it coarse. In a large skillet cook the onion in the butter over moderate heat, stirring, until it is softened. Add the kale and salt and pepper to taste and cook the mixture over low heat, stirring, for 1 minute.

In a large saucepan combine the potatoes, peeled and quartered, and enough cold water to cover them by 2 inches, bring the water to a boil, and simmer the potatoes, covered partially, for 15 to 20 minutes, or until they are tender. Drain the potatoes, force them while they are still warm through a food mill or ricer into the saucepan, and beat in the reserved kale cooking liquid, the scalded milk, and the kale mixture. Season the Kailkenny with salt and pepper. Serves 8.

SWEET-AND-SOUR BEETS WITH CARAWAY

- 2 pounds small beets, scrubbed and trimmed, leaving 2 inches of the stem ends intact
- 1/3 cup cider vinegar
- 2 teaspoons sugar
- 1/2 teaspoon dry mustard
- 1/2 teaspoon caraway seeds
- 2 tablespoons unsalted butter, cut into pieces

In a large saucepan combine the beets and enough cold water to cover them by 3 inches, bring the water to a boil, and simmer the beets, covered, for 15 to 35 minutes (depending on their size), or until they are tender. Drain the beets, slip off the skins and stems, and cut the beets into ¼-inch-thick slices.

In a small saucepan combine the vinegar, the sugar, the mustard, and the caraway seeds and boil the mixture until it is reduced to about 3 tablespoons. Add the butter and bring the sauce to a boil. In a serving dish toss the beets with the sauce and salt and pepper to taste. Serves 4.

BRAISED ESCAROLE IN TOMATO SAUCE

- 1 cup sliced onion
- 2 garlic cloves, minced
- 1/4 cup olive oil
- 2 pounds escarole, washed, trimmed, and chopped coarse
- 1 14 1/2- to 16-ounce can whole tomatoes, drained and chopped
- 1/2 teaspoon dried oregano, crumbled
- 1/2 teaspoon dried basil, crumbled
  dried hot red pepper flakes to taste
- 2 teaspoons balsamic vinegar, or to taste

In a large deep skillet or kettle cook the onion and the garlic in the oil over moderate heat, stirring, until the garlic is pale golden. Add the escarole, the tomatoes, the oregano, the basil, the red pepper flakes, and salt to taste, simmer the mixture, stirring, for 10 minutes, or until the escarole is tender, and stir in the vinegar. Serves 6 to 8.

The Flatiron Building, New York City

the mid-atlantic desserts

STRAWBERRY ICE-CREAM SODAS

- 1 1/2 cups milk
- 1 1/2 cups strawberry syrup (recipe follows)
- 1 quart strawberry ice cream (recipe follows)
- chilled seltzer to taste
- whipped cream for garnish

In each of 6 ice-cream soda glasses combine ¼ cup of the milk and ¼ cup of the syrup, add 2 or 3 scoops of the ice cream to each glass, and fill the glasses with the seltzer. Garnish the sodas with the whipped cream. **Serves 6.**

STRAWBERRY SYRUP

- 1 pound (about 1 1/4 pints) strawberries, hulled and sliced
- 1/2 cup sugar

In a food processor or blender purée the strawberries in batches, transfer the purée to a stainless-steel or enameled saucepan, and stir in the sugar and ½ cup water. Bring the mixture to a boil over moderate heat, stirring, and simmer it for 3 minutes. Force the mixture through a fine sieve into a bowl and chill it, covered, for at least 3 hours. **Makes 1 1/2 cups.**

STRAWBERRY ICE CREAM

- 1 pound (about 1 1/4 pints) strawberries, hulled and sliced
- 1 1/2 cups sugar
- 1 tablespoon fresh lemon juice
- 1 1/2 cups heavy cream
- 1 1/2 cups milk
- 4 large egg yolks
- 1 teaspoon vanilla, or to taste

In a food processor or blender purée the strawberries in batches and transfer the purée to a bowl. Stir in ½ cup of the sugar and the lemon juice and chill the mixture, covered, for 2 hours.

In a heavy saucepan combine the cream, the milk, and the remaining 1 cup sugar and scald the mixture over moderate heat, stirring. In a bowl beat the egg yolks until they are light and thick and pour in the milk mixture through a fine sieve in a stream, stirring. Transfer the custard to the pan and cook it over moderately low heat, stirring, until it coats the spoon. Transfer the custard to a metal bowl set in a bowl of ice and cold water, stir in the vanilla, and let the custard cool, covered with a buttered round of wax paper. Chill the custard for 2 hours, stir in the strawberry mixture, and freeze the mixture in an ice-cream freezer according to the manufacturer's instructions. **Makes 1 quart.**

BLUEBERRY CREAM CHEESE PIE

For the shell

- 1 1/2 cups fine graham cracker crumbs
- 1/2 cup finely ground walnuts
- 1/4 cup confectioners' sugar, sifted
- 1 stick (1/2 cup) unsalted butter, melted
- 1/2 teaspoon cinnamon

For the filling

- 8 ounces cream cheese, softened
- 1 tablespoon sour cream
- 2 tablespoons fresh lemon juice
- 1 1/2 tablespoons freshly grated lemon zest
- 3/4 cup confectioners' sugar, sifted
- 3 large eggs, beaten lightly

For the topping

- 1/4 cup granulated sugar
- 1 tablespoon cornstarch
- 2 tablespoons fresh lemon juice
- 2 cups blueberries, picked over

Preheat the oven to 350° F.

Make the shell: In a bowl combine well the graham cracker crumbs, the walnuts, the confectioners' sugar, the butter, and the cinnamon and press the mixture onto the bottom and up the side of a 9-inch pie plate.

Make the filling: In a bowl with an electric mixer beat the cream cheese with the sour cream, the lemon juice, and the zest until the mixture is smooth, beat in the confectioners' sugar, a pinch of salt, and the eggs, and beat the filling for 3 minutes, or until it is smooth and light.

Pour the filling into the shell and smooth the top. Bake the pie in the middle of the oven for 35 to 40 minutes, or until it is just set, and let it cool on a rack for 1 hour.

Make the topping: In a stainless-steel or enameled saucepan combine the sugar, the cornstarch, a pinch of salt, ½ cup water, the lemon juice, and the blueberries, bring the mixture to a simmer, stirring, and simmer it, stirring, for 3 minutes, or until the syrup is clear and thick. Let the topping cool for 10 minutes.

Spread the topping evenly over the pie.

MORAVIAN SUGAR COFFEECAKE

- 3/4 pound russet (baking) potatoes
- 1/4 cup plus 1 teaspoon granulated sugar
- 7 tablespoons unsalted butter, plus additional melted butter for brushing the dough
- 3 tablespoons lard
- 1/2 teaspoon salt
- 1 tablespoon active dry yeast
- 1 large egg, beaten lightly
- 3 1/2 cups unbleached flour, plus additional if necessary
- 1 1/2 tablespoons cinnamon
- 1 cup firmly packed light brown sugar
- 1/4 cup heavy cream

In a saucepan combine the potatoes, peeled and cubed, and 1 cup cold water and bring the water to a boil. Cook the potatoes, covered, over moderate heat for 15 minutes, or until they are tender, reserve 1 cup of the cooking water, and drain the potatoes. Force the potatoes through a food mill or ricer into a large bowl (there should be about 1 cup purée), add ½ cup of the reserved potato water, ¼ cup of the granulated sugar, 3 tablespoons of the butter, the lard, and the salt, and combine the mixture well. In a small bowl proof the yeast in 1/4 cup of the reserved lukewarm potato water with the remaining 1 teaspoon granulated sugar for 15 minutes, or until it is foamy. Add the yeast mixture and the egg to the potato mixture and combine the mixture well. Stir in 3½ cups of the flour, about 1 cup at a time, and combine the mixture well.

Transfer the dough to a floured surface and knead it, incorporating the additional flour if necessary to keep it from sticking, for 10 minutes, or until it is smooth and elastic. Form the dough into a ball, transfer it to a buttered bowl, and turn it to coat it with the butter. Let the dough rise, covered, in a warm place for 1½ hours, or until it is double in bulk. Punch down the dough, transfer it to a floured surface, and let it rest for 10 minutes. Roll out the dough ½ inch thick and fit it into a 15- by 10-inch jelly-roll pan. Brush the dough lightly with the melted butter and let it rise, covered, in a warm place for 30 minutes, or until it is puffy.

Preheat the oven to 400° F.

Punch indentations in the dough with your thumb and fill them with the remaining 4 tablespoons butter, cut into bits. Sprinkle the dough with the cinnamon and the brown sugar and drizzle it with the heavy cream. Bake the cake in the middle of the oven for 20 minutes, or until it is browned and bubbly. Let the cake cool for 5 minutes and cut it into squares.

MOCHA CREAM CHOCOLATE ROLL WITH MOCHA SAUCE

For the filling
- 1 1/2 cups well-chilled heavy cream
- 3 tablespoons instant espresso powder
- 1/4 cup sugar
- 1 1/2 teaspoons vanilla
- 1/4 cup shaved bittersweet or semisweet chocolate

For the chocolate roll
- 1/2 cup unsweetened cocoa powder
- 2 tablespoons cornstarch
- 2 tablespoons all-purpose flour
- 5 large eggs, separated
- 1/2 cup plus 3 tablespoons sugar
- 1/8 teaspoon salt
- 1/8 teaspoon cream of tartar

mocha sauce (recipe follows) as an accompaniment

Make the filling: In a chilled bowl with an electric mixer beat the cream with the espresso powder, the sugar, and the vanilla until it holds stiff peaks and stir in the shaved chocolate. Transfer the cream to a fine sieve set over a bowl and chill it, its surface covered with plastic wrap, for 2 hours.

Preheat the oven to 400° F. Line a lightly greased 15½- by 10½-inch jelly-roll pan with foil, leaving a 1-inch overhang on the short sides, and grease the foil. Line the foil with wax paper, grease the paper, and flour it lightly, shaking out the excess.

Make the chocolate roll: Into a bowl sift together the cocoa, the cornstarch, and the flour and in a large bowl with an electric mixer beat the egg yolks and ½ cup of the sugar for 5 minutes, or until the mixture is thick and pale and ribbons when the beater is lifted. In another bowl with cleaned beaters beat the egg whites with the salt until they are frothy, add the cream of tartar, and beat the whites until they hold soft peaks. Add the remaining 3 tablespoons sugar, a little at a time, and beat the whites until they barely hold stiff peaks. Fold one fourth of the whites into the yolk mixture, spoon the yolk mixture onto the remaining whites, and sift the cocoa mixture over the yolk mixture. Fold the mixture together gently but thoroughly, pour the batter into the prepared pan, and spread it evenly with a metal spatula. Bake the cake in the middle of the oven for 7 to 9 minutes, or until it is puffed and a tester comes out clean. Invert a sheet of wax paper and a baking sheet over the cake and invert the cake onto it. Peel off the top piece of wax paper carefully and fit another piece of wax paper over the cake, leaving a 1-inch overhang. Invert the cake (do not remove the wax paper) onto a rack, peel off the top piece of wax paper carefully, and let it cool.

Spread the cream filling over the cake, leaving a ¼-inch border all around, and with a long side facing you and using the wax paper as an aid, roll up the cake jelly-roll fashion, keeping it wrapped in the wax paper. (The cake may crack but it will hold together.) Chill the cake, wrapped in the wax paper, on the baking sheet for at least 4 hours or overnight.

Remove the wax paper from the cake and transfer the cake to a work surface. Trim the ends on the diagonal if desired, transfer the cake to a platter, and serve it with the mocha sauce.

BRANDY ALEXANDER MOUSSES

- 1 teaspoon unflavored gelatin
- 1/4 cup brandy
- 1/4 cup crème de cacoa
- 1/4 teaspoon freshly grated nutmeg
- 3 large egg yolks
- 1/2 cup sugar
- 1 cup well-chilled heavy cream
- 2 ounces fine-quality bittersweet (not unsweetened) chocolate, shaved with a vegetable peeler, for garnish

In a small heavy saucepan sprinkle the gelatin over the brandy and let it soften for 1 minute. Stir in the crème de cacoa, the nutmeg, the egg yolks, and the sugar, cook the mixture over moderately low heat, whisking constantly, until it is thickened slightly and a candy thermometer registers 160° F., and transfer it to a metal bowl set in a larger bowl of ice and cold water. Let the mixture chill, whisking occasionally, until it is cold and has the consistency of raw egg white, but do no let it set.

In a bowl beat the cream until it just holds stiff peaks and fold it into the custard mixture. Spoon the mousse into dessert glasses and chill it, covered loosely with plastic wrap, for at least 1 hour and up to 24 hours. Garnish the desserts with the chocolate. Serves 6.

MOCHA SAUCE

- 1/3 cup heavy cream
- 1 tablespoon instant espresso powder dissolved in 1/3 cup boiling water
- 1/3 cup firmly packed dark brown sugar
- 4 ounces semisweet chocolate, chopped
- 2 tablespoons unsalted butter
- 1/8 teaspoon salt
- 1 teaspoon vanilla

In a heavy saucepan heat the cream, the espresso, and the sugar over moderately low heat, stirring, until the sugar is dissolved. Add the chocolate, the butter, and the salt and cook the mixture, stirring, until it is smooth, but do not let it boil. Remove the pan from the heat, stir in the vanilla, and transfer the sauce to a bowl. *The sauce keeps, covered and chilled, for 2 weeks.* Makes about 1 1/3 cups.

On this page, a shady spot for a lazy afternoon on Key West and right, local color from a jacaranda tree in Fort Lauderdale, both in Florida

West Virginia, Virginia, Kentucky, Tennessee, North Carolina,

South Carolina, Arkansas, Louisiana, Mississippi, Alabama, Georgia, Florida

the south

the south

The South is both colorful and bountiful. Here mild winters turn into glorious springs with fairy-tale-like flowering gardens of azaleas and dogwoods, and hot summers are sweetened with the perfumes of gardenias and magnolias. Warm weather, adequate rainfall, and fertile land make this region a farmer's dream. Bordered on the east by the Atlantic and on the south by the Gulf of Mexico, the area is abundant in oysters, crabs, shrimp, and crayfish; from the rivers come catfish, trout, black bass, and bream.

Three distinct groups are responsible for the basics of Southern cooking: the native Algonquian peoples who introduced corn to the region; the British, who arrived in 1607 carrying recipes for pork (and the first pigs), beer, stews, and various desserts; and the slaves from Africa, who brought to the plantation kitchens their love for spices and developed the cooking traditions that evolved into soul food. In fact, it was the slave ships that carried black-eyed peas, okra, collard greens, and watermelons to these shores from Africa, and potatoes, tomatoes, and chilies (and the technique for barbecue) from the West Indies and South America. Later, the French introduced new flavors along the coastal areas from Charleston to Mobile, while the Spanish inspired the culinary tastes of Florida. The remarkable Creole and Cajun cuisines of New Orleans uniquely combine elements of both French and Spanish cooking.

A SOUTHERN COUNTRY SUPPER

SPICY FRIED CHICKEN WINGS

★

BUTTERMILK CORN BREAD

★

TOMATO ASPIC WITH HORSERADISH

★

DILLED SUMMER SQUASH SALAD

★

HERBED TWO-POTATO SALAD

★

OKRA, ONION, AND TOMATO SALAD

★

WATERMELON

★

LATTICE-CRUST PEACH PIE

★

LIMEADE

★

GUENOC ESTATE SELECTION CHARDONNAY 1992

Serves 8 to 12

**Lattice-Crust Peach Pie;
Limeade**

the south
menu

Our Southern Country Supper is a casual menu filled with regional tastes, both mild and spicy. Several of the dishes are easy make-ahead salads that are served chilled. One notable exception is our Herbed Two-Potato Salad that is typically served warm to meld the flavors of the potatoes and the mayonnaise dressing. Southerners love to cook with buttermilk, and both our Spicy Fried Chicken Wings and Buttermilk Corn Bread demonstrate how it is used to tenderize and enhance various foods. And because peaches are the pride of the South, we have included our Lattice-Crust Peach Pie. Buy only yellow or cream-colored peaches; red blush or green fruit will never fully ripen. If serving more than eight people, you may want to make a second pie.

SPICY FRIED CHICKEN WINGS

- 4 pounds chicken wings, third joint discarded
- 6 cups buttermilk
- 3 cups all-purpose flour
- 2 tablespoons plus 2 teaspoons salt
- 2 tablespoons dried thyme, crumbled
- 4 teaspoons black pepper
- 1 1/2 teaspoons cayenne
- vegetable oil for deep-frying the wings

In a bowl combine the wings with the buttermilk and chill them, covered, for at least 1 hour and up to 8 hours. In another bowl combine well the flour, the salt, the thyme, the black pepper, and the cayenne. Drain the wings in a colander set over a bowl, reserving the buttermilk, and dredge them in the flour mixture. Dip the wings in the reserved buttermilk, letting the excess drip off, and dredge them again in the flour mixture, shaking off the excess. Arrange the wings in a jelly-roll pan lined with wax paper and chill them, uncovered, for 30 minutes.

In a large deep fryer or large deep kettle heat 2 inches of the oil until it registers 375° F. on a deep-fat thermometer and in it fry the wings in batches, without crowding them, turning them, for 5 to 7 minutes, or until they are cooked through and golden. Transfer the wings with tongs to paper towels to drain and fry the remaining wings in the same manner, making sure the oil returns to 375° F. before adding each new batch. Sprinkle the wings with salt to taste and let them stand for 5 minutes. **Serves 8 to 12.**

Photo on page 68

BUTTERMILK CORN BREAD

- 1 1/3 cups yellow cornmeal
- 2/3 cup all-purpose flour
- 1 tablespoon sugar
- 2 teaspoons baking powder
- 1 teaspoon baking soda
- 1 teaspoon salt
- 2 large eggs
- 1 1/2 cups buttermilk
- 1 1/2 cups fresh corn kernels including the pulp scraped from the cobs (cut from about 3 ears)

Preheat the oven to 425° F. Grease a jelly-roll pan, 15½ by 10½ by 1 inch.

Into a bowl sift together the cornmeal, the flour, the sugar, the baking powder, the baking soda, and the salt. In a small bowl beat together the eggs and the buttermilk. To the cornmeal mixture add the buttermilk mixture and the corn, stir the batter until it is just combined, and pour it into the prepared pan, spreading it evenly. Bake the corn bread in the middle of the oven for 8 to 10 minutes, or until a tester comes out clean.

TOMATO ASPIC WITH HORSERADISH

- 2 pounds (exactly) tomatoes, chopped coarse
- 2 tablespoons fresh lemon juice
- 1/2 teaspoon sugar
- 2 envelopes (2 tablespoons) unflavored gelatin
- 1 1/2 teaspoons Tabasco
- 1 1/2 teaspoons Worcestershire sauce
- 1/4 cup drained bottled horseradish
- 1 cup sour cream combined with 3 tablespoons minced chives as an accompaniment if desired

In a large saucepan combine the tomatoes, the lemon juice, and the sugar, bring the mixture to a boil, and simmer it, covered, stirring occasionally, for 25 minutes. In a large metal bowl sprinkle the gelatin over ⅓ cup cold water and let it soften for 5 minutes. Force the hot tomato mixture through the medium disk of a food mill into the bowl and stir in the Tabasco, the Worcestershire sauce, the horseradish, and salt to taste, stirring until the gelatin is dissolved. Set the bowl in another bowl of ice and cold water and stir the mixture until it is the consistency of raw egg whites. Pour the mixture into a lightly oiled 4-cup ring mold and chill it, covered, for at least 3 hours or overnight. Serve the aspic with the sour cream mixture. **Serves 8 to 12.**

DILLED SUMMER SQUASH SALAD

- 1 1/2 pounds zucchini, cut into paper-thin slices
- 1 1/2 pounds yellow summer squash, cut into paper-thin slices
- 1 tablespoon salt
- 2/3 cup distilled white vinegar
- 1 1/2 teaspoons sugar
- 2 tablespoons snipped fresh dill

In a colander toss the zucchini and the yellow squash with the salt and let them drain for 1 hour. Refresh the squash under running cold water and drain it well. In a large ceramic or glass bowl combine the vinegar and the sugar, stirring until the sugar is dissolved, add the squash and the dill, and combine the mixture well. Chill the salad, covered, for at least 2 hours or overnight. Stir the salad and transfer it to a salad bowl. **Serves 8 to 12.**

HERBED TWO-POTATO SALAD

- 3 pounds sweet potatoes or yams, peeled and cut into 1/2-inch dice
- 3 pounds boiling potatoes, peeled, cut into 1/2-inch dice, and reserved in a bowl of cold water
- 2 cups mayonnaise
- 4 tablespoons fresh lemon juice
- 4 tablespoons honey
- 2/3 cup minced scallion
- 1/2 cup minced fresh parsley leaves
- 6 tablespoons minced fresh mint leaves

In a steamer set over boiling water steam the sweet potatoes or the yams for 6 to 8 minutes, or until they are just tender, and transfer them to a large bowl. In the steamer steam the boiling potatoes, drained, for 6 to 8 minutes, or until they are just tender, and transfer them to the bowl. In a small bowl whisk together the mayonnaise, the lemon juice, the honey, the scallion, the parsley, the mint, and salt and pepper to taste, add the dressing to the potatoes, and toss the salad until it is combined well. **Serves 8 to 12.**

OKRA, ONION, AND TOMATO SALAD

- 1 1/2 pounds small okra
- 1/2 cup minced red onion
- 1/3 cup distilled white vinegar
- 2 garlic cloves, minced
- 1 cup vegetable or olive oil
- 2 large tomatoes, seeded and chopped

In a large saucepan of boiling salted water boil the okra for 3 to 5 minutes, or until it is tender, drain it, and refresh it in a bowl of ice and cold water. Drain the okra well, transfer it to a shallow dish large enough to hold it in one layer, and add the onion. In a small bowl whisk together the vinegar, the garlic, and salt and pepper to taste, add the oil in a stream, whisking, and whisk the dressing until it is emulsified. Pour the dressing over the okra mixture, stir the mixture carefully until it is combined well, and chill the salad, covered, for 1 hour. Stir the tomatoes gently into the salad. **Serves 8 to 12.**

LATTICE-CRUST PEACH PIE

For the dough
- 3 cups all-purpose flour
- 3/4 teaspoon salt
- 1 cup cold lard, cut into bits
- about 1 tablespoon fresh lemon juice

For the filling
- 3 pounds peaches, peeled and sliced
- 1/4 cup fresh lemon juice, or to taste
- 5 tablespoons all-purpose flour
- 3/4 cup sugar
- 1/4 teaspoon salt
- a pinch of mace

- 2 tablespoons cold unsalted butter, cut into bits
- an egg wash made by beating 1 large egg yolk with 1 tablespoon water
- 1/4 cup apricot preserves

Make the dough: In a bowl combine the flour and the salt, add the lard, and blend the mixture until it resembles coarse meal. Stir in the lemon juice and ½ cup cold water, or enough to just form a dough, and knead the dough lightly to distribute the lard. Divide the dough into 2 balls, one slightly larger than the other, and chill it, wrapped in wax paper, for 30 minutes.

Make the filling: In a large bowl toss the peaches with the lemon juice. In a small bowl combine well the flour, the sugar, the salt, and the mace, add the mixture to the peaches, and toss the mixture until it is combined well.

Preheat the oven to 400° F. Line a baking sheet with foil.

Roll out the larger ball of dough ⅛-inch thick on a lightly floured surface, fit it into a 10-inch pie pan, and trim the edge, leaving a ½-inch overhang. Chill the shell while cutting the dough for the lattice crust. Roll out the other ball of dough ⅛-inch thick and with a knife or a fluted pastry wheel cut out ¾-inch strips. Transfer the strips to a baking sheet and chill them for 5 minutes, or until they are just firm enough to work with. (If the strips get too cold, they will be brittle and break.)

Spoon the filling into the shell, mounding it slightly in the center, dot it with the butter, and arrange the lattice strips on top. Trim the ends of the strips flush with the overhang of the shell and brush some of the egg wash between the ends of the strips and the overhang, pressing the dough together. Turn the edges of the dough under, pressing them against the inside of the pan, and brush the dough with some of the remaining egg wash. Bake the pie on the prepared baking sheet in the lower third of the oven for 25 minutes.

Reduce the oven temperature to 350° F. and bake the pie for 25 to 30 minutes more, or until the crust is golden brown and the juices are bubbling. Let the pie cool on a rack for 30 minutes and brush the filling with the preserves, heated and strained though a sieve. Serve the pie at room temperature.

Photo on page 63

LIMEADE

- 4 cups strained fresh lime juice
- 1 1/2 to 2 cups sugar

For the garnish
- 4 limes, cut into paper-thin slices
- mint sprigs
- whole strawberries

In a large bowl combine the lime juice, 1½ cups of the sugar, and 10 cups cold water, stir the mixture until the sugar is dissolved, and add more sugar if desired. *The limeade may be made up to 1 day in advance and kept covered and chilled.* To serve, transfer the limeade to two pitchers, stir about 2 cups ice cubes into each pitcher, and garnish the limeade with the lime slices, the mint sprigs, and the strawberries. **Makes about 16 cups.**

Photo on page 63

the south
starters

Spicy Fried Chicken Wings (page 64);
Green Onion Pancakes (page 77);
and Delta Dogs

DELTA DOGS
Spicy Deep-Fried Cornmeal Fritters

- 1 cup grated onion
- 1 cup grated sharp Cheddar
- 2 tablespoons chopped red or green bell pepper
- 1 cup cornmeal, plus additional if necessary
- 1 teaspoon cayenne
- 1 teaspoon black pepper
- 3/4 teaspoon salt
- vegetable shortening, vegetable oil, or lard for deep-frying the fritters

In a bowl toss together well the onion, the Cheddar, the bell pepper, 1 cup of the cornmeal, the cayenne, the black pepper, and the salt, stir in ¾ cup boiling water, and combine the batter well. In a deep fryer or large deep kettle heat 2 inches of the shortening, oil, or lard over moderately high heat until it registers 350° F. on a deep-fat thermometer. Test the batter by frying a heaping teaspoon of it in the fat for 2 to 3 minutes, or until it is golden brown. If the fritter disintegrates in the fat stir in some of the additional cornmeal. Fry heaping teaspoons of the batter in batches in the hot fat, making sure the fat returns to 375° F. before adding each new batch, for 2 minutes, or until the Delta dogs are golden brown, transferring them as they are cooked to brown paper or paper towels to drain. Serve the Delta dogs immediately. Makes about 28 Delta dogs.

FRIED OYSTERS WITH TARTAR SAUCE

For the tartar sauce
- 1 cup mayonnaise
- 1 teaspoon Dijon-style mustard
- 3 tablespoons minced scallion
- 3 tablespoons finely chopped sweet pickle
- 1 hard-boiled large egg, forced through a coarse sieve
- 1 1/2 tablespoons fresh lemon juice, or to taste

- 1 cup all-purpose flour
- 1/2 teaspoon cayenne
- 3 large eggs
- 3 tablespoons heavy cream
- 1 1/3 cups fine fresh bread crumbs
- 2/3 cup yellow cornmeal
- vegetable oil for deep-frying the oysters
- 36 shucked oysters, rinsed and drained well

Make the tartar sauce: In a bowl stir together the mayonnaise, the mustard, the scallion, the pickle, the egg, the lemon juice, and salt and pepper to taste and chill the sauce, covered.

Preheat the oven to 250° F. Line a baking sheet with paper towels.

In a shallow bowl stir together the flour, the cayenne, and salt and black pepper to taste. In a bowl whisk together the eggs and the cream and in another bowl stir together well the bread crumbs and the cornmeal. In a deep fryer or large deep kettle heat 1½ inches of the oil over moderately high heat until it registers 375° F. on a deep-fat thermometer. Working in batches of 6, dredge the oysters quickly in the flour mixture, shaking off the excess, dip them in the egg mixture, and roll them in the bread-crumb mixture, coating them completely. Fry the oysters in batches in the oil, making sure the oil returns to 375° F. before adding the next batch, for 1 to 2 minutes, or until they are golden and crisp, transferring them as they are fried to the prepared baking sheet, and keep them warm in the oven. Serve the oysters with the tartar sauce. Serves 6.

SHRIMP IN DILLED CUCUMBER SAUCE

- 1/2 cup peeled, seeded, and chopped cucumber, squeezed lightly in a kitchen towel, plus slices for garnish
- 3 tablespoons finely chopped red onion
- 1/4 cup sour cream
- 3 tablespoons chopped fresh dill, plus sprigs for garnish
- 2 teaspoons fresh lemon juice, or to taste
- 2 teaspoons Dijon-style mustard
- 1/8 to 1/4 teaspoon Tabasco
- 1 1/2 pounds small shrimp, shelled, cooked in boiling salted water for 1 to 2 minutes, drained, and cooled
- soft-leafed lettuce leaves for lining the plates

In a bowl combine the chopped cucumber, the onion, the sour cream, the chopped dill, the lemon juice, the mustard, the Tabasco, and salt to taste, add the shrimp, and toss the mixture. Serve the mixture on chilled salad plates lined with the lettuce and garnish it with the cucumber slices and the dill sprigs. **Serves 4**.

CHILLED CURRIED CARROT AND POTATO SOUP

- 1 1/2 cups chopped leek including 1 inch of the green part, washed well and drained
- 1/2 cup chopped onion
- 2 tablespoons unsalted butter
- 1 1/2 tablespoons curry powder
- 1 1/2 pounds carrots, sliced thin (about 4 cups), plus finely grated blanched carrot for garnish
- 1 pound boiling potatoes
- 1 teaspoon salt
- 2 1/2 cups chicken broth
- 1 cup milk
- 1 cup sour cream

In a heavy kettle cook the leek and the onion in the butter over moderately low heat, stirring, until the vegetables are softened. Stir in the curry powder and cook the mixture, stirring, for 2 minutes. Add the sliced carrots, the potatoes, peeled and cut into ½-inch pieces, the salt, the broth, and 2 cups water, bring the liquid to a boil, and simmer the mixture, covered, for 35 to 40 minutes, or until the potatoes and carrots are very soft. Force the mixture through a food mill fitted with the fine disk into a bowl and force the purée through a fine sieve into another bowl. Whisk in the milk, the sour cream, and salt and pepper to taste and chill the soup, covered, for at least 3 hours or overnight. Stir the soup before serving and garnish it with the grated carrot. **Makes about 8 cups, serving 6 to 8**.

ISLAND-STYLE SALT COD FRITTERS

- 1/2 pound thick cut salt cod
- 2 large eggs
- 1 cup milk
- 1 cup all-purpose flour
- 1/2 teaspoon baking powder
- 1/2 cup minced scallion
- 1 1/2 tablespoons minced peeled fresh gingerroot
- 2 teaspoons black pepper
- 1 1/2 teaspoons dried thyme, crumbled
- 1 cup steamed rice (recipe follows)
- vegetable oil for frying the fritters

In a ceramic or glass bowl let the salt cod soak in cold water to cover, changing the water several times, for 24 hours and drain it. In a kettle poach the cod in simmering water to cover for 25 minutes, or until it flakes easily when tested with a fork, drain it in a colander, and refresh it under cold water. Discard any skin and bones and break the cod into pieces. In a food processor purée the cod until it is smooth, add the eggs, the milk, the flour, and the baking powder, and blend the mixture until it is smooth. Transfer the mixture to a bowl, stir in the scallion, the gingerroot, the pepper, the thyme, and the rice, and if necessary add ¼ to ½ cup water to thin the batter to the consistency of a thick sauce.

Preheat the oven to 200° F. Line two baking sheets with paper towels.

In a heavy skillet heat enough of the oil to measure ¼ inch over moderately high heat until it registers 375° F. on a deep-fat thermometer and in it fry heaping tablespoons of the batter in batches, making sure the oil returns to 375° F. before adding each new batch, for 1 minute and 30 seconds on each side, or until the fritters are golden, transferring them as they are fried with a slotted spatula to the prepared baking sheets. (The fritters will be ¼ inch thick.)

Keep the fritters warm in the oven and serve them as an hors d'oeuvre. **Makes about 40 fritters.**

STEAMED RICE

- 1 tablespoon salt
- 2 cups long-grain rice

In a large saucepan bring 5 quarts water to a boil with the salt. Sprinkle in the rice, stirring until the water returns to a boil, and boil it for 10 minutes. Drain the rice in a large colander and rinse it. Set the colander over another large saucepan of boiling water and steam the rice, covered with a kitchen towel and the lid, for 15 minutes, or until it is fluffy and dry. **Makes about 6 cups.**

entrées
the south

Virginia's Hunt Country

PORK, RICE, AND TOMATO CASSEROLE

- 3 pounds boneless fresh pork butt, cut into 1 1/2-inch cubes
- 1/4 cup olive oil
- 2 large onions, sliced
- 1/2 cup dry white wine or dry vermouth
- 2 cups beef broth
- 1 cup drained and chopped canned tomatoes
- 3 garlic cloves, minced
- 1 bay leaf
- 1/2 teaspoon dried thyme, crumbled
- 1/2 teaspoon dried basil, crumbled
- 1/2 teaspoon ground cumin
- 1/4 teaspoon turmeric
- 1 tablespoon tomato paste
- 1 1/2 cups long-grain rice (not converted)
- 1/2 cup freshly grated Parmesan
- 6 large pimiento-stuffed olives, quartered
- 2 tablespoons minced fresh parsley leaves
- 1 tablespoon drained bottled capers

Preheat the oven to 350° F.

In a large flameproof casserole brown the pork, patted dry and seasoned with salt and pepper, in 2 tablespoons of the oil over moderately high heat and transfer it to a bowl. Add the onions to the casserole and cook them over moderate heat, stirring occasionally, until they are golden. Add the wine or the vermouth and cook the mixture over moderately high heat until the liquid is reduced by half. Add the pork, the broth, the tomatoes, the garlic, the bay leaf, the thyme, the basil, the cumin, the turmeric, and the tomato paste, bring the liquid to a boil, and braise the pork, covered, in the oven for 1½ hours. In a skillet cook the rice in the remaining 2 tablespoons oil over moderate heat, stirring, until it is transparent, stir it into the pork mixture, and braise the mixture, covered, in the oven for 25 to 30 minutes, or until the liquid is absorbed. Stir in the Parmesan, the olives, the parsley, the capers, and salt and pepper to taste and discard the bay leaf. Serves 8.

BARBECUE OXTAILS AND RED BEANS

- 6 pounds oxtails, trimmed
- all-purpose flour seasoned with salt and pepper for dredging the oxtails
- 6 tablespoons vegetable oil
- 3 cups finely chopped onion
- 3 large garlic cloves, minced
- 1 tablespoon grated peeled fresh gingerroot
- 2/3 cup firmly packed light brown sugar
- 1 1/2 cups ketchup
- 3 tablespoons Dijon-style mustard
- 1 cup cider vinegar
- 1/4 cup Worcestershire sauce
- 1/4 cup fresh lemon juice
- Tabasco to taste
- cayenne to taste
- 1 28-ounce can Italian tomatoes, drained, reserving the juice, and chopped
- 1 pound dried small red chili beans, soaked in enough cold water to cover them by 2 inches overnight, or quick-soaked (procedure follows), and drained
- chopped scallion greens for garnish

Dredge the oxtails in the flour, shaking off the excess. In a heavy kettle heat 4 tablespoons of the oil over moderately high heat until it is hot but not smoking and in it brown the oxtails in batches, transferring them with a slotted spoon as they are browned to a plate. To the kettle add the remaining 2 tablespoons oil, in it cook the onion, the garlic, and the gingerroot over moderately low heat, stirring, until the onion is softened, and stir in the sugar, the ketchup, the mustard, the vinegar, the Worcestershire sauce, the lemon juice, the Tabasco, the cayenne, the tomatoes with the reserved juice, and salt and black pepper to taste. Simmer the sauce, stirring occasionally, for 5 minutes, add the oxtails, and simmer the mixture, covered, stirring occasionally, for 2½ hours.

While the oxtails are cooking, in a large saucepan combine the beans with enough cold water to cover them by 2 inches, bring the water to a boil, and simmer the beans, covered, for 1 hour, or until they are tender. Drain the beans well and stir them into the oxtail mixture. Simmer the mixture, uncovered, stirring occasionally, for 30 minutes to 1 hour, or until the meat is very tender, and serve it sprinkled with the scallion greens. **Serves 6 to 8.**

to quick-soak dried beans

1 pound dried beans, picked over

In a colander rinse the beans under cold water and discard any discolored ones. In a kettle combine the beans with enough cold water to cover them by 2 inches, bring the water to a boil, and boil the beans for 2 minutes. Remove the kettle from the heat and let the beans soak, covered, for 1 hour.

CATFISH PO' BOYS

For the sauce
- 1 cup mayonnaise
- 3 tablespoons sweet pickle relish
- 2 tablespoons drained bottled capers, chopped fine
- 2 tablespoons finely chopped onion
- 1 tablespoon fresh lemon juice, or to taste
- 1/8 teaspoon cayenne, or to taste

- all-purpose flour seasoned with salt and pepper for dredging the fish
- 4 1/2-pound catfish fillets, halved crosswise
- vegetable oil for deep-frying the fish
- 8 4-inch pieces of French or Italian bread, halved horizontally (about 3 loaves)
- 3 tomatoes, sliced thin
- 2 cups shredded iceberg lettuce

Make the sauce: In a bowl stir together the mayonnaise, the relish, the capers, the onion, the lemon juice, the cayenne, and salt to taste and chill the sauce, covered.

Have the flour ready in a shallow dish. Dredge each catfish fillet in the flour, shaking off the excess, and transfer the fish to a wax paper-lined baking sheet. While coating the fish, in a kettle heat 1 inch of the oil until it registers 375° F. on a deep-fat thermometer. Fry the fish in batches in the oil for 2 to 4 minutes on each side, or until it is cooked through and golden, transferring it as it is fried with a slotted spatula to paper towels to drain.

Spread the bread halves with the sauce and top the bottom halves with the tomatoes, the fish, the lettuce, and the top halves. **Serves 8.**

BULGUR JAMBALAYA WITH HAM, CLAMS, AND VEGETABLES

- 1 large onion, chopped
- 3 tablespoons lard or vegetable oil
- 2 ribs of celery, chopped
- 1 green bell pepper, chopped
- 4 garlic cloves, minced
- 1/4 teaspoon ground allspice
- 1/4 teaspoon cayenne, or to taste
- 1/8 teaspoon ground cloves
- about 1 1/2 cups bottled clam juice
- 1 6 1/2-ounce can minced clams, drained, reserving the liquid in a measuring cup
- 1 17-ounce can Italian whole tomatoes, drained and chopped
- 1 10-ounce package frozen okra, thawed, drained, and cut crosswise into 1/2-inch pieces
- 1 pound smoked ham, cut into 1-inch cubes
- 1 1/2 cups *bulgur* (available at natural foods stores and most supermakets)
- 2 tablespoons minced fresh parsley leaves for garnish

Preheat the oven to 325° F.

In a large heavy stainless-steel or enameled casserole cook the onion in the lard or oil over moderate heat, stirring, until it is softened, add the celery and the bell pepper, and cook the mixture, stirring, for 3 minutes, or until the pepper is softened. Add the garlic and cook the mixture, stirring, for 1 minute. Add the allspice, the cayenne, and the cloves and cook the mixture, stirring, for 15 seconds. Add enough of the bottled clam juice to the reserved clam liquid to measure 2 cups total and add the liquid to the casserole. Add the tomatoes, the okra, the ham, and the clams, bring the liquid to a boil, stirring occasionally, and braise the mixture, covered tightly, in the oven for 45 minutes. Stir in the *bulgur* and salt to taste, bring the liquid to a boil over moderate heat, and braise the jambalaya, covered, in the oven for 15 to 20 minutes, or until the *bulgur* is tender and most of the liquid is absorbed. Transfer the jambalaya to a heated serving dish and garnish the dish with the minced parsley. **Serves 6.**

SPARERIBS WITH BOURBON MARINADE

- 1/3 cup bourbon
- 1/4 cup soy sauce
- 2 tablespoons unsulfured molasses
- 1 large onion, chopped
- 3 tablespoons Dijon-style mustard
- 1 teaspoon Worcestershire sauce
- 4 pounds lean spareribs, trimmed of excess fat

In a shallow ceramic or glass dish combine the bourbon, the soy sauce, the molasses, the onion, the mustard, and the Worcestershire sauce, add the spareribs, turning them to coat them with the marinade, and let them marinate, covered and chilled, turning them occasionally, for at least 6 hours or overnight.

Drain the spareribs, reserving the marinade, and in a saucepan boil the marinade for 5 minutes. Grill the spareribs on an oiled rack set about 4 inches above glowing coals for 15 minutes on each side and continue to grill them, basting them with the marinade, for 5 minutes on each side or until they are crisp on the outside and no longer pink within. Transfer the spareribs to a cutting board, cut them into serving portions, and arrange them on a heated platter. **Serves 4 to 6.**

CHICKEN AND AVOCADO SALAD WITH BACON DRESSING

- 3 cups chicken broth
- 3 whole boneless skinless chicken breasts, halved

For the dressing
- 8 slices of bacon, cut crosswise into 1/2-inch pieces
- 1 large hard-boiled egg yolk
- 2 tablespoons fresh lemon juice
- 1 tablespoon Dijon-style mustard
- 1/3 cup vegetable oil

- 2 avocados
- 2 tablespoons fresh lemon juice
- 3/4 cup thinly sliced celery
- 1/2 cup minced scallion
- lettuce leaves for lining the plates
- tomato slices for garnish

In a skillet bring the broth to a boil, add the chicken breasts in one layer, reducing the heat to keep the broth at a bare simmer, and simmer them, turning them once, for 7 minutes. Remove the skillet from the heat and let the chicken cool in the broth for 30 minutes.

Make the dressing: In a heavy skillet cook the bacon over moderate heat, stirring, until it is crisp, transfer it to paper towels to drain, and reserve 2 tablespoons of the fat. In a food processor or blender blend well the egg yolk, the lemon juice, the mustard, the reserved bacon fat, the oil, and salt and pepper to taste. Add the bacon and blend the dressing for 5 seconds.

Transfer the chicken with a slotted spatula to a cutting board, reserving the broth for another use, pat it dry, and cut it into bite-size cubes. Cut the avocado into cubes and in a bowl combine it with the lemon juice, the chicken, the celery, and the scallion, pour the dressing over the mixture, and toss the salad gently. Serve the salad on plates lined with the lettuce and garnish it with the tomato slices. **Serves 6.**

side dishes
the south

Roasted Vidalia Onion "Flowers" with Pecans

ROASTED VIDALIA ONION "FLOWERS" WITH PECANS

- 6 large Vidalia onions* (about 3 1/2 pounds)
- 3/4 stick (6 tablespoons) unsalted butter, melted
- 1/4 cup chopped pecans

*available by mail order from Bland Farms, tel. (800) 843-2542, or G & R Farms of Georgia, Inc., tel. (912) 654-1534

Preheat the oven to 350° F. Lightly butter a shallow baking dish large enough to let the onions open, or "flower."

With a sharp knife trim the root end of each onion carefully so that it is still intact. Standing each onion on its root end, cut parallel vertical slices at ¼-inch intervals into but not through the onion, stopping about ½ inch above the root end. Rotate each onion 90 degrees and cut parallel vertical slices in the same manner to form a crosshatch pattern, keeping the onions intact. Arrange the onions, root ends down, in the prepared baking dish, drizzle them with the butter, and season them with salt and pepper. Bake the onions in the middle of the oven, basting them occasionally, for 1 hour, sprinkle them with the pecans, and bake them for 30 minutes more. Serves 6.

GREEN ONION PANCAKES

- 1 cup cornmeal
- 1/2 cup all-purpose flour
- 1 teaspoon sugar
- 2 teaspoons baking powder
- 1/2 teaspoon baking soda
- 1/2 teaspoon salt
- 2 large eggs, beaten lightly
- 1 1/4 cups buttermilk
- 2 tablespoons unsalted butter, melted and cooled
- 2/3 cup finely chopped scallion
- bacon fat or vegetable oil for frying the pancakes

Into a bowl sift together the cornmeal, the flour, the sugar, the baking powder, the baking soda, and the salt. In another bowl beat together the eggs, the buttermilk, and the butter. Add the egg mixture to the cornmeal mixture and stir the batter until it is smooth. Let the batter stand for 10 minutes.

Stir the scallion into the pancake batter. In a heavy skillet heat ⅛ inch of the fat or oil over moderately high heat until it is hot but not smoking and in it fry tablespoons of the batter in batches, adding more fat as necessary, for 1 minute, or until the undersides are golden. Turn the pancakes, fry them for 1 minute more, or until the undersides are golden, and transfer them as they are cooked to a heated platter. Serve the green onion pancakes as an accompaniment to fried chicken. **Makes about 24 pancakes.**

Photo on page 68

COLESLAW WITH BUTTERMILK DRESSING

- 1 cup mayonnaise
- 2 teaspoons fresh lemon juice
- 2 teaspoons Dijon-style mustard
- 1 cup buttermilk
- 2 tablespoons sugar
- 1 1/2 pounds cabbage, cored
- 1/2 pound carrots
- 1 cup raisins

In a blender or food processor combine the mayonnaise, the lemon juice, the mustard, the buttermilk, the sugar, and salt and pepper to taste and blend the dressing until it is smooth. Grate the cabbage and the carrots and in a salad bowl combine the vegetables with the raisins. Stir in the dressing and add salt and pepper to taste. Chill the coleslaw, covered, for 1 hour. Serves 8 to 10.

HOPPIN' JOHN

- 1 pound dried black-eyed peas, picked over
- 2 onions, quartered
- 1/2 bay leaf
- 1 smoked ham hock
- 2 large garlic cloves, chopped
- 1/2 teaspoon dried hot red pepper flakes
- 1 tablespoon white-wine vinegar, or to taste
  steamed rice (page 71) as an accompaniment
- 1 cup thinly sliced scallion greens

In a kettle combine the black-eyed peas with enough cold water to cover them by 2 inches, bring the water to a boil, and boil the black-eyed peas for 2 minutes. Remove the kettle from the heat and let the black-eyed peas soak for 1 hour. Drain the black-eyed peas in a colander, rinse them, and in the kettle combine them with the onions, the bay leaf, 8 cups cold water, the ham hock, the garlic, and the red pepper flakes. Simmer the mixture, covered, stirring occasionally, for 1 hour. Simmer the mixture, uncovered, stirring frequently, for 45 minutes, or until the mixture is thickened. Discard the bay leaf and remove the meat from the ham hock, returning it to the kettle. Stir in the vinegar and salt and pepper to taste. Serve the mixture over the rice and sprinkle it with the scallion greens. **Serves 8.**

BAKED RICE WITH PEAS, CELERY, AND ALMONDS

- 1 small onion, minced
- 1/2 stick (4 tablespoons) unsalted butter
- 2 ribs of celery, cut into 1/4-inch slices
- 1 cup long-grain rice
- 2 cups simmering chicken broth
- 1/3 cup sliced almonds
- 1 cup cooked fresh or thawed frozen peas

Preheat the oven to 375° F.

In a flameproof casserole cook the onion in 3 tablespoons of the butter over moderately low heat, stirring, until it is softened. Add the celery and the rice and cook the mixture, stirring, until the rice is coated well with the butter. Stir in the broth, bring it to a boil, and bake the mixture, covered, in the oven for 15 minutes. While the rice is baking, sauté the almonds in the remaining 1 tablespoon butter over moderately high heat, stirring, until they are golden. Stir the almonds, the peas, and salt and pepper to taste into the rice and bake the mixture, covered, in the oven for 5 minutes, or until the rice is tender and all the liquid has been absorbed. Let the rice stand, covered, for 5 minutes and fluff it with a fork. **Serves 6.**

Peanut Sesame Noodles

PEANUT SESAME NOODLES

- 1/2 pound thin spaghetti or *vermicelli*
- 4 tablespoons Asian sesame oil*
- 1 bunch of scallions (about 6), chopped fine
- 2 garlic cloves, minced
- 1/4 teaspoon dried hot red pepper flakes, or to taste
- 1 tablespoon rice vinegar*
- 1 teaspoon sugar
- 1 tablespoon soy sauce
- 1/2 cup finely chopped salted dry-roasted peanuts
- 1/3 cup finely chopped fresh coriander, plus a coriander sprig for garnish

*available at Asian markets and some specialty foods shops and supermarkets

In a kettle of boiling salted water cook the noodles until they are *al dente*, drain them in a colander, and rinse them briefly under cold water. Drain the noodles well and in a bowl toss them with 2 tablespoons of the oil. In a large skillet cook the scallions, the garlic, and the red pepper flakes in the remaining 2 tablespoons oil over moderate heat, stirring, until the scallions are just softened, add the noodles, the vinegar, the sugar, and the soy sauce, and heat the mixture, tossing it to combine it well, until the noodles are heated through. Stir in the peanuts, the chopped coriander, and salt to taste and serve the mixture garnished with the coriander sprig. **Serves 4.**

FRIED RIPE AND GREEN TOMATOES

- 1 pound ripe tomatoes, cored
- 1 pound green tomatoes, cored
- 2 large eggs
- 1/4 cup milk
- 2 cups saltine cracker crumbs
- 1 cup all-purpose flour
  vegetable oil for frying the tomatoes
- 2 tablespoons bacon fat if desired

Cut the ripe and green tomatoes into ⅓-inch slices, pat them dry, and sprinkle both sides of the slices with salt and pepper. In a bowl beat the eggs with the milk, ¼ cup water, and salt and pepper to taste. Have the cracker crumbs and the flour ready in separate shallow dishes.

In a large skillet heat ½ inch of the oil with the bacon fat (omit bacon fat if desired) over moderate heat until it registers 375° F. on a deep-fat thermometer. Dredge the tomatoes in the flour, shaking off the excess, and dip them in the egg mixture, letting the excess drip off. Coat the tomatoes with the cracker crumbs, fry them, a few at a time, turning them carefully, for 30 seconds on each side, or until they are golden, transferring them with a slotted spatula as they are cooked to paper towels to drain, and keep them warm. Arrange the tomatoes, alternating 1 red and 1 green, on a heated platter and serve them with scrambled eggs or grilled meats. **Serves 4 to 6.**

the south
desserts

SWEET POTATO MERINGUE PIE

	pastry dough (page 15)
	raw rice for weighting the shell
1 1/2	cups mashed cooked sweet potatoes or yams, cooled
1/2	cup firmly packed light brown sugar
1/4	cup heavy cream
2	large eggs, separated and the yolks beaten lightly
1/2	teaspoon cinnamon
1/2	teaspoon ground ginger
1/4	teaspoon ground allspice
1/4	teaspoon salt
	a pinch of freshly grated nutmeg
	a pinch of cream of tartar
3	tablespoons granulated sugar

Preheat the oven to 425° F.

Roll the dough into a round ⅛ inch thick on a floured surface, fit it into a 9-inch pie plate, and crimp the edge decoratively. Prick the bottom of the shell with a fork and chill the shell for 30 minutes. Line the shell with wax paper, fill the paper with the rice, and bake the shell in the middle of the oven for 10 minutes. Remove the rice and the paper carefully, bake the shell for 10 minutes more, or until it is golden, and let it cool on a rack.

Reduce the oven temperature to 350° F. In a bowl combine well the sweet potatoes or the yams, the brown sugar, the heavy cream, the egg yolks, the cinnamon, the ginger, the allspice, the salt, and the nutmeg and spread the mixture evenly in the shell. In another bowl beat the egg whites with the cream of tartar and a pinch of salt until they hold soft peaks, beat in the granulated sugar, 1 scant teaspoon at a time, and beat the meringue until it holds stiff peaks. Spread the meringue over the filling and the crust, covering them completely, and bake the pie in the middle of the oven for 15 minutes, or until the meringue is set and pale golden. Let the pie cool on the rack.

KEY LIME PIE WITH PECAN CRUMB CRUST

For the crust

- 2/3 cup pecans, toasted lightly and cooled completely
- 1 cup zwieback or graham cracker crumbs
- 1/4 cup sugar
- 1/2 stick (1/4 cup) unsalted butter, melted and cooled

- 2 large egg yolks
- 1 14-ounce can sweetened condensed milk
- 1/2 cup bottled Key lime juice* or fresh lime juice (about 3 limes)
- 1/2 cup well-chilled heavy cream
- 1 tablespoon sugar
- 2 teaspoons light rum

*available at specialty foods shops or by mail order from Adriana's Bazaar, New York City, tel. (212) 877-5757

Preheat the oven to 350° F.

Make the crust: In a food processor grind the pecans fine with the crumbs and the sugar and blend in the butter. Press the mixture onto the bottom and up the side of a 9-inch pie plate and bake the shell in the middle of the oven for 8 minutes, or until it is browned lightly. Let the shell cool on a rack.

In a large bowl beat the egg yolks with the condensed milk, stir in the lime juice, a little at a time, stirring to combine the filling well, and spoon the filling into the shell. Bake the pie in the middle of the oven for 15 minutes, or until the filling is set, let the pie cool on a rack, and chill it for 1 hour. In a bowl beat the cream with the sugar until it holds stiff peaks and beat in the rum. Serve the pie with the whipped cream.

Limeade and
Lattice-Crust Peach Pie
(both on page 67)

BANANAS FOSTER

- 1/2 stick (1/4 cup) unsalted butter, cut into pieces
- 1/3 cup firmly packed dark brown sugar
- 3/4 teaspoon cinnamon
- 4 firm-ripe bananas
- 1/3 cup banana-flavored liqueur
- 1/4 cup light rum
- vanilla ice cream as an accompaniment

In a large skillet melt the butter over moderate heat, add the sugar and the cinnamon, and whisk the mixture until it is combined well. Add the bananas, cut diagonally into 1-inch pieces, cook them, turning them carefully, for 1 to 2 minutes, or until they begin to soften, and stir in the liqueur. Cook the mixture, stirring gently, for 1 minute, add the rum, heated, and ignite it, shaking the skillet gently until the flames go out. Serve the banana sauce over the ice cream. **Serves 6.**

RICE PUDDING À L'ORANGE

- 3 1/2 cups milk
- 5 tablespoons sugar
- 1/2 teaspoon salt
- 1/2 cup long-grain rice
- 2 large egg yolks
- 1 1/2 teaspoons vanilla
- 1 cup golden raisins, plumped in boiling-hot water for 5 minutes and drained
- 1 tablespoon freshly grated orange zest
- 1 tablespoon freshly grated lemon zest

In a saucepan combine 2½ cups of the milk, the sugar, the salt, and the rice, bring the mixture to a bare simmer, stirring, and simmer it, stirring, for 5 minutes. Transfer the mixture to the top of a double boiler set over simmering water and cook it, covered, stirring occasionally, for 1 hour, or until most of the milk is absorbed.

Preheat the oven to 300° F. Butter a 2-quart casserole.

In a bowl whisk together lightly the egg yolks, the remaining 1 cup milk, and the vanilla. Stir one third of the rice mixture into the yolk mixture and stir the yolk mixture into the remaining rice mixture. Stir in the raisins and the zests and pour the pudding into the prepared casserole. Set the casserole in a baking pan, add enough hot water to the pan to reach halfway up the side of the casserole, and bake the pudding, covered, in the oven for 1½ hours, or until a knife inserted in the center comes out clean. Serve the pudding warm or at room temperature. **Serves 8.**

PECAN LEMON POUND CAKE

For the cake

- 1/3 cup milk
- 6 large eggs
- 1 tablespoon vanilla
- 2 2/3 cups all-purpose flour
- 1 teaspoon baking powder
- 3/4 teaspoon ground cardamom
- 1 1/4 teaspoons salt
- 3 sticks (1 1/2 cups) unsalted butter, softened
- 1/2 cup granulated sugar
- 3/4 cup firmly packed dark brown sugar
- 2 tablespoons freshly grated lemon zest
- 2 cups pecans, toasted lightly and chopped

For the syrup

- 1/3 cup fresh lemon juice
- 3 tablespoons bourbon
- 1/2 cup granulated sugar

Preheat the oven to 350° F. Grease and flour a 10-inch (3-quart) bundt pan.

Make the cake: In a small bowl whisk together the milk, the eggs, and the vanilla. Into a bowl sift together the flour, the baking powder, the cardamom, and the salt. In a large bowl with an electric mixer cream the butter with the sugars and the zest until the mixture is light and fluffy, add the flour mixture alternately in batches with the egg mixture, beginning and ending with the flour mixture and beating the batter after each addition until it is just combined, and fold in the pecans. Spoon the batter into the prepared pan, spreading it evenly, and bake the cake in the middle of the oven for 50 minutes to 1 hour, or until it is golden and a tester comes out clean.

Make the syrup while the cake is baking: In a small saucepan combine the lemon juice, the bourbon, and the sugar, bring the mixture to a boil, stirring until the sugar is dissolved, and remove the pan from the heat.

Remove the cake from the oven, poke the top immediately all over with a wooden skewer, and brush it with half the syrup. Let the cake cool in the pan on a rack for 10 minutes, invert it onto the rack, and poke it all over with the skewer. Brush the cake with the remaining syrup and let it cool completely.

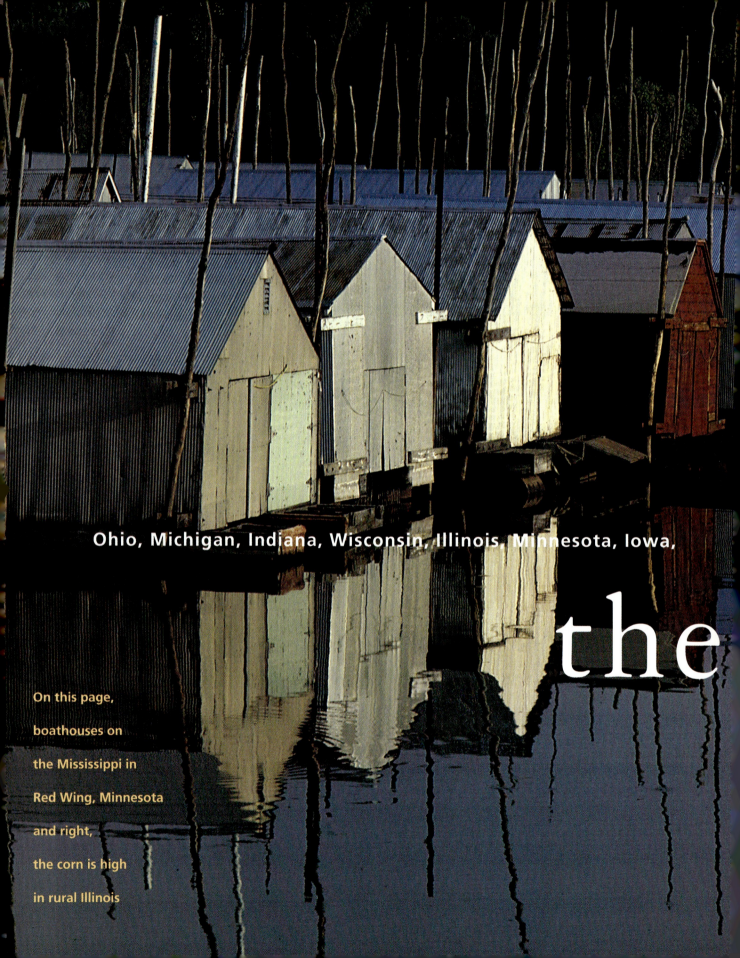

Ohio, Michigan, Indiana, Wisconsin, Illinois, Minnesota, Iowa, the

On this page, boathouses on the Mississippi in Red Wing, Minnesota and right, the corn is high in rural Illinois

Missouri, North Dakota, South Dakota, Nebraska, Kansas, Oklahoma

heartland

the heartland

Spanning from Ohio to Iowa in the Midwest, and continuing from North Dakota south to Oklahoma in the Plains States, the Heartland is the geographic center of America. This massive area is the home of the mighty Mississippi River, nineteen million acres of forest, and sturdy farmhouses dotting vast stretches of corn and grain fields. Here, too, is the heart of the country's homey style of cooking, which includes comforting pot pies, fresh breads and biscuits, and hearty meat-and-potato dishes.

Hundreds of years ago the Great Lakes and numerous rivers provided natives with ample trout, bass, perch, pike, and smelt, and to this day, the Chippewa people harvest the area's wild rice in canoes with cedar sticks. In the 1600s, French explorers traveled south from Canada searching for the northwest passage to the Orient. Instead they discovered excellent farmland (throughout Michigan they planted cherry pits from Normandy) and natives eager to engage in fur trading.

In the late eighteenth century, Revolutionary War veterans were granted land in Ohio in recognition of their service. They planted yellow corn seed, which became the cornerstone of the pioneer diet, squash, beans, and cabbage. In the 1830s, Amish and Mennonite groups also began to move westward, and they brought cows and pigs with them (today there are 33,000 dairy farms in Wisconsin). The Ukrainian Mennonites moved farther west still and planted the drought-resistant wheat that transformed Kansas into America's bread basket. By the 1890s, the Midwest was filled with European immigrants: the Germans introduced sausages and sauerkraut, the Scandinavians baked hearty rye breads and kuchen, the Dutch made almond-filled strudel pastries, and the Irish planted potatoes.

A FARMHOUSE SUPPER

SCALLION NOODLE SOUP
★
CHICKEN IN SUCCOTASH
★
CREAM BISCUITS
★
CUCUMBER AND TOMATO SALAD WITH BUTTERMILK DRESSING
★
BLACKBERRY JAM CAKE WITH PENUCHE FROSTING
★

MONTELLE MISSOURI DRY VIGNOLES 1993
OR
ADELSHEIM VINEYARD WILLAMETTE VALLEY, OREGON, PINOT GRIS 1993

Serves 4

Chicken in Succotash;
Cream Biscuits

the heartland menu

Life on the prairie was difficult, and with few amenities pioneer women had the task of cooking hearty food that was easy to prepare, eat, and store. One-pot meals that could be made on the open hearth were best, and at the center of our Farmhouse Supper is just such a dish — Chicken in Succotash — a combination of chicken, corn, and lima beans. We begin with a light soup that pairs scallions and egg noodles, and supplement our entrée with comforting cream biscuits that can be made in minutes and a simple salad drizzled with creamy buttermilk dressing. For dessert, our moist blackberry jam cake is filled with raisins, pecans, and spices.

SCALLION NOODLE SOUP

- 1 3/4 cups thinly sliced scallion
- 1 garlic clove, minced
- 2 tablespoons unsalted butter
- 4 cups chicken broth
- 1 cup fine egg noodles
- 1 large egg, plus 2 large egg yolks
- 3 tablespoons fresh lemon juice

In a skillet cook the scallion and the garlic in the butter over moderately low heat, stirring, for 5 to 7 minutes, or until they are just softened.

In a stainless-steel or enameled saucepan bring the broth to a boil, add the egg noodles, and boil them for 3 minutes, or until they are *al dente*. In a heatproof bowl beat the egg and the egg yolks, add the lemon juice in a stream, whisking, and whisk the mixture until it is combined well. Add 1 cup of the hot broth in a stream, whisking vigorously, pour the mixture into the saucepan, whisking, and heat the mixture over low heat, stirring, but do not let it boil. Stir in the scallion mixture, season the soup with salt and pepper, and heat it, stirring, until it is thickened slightly and heated through. Ladle the soup into heated bowls. **Serves 4.**

CHICKEN IN SUCCOTASH

1	3 1/2-pound chicken, cut into serving pieces, including the neck, back, and giblets (excluding the liver)
2	tablespoons bacon fat or a mixture of 1 tablespoon butter and 1 tablespoon vegetable oil
1	onion, chopped
3/4	cup chicken broth
1	10-ounce package frozen baby lima beans, thawed, or 2 cups fresh shelled lima beans
1	sprig of fresh thyme or 1/4 teaspoon dried, crumbled, plus additional sprigs for garnish
1	sprig of fresh chervil or 1/4 teaspoon dried, crumbled, plus additional sprigs for garnish
1 1/3	to 1 1/2 cups heavy cream
1 1/2	cups corn (cut from about 3 ears)
	fresh lemon juice to taste
2	tablespoons minced fresh parsley leaves
2	tablespoons chopped fresh chives
	cream biscuits (recipe follows) as an accompaniment if desired

Pat the chicken dry and season it with salt and pepper. In a large skillet heat the fat over moderate heat until it is hot but not smoking, in it cook the chicken, including the neck, back, and giblets, in batches for 10 to 12 minutes, or until it is golden on both sides, and transfer it to paper towels to drain. Pour off all but 1 tablespoon of the fat from the skillet, add the onion, and cook it over moderate heat, stirring, for 2 minutes. Add the broth and deglaze the skillet over high heat, scraping up any brown bits. Arrange the chicken in the skillet, putting the breast pieces on top, and simmer it, covered, over moderately low heat for 10 minutes. Add the lima beans, the thyme sprig, and the chervil sprig, and simmer the mixture, covered, for 8 to 10 minutes, or until the chicken is tender. Transfer the chicken with tongs to a platter, reserving the neck, back, and giblets for another use.

Add 1 1/3 cups of the cream to the skillet, boil the liquid until it is thickened slightly, skimming any fat that has accumulated around the edge, and stir in the corn. Simmer the mixture for 1 minute, return the chicken to the skillet, and simmer the mixture for 3 to 5 minutes, or until the chicken is heated through. Discard the thyme and chervil sprigs, add enough of the remaining cream to thin the sauce to the desired consistency, and add the lemon juice and salt and pepper to taste. Remove the skillet from the heat and stir in the parsley and the chives. Transfer the mixture to a serving dish, garnish it with the additional thyme sprigs and chervil sprigs, and serve it with the cream biscuits. **Serves 4.**

Photo on page 89

CREAM BISCUITS

2	cups all-purpose flour
1	tablespoon baking powder
3	tablespoons sugar if desired
1/2	teaspoon salt
1 1/4	cups heavy cream
	milk for brushing the biscuits

Preheat the oven to 425° F.

Into a bowl sift together the flour, the baking powder, the sugar, and the salt, add the cream, and stir the mixture until it just forms a dough.

Gather the dough into a ball, knead it gently 6 times on a lightly floured surface, and roll or pat it out 1/2 inch thick. Cut out as many rounds as possible with a 2 1/2-inch round cutter dipped in flour and transfer them to an ungreased baking sheet. Gather the scraps, reroll the dough, and cut out more rounds in the same manner until there are 10 in all. Brush the tops of the rounds with the milk and bake the biscuits in the middle of the oven for 15 minutes, or until they are pale golden. Transfer the biscuits to a rack and let them cool for 5 minutes. **Makes 10 biscuits.**

Photo on page 89

Carl Sandburg's birthplace, Galesburg, Illinois

CUCUMBER AND TOMATO SALAD WITH BUTTERMILK DRESSING

- 1/2 cup mayonnaise
- 1 tablespoon distilled white vinegar
- 2 teaspoons Dijon-style mustard
- 1 teaspoon dried dill, crumbled
- 3/4 teaspoon salt
- 1 small garlic clove, crushed
- 1/2 teaspoon dried thyme, crumbled
- 1/2 teaspoon dried marjoram, crumbled
- 1/2 teaspoon dried basil, crumbled
- 1/2 teaspoon celery salt
- 1/2 cup vegetable oil
- 1 cup buttermilk
- 4 medium tomatoes (about 2 pounds), sliced
- 1 seedless cucumber, ends trimmed, quartered

In a blender or food processor put the mayonnaise, the vinegar, the mustard, the dill, the salt, the garlic, the thyme, the marjoram, the basil, and the celery salt and turn the motor on and immediately off. With the motor running add the oil and the buttermilk in a stream and pepper to taste. The dressing will be thin.

Divide the tomato slices among 4 salad plates, arrange the cucumber in the center of the tomatoes, and drizzle some of the dressing over the salad. Serve the remaining dressing on the side. Serves 4.

BLACKBERRY JAM CAKE WITH PENUCHE FROSTING

For the cake
- 1 1/4 cups all-purpose flour
- 1 teaspoon baking powder
- 1 teaspoon salt
- 1 teaspoon cinnamon
- 1/2 teaspoon freshly grated nutmeg
- 1/4 teaspoon ground cloves
- 1 stick (1/2 cup) unsalted butter, softened
- 1 cup firmly packed light brown sugar
- 2 large eggs
- 1 teaspoon vanilla
- 1/2 cup buttermilk
- 1/2 cup blackberry jam
- 1/2 cup raisins
- 3/4 cup chopped pecans

For the frosting
- 1 cup firmly packed light brown sugar
- 1/3 cup heavy cream
- 3 tablespoons unsalted butter

Preheat the oven to 350° F. Butter and flour a loaf pan, 9 by 5 by 3 inches.

Make the cake: Into a bowl sift together the flour, the baking powder, the salt, the cinnamon, the nutmeg, and the cloves. In another bowl with an electric mixer cream the butter with the sugar until the mixture is light and fluffy, add the eggs, 1 at a time, beating well after each addition, and beat in the vanilla. Add the flour mixture to the butter mixture in batches alternately with the buttermilk, beginning and ending with the flour mixture and beating well after each addition, and stir in the jam, the raisins, and the pecans. Pour the batter into the prepared pan and bake the cake in the middle of the oven for 55 minutes to 1 hour, or until a tester comes out clean. Let the cake cool in the pan on a rack for 5 minutes and turn it out onto the rack to cool completely.

Make the frosting: In a saucepan combine the sugar, the cream, and the butter, cook the mixture over moderate heat, stirring, until the sugar is dissolved, and boil it, without stirring, washing down any sugar crystals clinging to the side of the pan with a brush dipped in cold water, until it registers 238° F. on a candy thermometer. Transfer the frosting to a bowl and beat it until it is just of spreading consistency. (The frosting will still be warm.)

Working quickly, spread the frosting over the top and side of the cake.

the heartland
starters

Butternut Squash Tartlets with Cheese Lattice and Sunflower Seed Crust

BUTTERNUT SQUASH TARTLETS WITH CHEESE LATTICE AND SUNFLOWER SEED CRUST

For the shells
- sunflower seed pastry dough (recipe follows)
- raw rice for weighting the shells

For the filling
- 1 cup puréed steamed butternut squash (procedure follows)
- 1/4 cup heavy cream
- 1 large egg, beaten lightly
- 3/4 teaspoon salt, or to taste
- 1/4 teaspoon black pepper, or to taste

about 1/4 pound thinly sliced Gruyère, cut into thirty-six 1/8-inch strips, for the lattice

Preheat the oven to 425° F.

Make the shells: Roll out the dough 1/8 inch thick on a lightly floured surface and with a 4½-inch round cutter cut out 6 rounds, gathering and rerolling the scraps as necessary. Press each round into a fluted metal tartlet pan, 3¼ inches across the bottom and 5/8 inch deep, prick the shells lightly with a fork, and chill them for 30 minutes or freeze them for 15 minutes. Line the shells with foil, fill the foil with the rice, and bake the shells in a jelly-roll pan in the lower third of the oven for 15 minutes. Remove the rice and foil carefully and bake the shells for 5 to 7 minutes more, or until they are golden. Let the shells cool in the pans on a rack. *The shells may be made 1 day in advance and kept in an airtight container at room temperature.*

Reduce the oven temperature to 375° F.

Make the filling: In a food processor or bowl with a whisk blend the squash with the cream, the egg, the salt, and the pepper.

Divide the filling among the tartlet shells, smoothing it, and arrange 6 strips of Gruyère, trimming them to fit, in a lattice pattern on each tartlet.

Bake the tartlets in the jelly-roll pan in the middle of the oven for 20 to 25 minutes, or until the filling is puffed slightly and the cheese is melted, and serve them immediately. **Serves 6.**

SUNFLOWER SEED PASTRY DOUGH

- 1/4 cup salted roasted sunflower seeds
- 1 cup all-purpose flour plus additional for dusting the dough
- 3/4 stick (6 tablespoons) cold unsalted butter, cut into bits

In a food processor grind fine the sunflower seeds with 1 cup of the flour, add the butter, and blend the mixture until it just resembles coarse meal. Transfer the mixture to a bowl and toss it with 2 to 3 tablespoons ice water, or enough to just form a dough. Knead the dough lightly with the heel of the hand against a smooth surface, distributing the butter evenly, for a few seconds and form it into a ball. Dust the dough with the additional flour, flatten it slightly, and chill it, wrapped in wax paper, for at least 1 hour or overnight.

to *steam and purée butternut squash*

Cut the squash into 2-inch pieces, discard the seeds and strings, and in a steamer set over boiling water steam the squash, covered, checking the water level every 10 minutes and adding more water as necessary, for 30 to 40 minutes, or until it is very tender. Let the squash cool until it can be handled, scrape the flesh from the skins into a food processor, discarding the skins, and purée it. If the purée is watery, drain it in a sieve lined with paper towels set over a bowl for 10 to 15 minutes. **One pound raw squash makes about 1 cup purée.**

the heartland starters

BLUE-CHEESE-STUFFED RADISHES

- 1 pound radishes (about 18, each about 1 1/4 inches in diameter), halved crosswise
- 5 ounces (about 2/3 cup packed) fine-quality blue cheese such as Gorgonzola, Maytag, Stilton, or Roquefort, softened
- 2 tablespoons unsalted butter, softened
- about 36 drained bottled capers

Trim the narrow end of each radish half so that the half will stand upright and with a small melon-ball cutter hollow out a ¾-inch cavity in each half, dropping the halves as they are hollowed into a bowl of ice and cold water. In a bowl cream together the blue cheese and the butter with a fork until the mixture is smooth and transfer it to a pastry bag fitted with a ½-inch plain tip. Transfer the radishes, hollowed sides down, to paper towels, let them drain for 5 minutes, and pipe the mixture into them. Arrange the radishes on a plate and top each with a caper. Makes about 36 hors d'oeuvres.

ONION, PEACH, AND RAISIN COMPOTE

- 1 1/2 pounds pearl onions, about 1 inch in diameter, blanched, peeled, and stems trimmed
- 1/2 cup olive oil
- 1/2 cup dry white wine or dry vermouth
- 2 peaches, pitted and cut into 1-inch chunks
- 2 cups raisins
- 1 1-pound can crushed tomatoes
- 2 tablespoons tomato paste
- 1 teaspoon ground ginger
- 1 tablespoon mustard seeds
- 1/4 teaspoon dried hot red pepper flakes
- 1 tablespoon firmly packed light brown sugar
- 2 garlic cloves, minced
- 1 bay leaf
- 2 tablespoons fresh lemon juice, or to taste
- minced fresh parsley leaves for garnish
- French or Italian bread, cut into rounds and toasted as an accompaniment
- Cheddar as an accompaniment

In a saucepan cook the onions in the oil over moderate heat for 5 to 10 minutes, stirring occasionally, until they are golden and add the wine or the vermouth, the peaches, the raisins, the tomatoes, the tomato paste, the ginger, the mustard seeds, the red pepper flakes, the sugar, the garlic, the bay leaf, the lemon juice, and salt to taste. Add enough water to just cover the onions, bring the liquid to a boil, and simmer the mixture, stirring occasionally, for 30 minutes, or until the onions are just tender and the mixture is thickened. Discard the bay leaf and transfer the mixture to a serving dish. Let the compote cool and sprinkle it with the parsley. Serve the compote with the bread rounds and the cheese. Serves 6 as an hors d'oeuvre or as an accompaniment to roast meats, game, or poultry.

CELERY AND KIELBASA CREAM KUCHEN

For the dough
- 5 teaspoons (two 1/4-ounce packages) active dry yeast
- 1 cup lukewarm milk
- 3 1/2 to 4 cups all-purpose flour
- 1 teaspoon sugar
- 2 large eggs, beaten lightly
- 1/2 stick (1/4 cup) unsalted butter, softened
- 2 teaspoons salt

- 3/4 pound smoked *kielbasa,* cut into 1/4-inch dice (about 3 cups)
- 3 tablespoons unsalted butter
- 1 pound onions, sliced thin
- 3 cups thinly sliced celery
- 1 tablespoon distilled white vinegar

1/2 cup heavy cream
1 tablespoon Dijon-style mustard, or to taste
1 1/4 cups coarsely grated Gruyère
1/2 teaspoon celery seeds

Make the dough: In a measuring cup proof the yeast in ½ cup of the milk with 1 tablespoon of the flour and the sugar for 10 minutes, or until it is foamy. In a large bowl combine well the yeast mixture, the remaining ½ cup milk, and the eggs and stir in 3½ cups of the remaining flour, the butter, and the salt. Beat the dough with an electric mixer fitted with a dough hook, adding more of the remaining flour if necessary, for 5 minutes, or until it is smooth and elastic. (Alternatively, knead the dough on a floured surface, adding more of the remaining flour if necessary, for 10 minutes, or until it is smooth and elastic.) Put the dough in a buttered bowl, turn it to coat it with the butter, and let it rise, covered with plastic wrap, in a warm place for 1 hour, or until it is double in bulk.

Preheat the oven to 550° F. Butter and flour a jelly-roll pan.

In a large skillet cook the *kielbasa* over moderately high heat, stirring, until it is golden brown and transfer it to paper towels to drain. Pour off the fat from the skillet, add the butter, the onions, the sliced celery, and salt and pepper, and cook the mixture, stirring occasionally, until the onions are golden. Add the vinegar and boil the mixture, stirring, until the liquid is evaporated. Add the cream and boil the mixture, stirring, for 5 minutes, or until it is thickened. Add the mustard, ½ cup of the Gruyère, the celery seeds, and salt and pepper, stir in the *kielbasa,* and let the mixture cool.

Roll the dough into an 18- by 13-inch rectangle, fitting it into the bottom and up the sides of the jelly-roll pan, and prick it lightly with a fork. Spread the *kielbasa* mixture on the dough, sprinkle the remaining ¾ cup Gruyère evenly on top, and bake the kuchen in the oven for 10 to 15 minutes, or until the top is golden brown and bubbling. **Serves 12 as an hors d'oeuvre.**

PORT AND BLACK-WALNUT CHEESE SPREAD

1 cup chopped onion
2 tablespoons unsalted butter
1/3 cup Tawny Port
4 ounces sharp Cheddar, sliced
2 ounces cream cheese at room temperature
3 tablespoons sour cream
1/4 cup black walnuts*
    crackers as an accompaniment

* available at some specialty foods shops and by mail order from Missouri Dandy Pantry, tel. (800) 872-6879

In a large skillet cook the onion in the butter over moderately low heat, stirring, until it is softened but not browned. Add the Port and boil the mixture over high heat until almost all the liquid is evaporated. Season the mixture with salt and pepper and let it cool to room temperature. In a food processor grind the Cheddar fine, add the cream cheese and the sour cream, and blend the mixture until it is smooth. Add the Port mixture and blend the mixture well. Add the walnuts and pulse the motor until they are just combined. Serve the cheese spread with the crackers. **Makes about 1 1/2 cups.**

the heartland entrées

Beer-Braised Brisket with Root Vegetables

BEER-BRAISED BRISKET WITH ROOT VEGETABLES

- 4 slices of bacon, chopped
- 1 2 1/2-pound beef brisket
- 3 onions, sliced thin
- 4 12-ounce bottles of beer (not dark)
- 1 large rutabaga (about 2 pounds), peeled and cut into 1/2-inch pieces
- 6 carrots, cut crosswise into 1 1/2-inch-thick pieces
- 6 boiling potatoes, cut into 1-inch pieces
  a *beurre manié* made by blending 2 tablespoons softened unsalted butter with 2 tablespoons all-purpose flour
  cooked noodles as an accompaniment
- 1/2 cup minced fresh parsley leaves

Preheat the oven to 350° F.

In a kettle cook the bacon over moderate heat, stirring, until it is crisp, transfer it to paper towels to drain, and pour off all but 2 tablespoons of the fat. Heat the fat remaining in the kettle over moderately high heat until it is hot but not smoking, in it brown the brisket, patted dry and seasoned with salt and pepper, and transfer it to a platter. Add the onions to the kettle, sauté them until they are golden, and add the bacon, the brisket, and the beer. Bring the beer to a boil and braise the brisket, covered, in the oven for 2 hours. Stir in the rutabaga, the carrots, and the potatoes and braise the mixture for 45 minutes, or until the vegetables are tender.

Transfer the brisket and the vegetables with a slotted spoon to a plate and keep them warm, covered. Bring the braising liquid to a boil, boil it until it is reduced to about 3 cups, and whisk in the *beurre manié*, bit by bit, whisking well after each addition. Simmer the sauce for 3 minutes and season it with salt and pepper. Slice the brisket and arrange it and the vegetables with the noodles on a platter. Spoon some of the sauce over the brisket and the vegetables, sprinkle the dish with the parsley, and serve the remaining sauce separately. **Serves 6 to 8.**

CIDER-BRAISED PORK SHOULDER WITH CHERRIES

- 1 6-pound pork picnic shoulder
- 2 tablespoons all-purpose flour
- 1 teaspoon salt
- 1 teaspoon black pepper
- 1 teaspoon dried thyme, crumbled
- 3 tablespoons vegetable oil
- 3 medium onions, sliced (about 3 1/2 cups)
- 1/3 cup dried sour cherries (available at specialty foods shops)
- 1 bay leaf
- 2 cups apple cider
- 1/2 cup dry red wine
- 1 tablespoon fresh lemon juice, or to taste

Preheat the oven to 325° F.

Trim all but a thin layer of fat from the pork. In a small bowl combine the flour, the salt, the pepper, and the thyme and rub the mixture on the pork. In an ovenproof kettle measuring 12 inches across the top and 5 inches deep heat the oil over moderately high heat until it is hot but not smoking, in it brown the pork, and transfer the pork to a plate. Add the onions to the kettle and cook them over moderate heat, stirring, until they begin to brown. Add the cherries, the bay leaf, the cider, and the wine, bring the liquid to a boil, and return the pork to the kettle.

Braise the pork, covered, in the oven for about 2¼ hours, or until it is tender when pierced with a fork. Transfer the pork to a platter and keep it warm, covered. Skim the fat from the cooking liquid, discard the bay leaf, and in a blender blend the sauce until it is smooth. Season the sauce with the lemon juice and salt and pepper. Slice the pork across the grain, pour some of the sauce over it, and serve the remaining sauce separately. **Serves 6 to 8.**

STUFFED CABBAGE ROLLS

- 1   2 1/2- to 3-pound cabbage, cored

For the filling
- 2   slices of homemade-type white bread, torn into pieces
- 1/4 cup milk
- 1/2 cup long-grain rice
- 2   onions, chopped
- 1   green bell pepper, chopped
- 2   tablespoons vegetable oil
- 1 1/2 tablespoons sweet paprika
- 1   pound ground chuck
- 1   large egg, beaten lightly
- 1   tablespoon tomato paste

- 9   slices of lean bacon, halved crosswise
- 1   cup dry white wine or dry vermouth

For the sauce
- 1   tablespoon flour
- 2   tablespoons vegetable oil
- 2   tablespoons sweet paprika
- 1/2 cup beef broth
- 1   cup tomato sauce
- 1   cup sour cream

In a kettle of boiling salted water boil the cabbage for 10 minutes, or until it is softened, transfer it with slotted spoons to a colander, and remove 18 of the leaves carefully. (If the inner leaves are not softened, return the cabbage to the kettle and continue to boil it until the leaves are softened.) Drain the leaves, trim any tough ribs, and chop enough of the remaining cabbage to measure 2 cups.

Preheat the oven to 350° F.

Make the filling: In a large bowl let the bread soak in the milk until it is softened. In a saucepan of boiling water boil the rice, stirring occasionally, for 10 minutes, drain it, and transfer it to the bowl of bread. In a large heavy skillet cook the onions, the bell pepper, and the chopped cabbage in the oil over moderate heat, stirring, until the vegetables are softened, stir in the paprika, and cook the mixture, stirring, for 1 minute. Add the cabbage mixture to the rice mixture and let the mixture cool. Add the chuck, the egg, the tomato paste, and salt and pepper to taste and blend the filling well. (Test the seasoning by cooking a small amount of the filling.)

Arrange 1/3 cup of the filling along the rib end of each cabbage leaf, roll it up in the leaf, tucking in the sides to enclose it completely, and wrap a piece of bacon around the center of each roll. Arrange the rolls seam side down in a baking pan just large enough to hold them in one layer, pour the wine or the vermouth over them, and bake the rolls, covered, in the oven for 30 minutes. Continue to bake the rolls, uncovered, for 1 hour and 15 minutes. (The leaves will brown slightly.)

Make the sauce while the cabbage is baking: In a heavy saucepan cook the flour in the oil over moderately low heat, stirring, for 3 minutes, stir in the paprika, and cook the mixture, stirring, for 1 minute. Add the broth and the tomato sauce and bring the mixture to a boil, stirring. Simmer the sauce, stirring, for 1 minute and stir in the sour cream.

Pour the sauce over the cabbage rolls and bake the mixture for 15 minutes. *The dish may be made 1 day in advance and kept covered and chilled.* **Serves 6.**

ROAST TURKEY WITH CRANBERRY GRAVY

- 1 12- to 14-pound turkey, the neck and giblets (excluding the liver) reserved for making turkey giblet stock (recipe follows)
- 2 apples, cut into chunks
- 1 orange, peeled and cut into chunks
- 2 onions, cut into chunks
- 1 stick (1/2 cup) unsalted butter, softened

For the gravy

- 4 cups turkey giblet stock (recipe follows)
- 1 cup cranberries, picked over and chopped coarse
- 1/4 cup firmly packed brown sugar
- 3 tablespoons all-purpose flour

Preheat the oven to 425° F.

Rinse the turkey, pat it dry, and season it inside and out with salt and pepper. Pack the neck and body cavities with the apples, the orange, and the onions and truss the turkey. Spread the turkey with the butter and roast it on a rack in a roasting pan in the oven for 30 minutes.

Reduce the oven temperature to 325° F. Baste the turkey with the pan juices, add 1 cup water to the pan, and roast the turkey, basting it every 20 minutes, for 2½ to 3 hours more, or until a meat thermometer inserted in the fleshy part of a thigh registers 180° F. and the juices run clear when the thigh is pierced. Transfer the turkey to a heated platter, reserving the juices in the roasting pan, discard the string, and keep the turkey warm, covered loosely with foil.

Make the gravy: Skim all the fat from the roasting pan juices, reserving 3 tablespoons of the fat, and add 1 cup of the stock to the pan. Deglaze the pan over moderately high heat, scraping up the brown bits. In a small heavy stainless-steel or enameled saucepan cook the cranberries with the sugar over high heat, stirring, until the sugar is dissolved, cook the mixture, covered, over low heat for 3 minutes, and cook it, uncovered, for 3 minutes more. In a saucepan combine the reserved fat and the flour and cook the *roux* over moderately low heat, whisking, for 3 minutes. Add the deglazing mixture and the remaining 3 cups stock in a stream, whisking, stir in the cranberry mixture, and bring the mixture to a boil, whisking. Simmer the gravy, stirring occasionally, for 10 minutes, season it with salt and pepper, and transfer it to a heated sauceboat. **Serves 8.**

TURKEY GIBLET STOCK

- the neck and giblets (excluding the liver) from a 12- to 14-pound turkey
- 5 cups chicken broth
- 1 rib of celery, chopped
- 1 carrot, chopped
- 1 onion, quartered
- 1 bay leaf
- 1/2 teaspoon dried thyme, crumbled
- 1 teaspoon black peppercorns

In a large saucepan combine the neck and giblets, the broth, 5 cups water, the celery, the carrot, and the onion and bring the liquid to a boil, skimming the froth. Add the bay leaf, the thyme, and the peppercorns, cook the mixture at a bare simmer for 1½ to 2 hours, or until the liquid is reduced to about 4 cups, and strain the stock through a fine sieve into a bowl. *The stock may be made 2 days in advance, cooled, uncovered, and kept chilled or frozen in an airtight container.* **Makes about 4 cups.**

RABBIT AND SAUSAGE WITH MORELS

- 2   2 1/2- to 3-pound rabbits, thawed if frozen, cut into 8 serving pieces, reserving the giblets for another use
- 1/2   cup all-purpose flour seasoned with salt and pepper for dredging the rabbit
- 7   tablespoons olive oil
- 2   cups chopped onion (about 2 medium onions)
- 1   tablespoon minced garlic
- 1/2   pound fresh morels* or 1 ounce dried morels soaked in 1 cup warm water for 15 minutes, drained, reserving 3/4 cup strained liquid if desired
- 1/4   cup tomato paste
- 2   cups chopped tomatoes
- 1   cup dry white wine or dry vermouth
- 4   cups chicken broth or 3 1/4 cups chicken broth and 3/4 cup reserved strained mushroom liquid
- 1   bay leaf
- 1   teaspoon dried rosemary, crumbled
- 1   teaspoon dried thyme, crumbled
- 1   pound Italian sweet sausage, cut into 2-inch lengths
- 1/4   cup minced fresh parsley leaves
    cooked wide egg noodles as an accompaniment

* available in the spring at specialty produce markets and some supermarkets

Preheat the oven to 350° F.

Pat the rabbit dry and dredge it in the seasoned flour, shaking off the excess. In a large heavy ovenproof kettle heat 4 tablespoons of the oil over moderately high heat until it is hot but not smoking and in it brown the rabbit, patted dry, in batches, adding the remaining 3 tablespoons oil as needed and transferring the rabbit as it is browned to a plate. Add the onion and the garlic to the kettle and cook them over moderately low heat, stirring, until the onion is softened. Add the morels, the tomato paste, the tomatoes, the wine or the vermouth, the broth or the broth and mushroom liquid, the bay leaf, the rosemary, the thyme, the sausage, and the rabbit with any juices, and bring the mixture to a boil, stirring. Braise the mixture, covered, in the middle of the oven for 1½ hours, or until the rabbit is tender, and transfer the rabbit and the sausage with tongs to a serving platter. Boil the sauce, stirring, until it is thickened slightly, stir in the parsley and salt and pepper to taste, and spoon the sauce over the meats. Serve the meats with the sauce over the noodles. **Serves 6.**

CINCINNATI-STYLE CHILI "FIVE WAY"

- 2 large onions, chopped
- 3 tablespoons vegetable oil
- 4 garlic cloves, minced
- 3 pounds ground chuck
- 4 tablespoons chili powder
- 2 teaspoons ground cumin
- 2 teaspoons sweet paprika
- 3/4 teaspoon cayenne
- 1/4 teaspoon ground allspice
- 1/4 teaspoon cinnamon
- 1/4 teaspoon turmeric
- 1/4 teaspoon ground coriander
- 1/4 teaspoon ground cardamom
- 2 8-ounce cans tomato sauce
- 2 tablespoons unsweetened cocoa powder
- 1 tablespoon molasses
- 3 cups beef broth
- 2 tablespoons cider vinegar, or to taste

Accompaniments
cooked spaghetti
cooked red kidney beans
chopped onion
finely grated Cheddar
oyster crackers

In a heavy kettle cook the onions in the oil over moderate heat, stirring, until they are softened, add the garlic, and cook the mixture, stirring, for 1 minute. Add the chuck and cook it, stirring and breaking up the lumps, until it is no longer pink. Add the chili powder, the cumin, the paprika, the cayenne, the allspice, the cinnamon, the turmeric, the coriander, and the cardamom, cook the mixture, stirring, for 1 minute, and stir in the tomato sauce, the cocoa powder, the molasses, the broth, the vinegar, 3 cups water, and salt and pepper to taste. Bring the liquid to a boil and simmer the mixture, stirring occasionally, for 1½ hours, or until it is thickened but soupy enough to be ladled. (The chili will improve in flavor if cooled completely, uncovered, and chilled, covered, overnight. Add more water as necessary when reheating the chili.) *The chili may be made 3 days in advance.* To serve the chili "Five Way," ladle it over individual bowls of the spaghetti and top it with the kidney beans, the onion, the Cheddar, and the crackers. **Serves 6.**

the heartland entrées

the heartland
side dishes

Apple Cheese Quick Bread;
Chunky Lemon Applesauce

APPLE CHEESE QUICK BREAD

1	stick (1/2 cup) unsalted butter, softened
1/3	cup sugar
1/3	cup honey
2	large eggs
1	cup whole-wheat flour
1	cup all-purpose flour
1	teaspoon baking powder
1/2	teaspoon baking soda
1/2	teaspoon salt
1 1/2	cups grated Granny Smith apples (about 2)
1/2	cup grated Swiss cheese
1/2	cup chopped walnuts
	cream cheese as an accompaniment

Preheat the oven to 350° F. Butter a loaf pan, 9 by 5 by 3 inches.

In a large bowl cream together the butter and the sugar and beat in the honey and the eggs. Into the butter mixture sift together the flours, the baking powder, the baking soda, and the salt, stir the mixture until it is combined well, and stir in the apples, the cheese, and the walnuts. Spoon the batter into the prepared pan and bake it in the middle of the oven for 50 to 60 minutes, or until a tester comes out clean. Turn the bread out onto a rack, let it cool completely, and serve it, sliced, with the cream cheese.

CHUNKY LEMON APPLESAUCE

3 1/2	pounds McIntosh apples (about 10), peeled, cored, and quartered
3/4	cup fresh lemon juice
3/4	to 1 cup sugar, or to taste

In a large heavy saucepan combine the apples, ¾ cup water, the lemon juice, and the sugar, bring the liquid to a boil, and simmer the mixture, stirring occasionally and breaking up the apples, for 20 minutes, or until the apples are tender and the mixture is the consistency of a chunky purée. Increase the heat and boil the mixture, stirring, for 4 minutes, or until it is thickened. (The mixture will splatter.) Serve the applesauce warm or chilled. **Makes about 5 cups.**

CHEESE PUDDING WITH ZUCCHINI AND LEEK

1 1/2	cups thinly sliced white and pale green parts of leek (1 large), washed and drained well
2 1/2	cups thinly sliced zucchini (about 2 medium)
3	tablespoons unsalted butter
1/3	cup chopped well-drained bottled pimientos
18	slices of homemade-type white bread, buttered lightly
1	pound sliced Münster or Brick cheese
5	large eggs, beaten lightly
1 1/2	tablespoons Dijon-style mustard
3	cups milk
1	teaspoon salt
1/2	teaspoon black pepper
1/4	cup fine fresh bread crumbs
1/3	cup freshly grated Parmesan

Butter a baking dish, 13 by 9 by 2 inches.

In a skillet cook the leek and the zucchini in 1 tablespoon of the butter over moderate heat, stirring, until the vegetables are tender and the liquid they give off is evaporated and stir in the pimientos. In the prepared baking dish arrange in alternate layers the bread, the cheese, and the vegetable mixture. In a bowl whisk the eggs with the mustard until the mixture is combined and whisk in the milk, the salt, and the black pepper. Pour the egg mixture into the baking dish slowly and let the mixture stand for 30 minutes.

Preheat the oven to 350° F.

In a small bowl combine the bread crumbs and the Parmesan, sprinkle the pudding evenly with the mixture, and dot it with the remaining 2 tablespoons butter, cut into bits. Bake the pudding in the oven for 45 minutes, or until it is puffed and golden brown. **Serves 8.**

LIMPA
Swedish Rye Bread

2	packages (about 5 teaspoons) active dry yeast
1 1/2	cups milk
1/3	cup molasses
1/2	stick (1/4 cup) unsalted butter
1	tablespoon aniseed
1	tablespoon caraway seeds if desired
1	tablespoon salt
1 1/2	teaspoons freshly grated orange zest
2	cups rye flour
3	to 4 cups unbleached all-purpose flour

In a small bowl proof the yeast in ½ cup warm water for 5 minutes, or until the mixture is foamy. In a small saucepan heat the milk with the molasses and the butter until the mixture is just lukewarm and the butter is melted and remove the pan from the heat. In a large bowl stir together the yeast mixture, the milk mixture, the aniseed, the caraway seeds, the salt, the zest, the rye flour, and 3 cups of the unbleached flour until the mixture is combined well, turn the dough out onto a floured surface, and knead it for 8 minutes, adding as much of the remaining 1 cup unbleached flour as necessary, or until it is smooth and elastic.

Butter a large bowl and a large baking sheet.

Transfer the dough to the prepared bowl, turning it to coat it with the butter, and let it rise, covered with plastic wrap, in a warm place for 1½ hours, or until it is double in bulk. Punch down the dough, turn it out onto a floured surface, and knead it a few times. Divide the dough in half, form each half into a round loaf, and transfer the loaves to the prepared baking sheet. Let the loaves rise, covered with a kitchen towel, in a warm place for 1 hour, or until they are almost double in bulk.

Preheat the oven to 375° F.

Prick the loaves with a fork to form a decorative pattern and bake them in the middle of the oven for 30 to 40 minutes, or until they are browned and sound hollow when the bottoms are tapped. Transfer the loaves to a rack and let them cool. **Makes 2 loaves.**

Cream Biscuits
(page 91)

WILD RICE TABBOULEH
Wild Rice, Bulgur, and Herb Salad

- 1/2 cup coarse *bulgur* (available at natural foods stores)
- 3/4 cup wild rice
- 6 tablespoons olive oil
- 1/4 cup fresh lemon juice plus additional to taste
- 1 to 1 1/2 cups minced fresh parsley leaves
- 1/2 cup minced fresh mint leaves
- 1/2 cup minced scallion
- whole romaine leaves for lining the bowl

In a heatproof bowl cover the *bulgur* with 1½ cups boiling water and let it soak, covered with plastic wrap, for 2 hours, or until it is tender. Drain the *bulgur* in a colander, pressing on it gently to extract the excess liquid.

In a saucepan bring 2¼ cups salted water to a boil, add the wild rice, and simmer it, covered, for 45 to 50 minutes, or until it is just tender and most of the water is absorbed. Pour off any excess water or drain the wild rice in the colander and transfer it to a bowl. Add the oil, ¼ cup of the lemon juice, and salt and pepper to taste, toss the mixture, and let it cool. Add the *bulgur,* the parsley, the mint, the scallion, the additional lemon juice, and salt and pepper to taste, toss the salad, and transfer it to a serving bowl lined with the romaine leaves. **Serves 6 to 8.**

RYE BREAD STUFFING WITH SAUERKRAUT, BACON, AND RAISINS

- 1/2 pound sliced bacon
- 1 stick (1/2 cup) unsalted butter plus 2 additional tablespoons if baking the stuffing separately
- 2 cups finely chopped onion
- 1 cup finely chopped celery
- 1 garlic clove, minced
- 1 cup raisins
- 2 tablespoons firmly packed light brown sugar
- 2 teaspoons caraway seeds
- 1/4 cup cider vinegar
- 1 1-pound bag sauerkraut, rinsed and drained well
- 10 slices of rye bread, cut into 1/2-inch cubes, toasted, and cooled (about 7 1/2 cups)
- 1 cup chicken broth if baking the stuffing separately

In a large skillet cook the bacon over moderate heat until it is crisp, transfer it to paper towels to drain, and pour off all the fat from the skillet. Add 1 stick of the butter and in it cook the onion, the celery, and the garlic over moderately low heat, stirring occasionally, until the vegetables are softened. Add the raisins and the sugar and cook the mixture over moderate heat, stirring occasionally, for 5 minutes. Stir in the caraway seeds, the vinegar, and the sauerkraut and cook the mixture, stirring, for 3 minutes. Transfer the mixture to a large bowl, add the toasted bread cubes, the bacon, crumbled, and salt and pepper to taste, and combine the stuffing gently but thoroughly. Let the stuffing cool completely before using it to stuff a 12- to 14-pound turkey.

(Alternatively, the stuffing may be baked separately: Preheat the oven to 325° F. Butter a 3- to 4-quart casserole. Spoon the stuffing into the prepared casserole, drizzle it with the broth, and dot the top with the additional 2 tablespoons butter, cut into bits. Bake the stuffing, covered, in the middle of the oven for 30 minutes and bake it, uncovered, for 30 minutes more.) **Serves 8 to 10.**

the heartland
desserts

APPLE PIE

- 2 recipes pastry dough (page 15)
- 3 pounds McIntosh apples (about 8)
- 3/4 cup plus 1 tablespoon sugar
- 2 tablespoons all-purpose flour
- 1 teaspoon cinnamon
- 1/4 teaspoon freshly grated nutmeg
- 1/4 teaspoon salt
- 1 tablespoon fresh lemon juice
- 2 tablespoons cold unsalted butter, cut into bits
- milk for brushing the crust

Preheat the oven to 450° F.

Roll out half the dough ⅛ inch thick on a lightly floured surface, fit it into a 9-inch (1-quart) glass pie plate, and trim the edge, leaving a ¾-inch overhang. Chill the shell and the remaining dough while making the filling. In a large bowl toss together the apples, each peeled, cored, and cut into eighths, ¾ cup of the sugar, the flour, the cinnamon, the nutmeg, the salt, and the lemon juice until the mixture is combined well, transfer the filling to the shell, and dot it with the butter.

Roll out the remaining dough into a 13- to 14-inch round on a lightly floured surface, drape it over the filling, and trim it, leaving a 1-inch overhang. Fold the overhang under the bottom crust, pressing the edge to seal it, and crimp the edge decoratively. Brush the crust lightly with the milk, cut slits in it with a sharp knife, forming steam vents, and sprinkle the pie evenly with the remaining 1 tablespoon sugar. Bake the pie on a large baking sheet in the middle of the oven for 20 minutes, reduce the temperature to 350° F., and bake the pie for 20 to 25 minutes more, or until the crust is golden and the apples are tender.

BLUEBERRY TART

For the shell

- 1 1/3 cups all-purpose flour
- 1 tablespoon sugar
- 1/2 teaspoon baking powder
- 1 1/2 teaspoons cinnamon
- 1 stick (1/2 cup) cold unsalted butter, cut into bits
- 1 large egg, beaten lightly

For the filling

- 1 tablespoon unsalted butter
- 1/4 cup honey
- 1/2 cup sugar
- 4 cups blueberries, picked over
- 3 tablespoons fresh lemon juice
- 2 tablespoons cornstarch

- 1 cup well-chilled heavy cream

Preheat the oven to 450° F.

Make the shell: Into a bowl sift together the flour, the sugar, the baking powder, the cinnamon, and a pinch of salt. Add the butter, blend the mixture until it resembles coarse meal, and stir in the egg. Knead the dough until it is combined well, press it into the bottom and halfway up the sides of a baking pan, 13 by 9 by 2 inches, and chill the shell for 1 hour. Bake the shell in the middle of the oven for 10 minutes.

Reduce the oven temperature to 375° F.

Make the filling: In a stainless-steel or enameled saucepan melt the butter with the honey and the sugar over moderately low heat, stirring, and add the blueberries, a pinch of salt, the lemon juice, and the cornstarch. Bring the mixture to a simmer, stirring, and simmer it for 3 minutes, or until the syrup is clear and thick.

Spread the filling in the shell and bake the tart in the middle of the 375° F. oven for 10 minutes. Let the tart cool in the pan on a rack and chill it for 30 minutes, or until the filling is set. In a chilled bowl beat the cream until it holds stiff peaks, transfer it to a pastry bag, and pipe it decoratively over the tart. **Serves 8.**

BROWNIE PUDDING CAKE

- 1 cup all-purpose flour
- 2/3 cup unsweetened cocoa powder
- 3/4 teaspoon baking powder
- 3/4 teaspoon salt
- 2 large eggs
- 1 cup granulated sugar
- 3/4 stick (6 tablespoons) unsalted butter, melted and cooled
- 1/2 cup milk
- 1 teaspoon vanilla
- 1/2 cup chopped walnuts
- 3/4 cup firmly packed light brown sugar
  coffee ice cream as an accompaniment

Preheat the oven to 350° F.

Into a bowl sift together the flour, 1/3 cup of the cocoa powder, the baking powder, and the salt. In another bowl whisk together the eggs, the granulated sugar, the butter, the milk, and the vanilla, add the flour mixture, and stir the batter until it is just combined. Stir in the walnuts and spread the batter evenly in an ungreased 8-inch-square baking pan. In another bowl whisk together the remaining 1/3 cup cocoa powder, the brown sugar, and 1 1/3 cups boiling water, pour the mixture over the batter, and bake the cake in the middle of the oven for 35 to 40 minutes, or until a tester comes out with crumbs adhering to it. Serve the cake hot with the ice cream.

NECTARINE AND BROWN SUGAR ICE CREAM

- 2 pounds nectarines (about 4), pitted and chopped
- 3/4 cup firmly packed light brown sugar
- 2 teaspoons fresh lemon juice
- 2 tablespoons bourbon liqueur
- 2 cups heavy cream
- 1 cup milk
- 3 large egg yolks
- 1 large whole egg
- 1 teaspoon vanilla

In a saucepan combine the nectarines, ¼ cup of the sugar, ¼ cup water, and the lemon juice and cook the mixture at a high simmer, covered, for 5 minutes. Simmer the mixture, uncovered, for 5 to 10 minutes, or until the nectarines are soft. Purée the mixture in a food processor or blender with the bourbon liqueur. In a heavy saucepan scald the cream and the milk with a pinch of salt. In a large bowl with an electric mixer beat the egg yolks and the whole egg with the remaining ½ cup sugar until the mixture is thick and pale, beat in the cream mixture, and pour the mixture into the heavy saucepan. Cook the mixture over moderately low heat, stirring with a wooden spoon, until it registers 175° F. on a candy thermometer. Strain the custard through a fine sieve into a large bowl and stir in the nectarine purée and the vanilla. Set the bowl in another bowl of ice and cold water and stir the mixture until it is cold. Freeze the mixture in an ice-cream freezer according to the manufacturer's instructions. Makes about 2 quarts.

RHUBARB CUSTARD PIE

- 2 recipes pastry dough (page 15)
- 2 large eggs
- 1 cup sugar
- 2 tablespoons unsalted butter, cut into bits and softened
- 1/4 cups all-purpose flour
- 1/2 teaspoon freshly grated nutmeg
- 1/2 teaspoon cinnamon
- 1 teaspoon freshly grated lemon zest
- 1 pound rhubarb, trimmed and cut into 1-inch pieces (about 4 cups)
- 2 cloves

    an egg wash made by beating 1 large egg with 1 teaspoon water

Roll out half the dough ⅛ inch thick on a floured surface, fit it into a 9-inch pie plate, and trim it flush with the edge. Chill the shell for at least 30 minutes.

Preheat the oven to 450° F.

In a bowl with an electric mixer beat the eggs until they are combined well, add the sugar, a little at a time, beating, and beat the mixture until it is light and fluffy. Beat in the butter, the flour, the nutmeg, the cinnamon, and the zest. Arrange the rhubarb in the shell with the cloves and pour the egg mixture over it.

Roll out the remaining dough ⅛ inch thick on a floured surface and drape it over the filling. Trim the top crust, leaving a ½-inch overhang, fold it under the bottom crust, pressing the edge to seal it, and crimp the edge decoratively. Brush the dough with the egg wash and cut slits in the top crust with a sharp knife to form steam vents. Bake the pie on a baking sheet in the oven for 10 minutes, reduce the oven temperature to 350° F., and bake the pie for 30 to 40 minutes more, or until the crust is golden. Serve the pie warm or at room temperature.

CHOCOLATE PEANUT BUTTER SWIRL BROWNIES

- 4 ounces unsweetened chocolate
- 3/4 stick (6 tablespoons) unsalted butter
- 6 large eggs
- 2 cups granulated sugar
- 1 teaspoon vanilla
- 1/2 teaspoon salt
- 3/4 cup all-purpose flour
- 2/3 cup semisweet chocolate chips
- 3/4 cup smooth peanut butter
- 1/4 cup confectioners' sugar

Preheat the oven to 350° F. Butter and flour a 13- by 9-inch baking pan.

In a metal bowl set over simmering water melt the unsweetened chocolate with the butter, stirring, and let it cool. In a bowl with an electric mixer beat 4 of the eggs with the granulated sugar, the vanilla, and the salt until the mixture is thick and pale. Stir in the chocolate mixture until it is just combined and add the flour and the chocolate chips, stirring until the batter is just combined. Spread the batter in the prepared baking pan. In a small bowl with the electric mixer cream together the peanut butter and the confectioners' sugar, add the remaining 2 eggs and 1 tablespoon water, and beat the mixture until it is smooth. Drop the mixture by heaping tablespoons on the brownie mixture, pull the back of a spoon through the peanut butter mixture to swirl the mixtures, and bake the brownies in the middle of the oven for 30 to 35 minutes, or until they spring back when touched lightly. Let the brownies cool completely in the pan on a rack and cut them into squares.

OATMEAL RAISIN COOKIES

- 1 cup raisins
- 1 stick (1/2 cup) plus 3 tablespoons unsalted butter, softened
- 1 cup firmly packed light brown sugar
- 1/3 cup granulated sugar
- 2 large eggs
- 1 teaspoon vanilla
- 1 1/4 cups all-purpose flour
- 2 cups old-fashioned rolled oats
- 1/2 teaspoon baking soda
- 3/4 teaspoon cinnamon
- 1/4 teaspoon ground cloves
- 1 teaspoon salt

Preheat the oven to 350° F. Butter baking sheets.

In a small bowl let the raisins soak in 1 cup hot water, covered, for 30 minutes, or until they are plump, and drain them well. In a bowl with an electric mixer cream the butter with the sugars, add the eggs, one at a time, beating well after each addition, and beat in the vanilla. In another bowl whisk together well the flour, the oats, the baking soda, the cinnamon, the cloves, and the salt, stir the mixture into the butter mixture, and stir in the raisins.

Drop tablespoons of the batter about 2 inches apart onto the prepared baking sheets, bake the cookies in the middle of the oven for about 15 minutes, or until they are golden, and let them cool on the baking sheets for no more than 5 minutes. Transfer the cookies to racks and let them cool completely. **Makes about 36 cookies.**

the moun

On this page, a fresh snowfall at Bridger Bowl and right, fly fishing the Yellowstone River, both in Montana

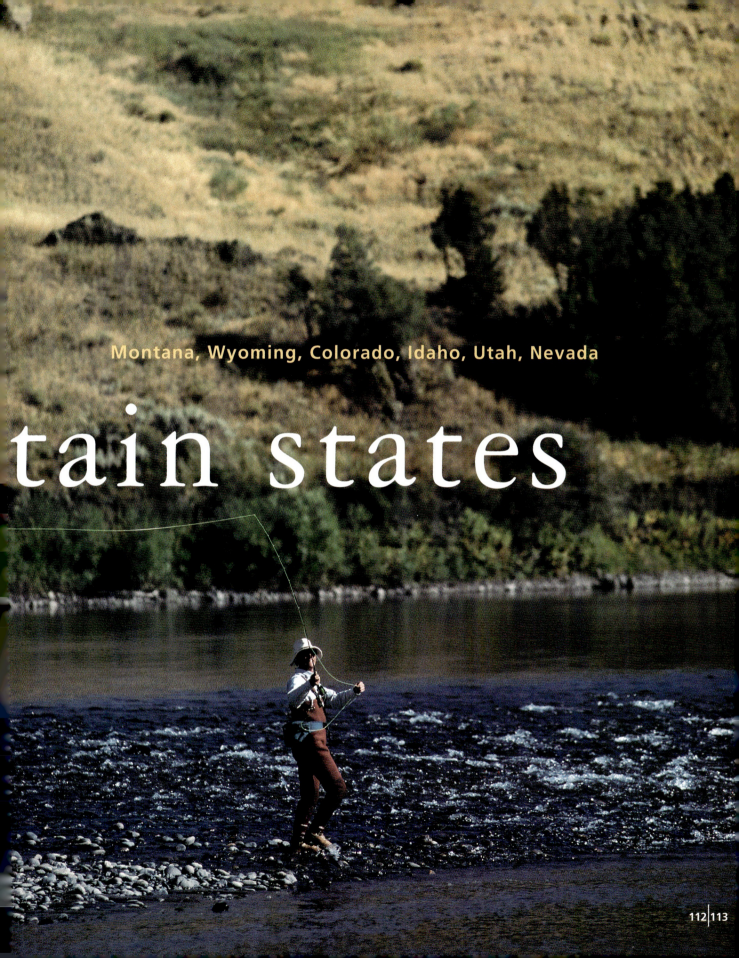

Montana, Wyoming, Colorado, Idaho, Utah, Nevada

tain states

the mountain states

Snow-capped Rocky Mountains, verdant valleys, barren desert, and jagged canyons — this vast area is one of spectacular contrasts. But it was the gold, silver, and beaver skins that lured early settlers, and the promise of land that later enticed homesteaders. To this day, the spirit of these rugged, adventuresome people is captured in the hearty regional cuisine.

For hundreds of years the native Anasazi hunted buffalo and wild game, fished for trout, cultivated beans, and foraged for pine nuts and edible berries — foods still enjoyed today. Spanish explorers arrived in 1540, but it was not until 1804 that Lewis and Clark began to chart the territory. During these early years fur trappers, living on buffalo meat, traversed the mountains.

Then, in the mid-1800s, the Mormons came in search of religious freedom. These adept farmers planted fields of wheat, barley, and potatoes and brought recipes for whole-wheat bread and hearty stews. Later, homesteaders came by wagon train carrying with them various fruit and vegetable cuttings from their Eastern farms. When gold and silver were discovered in Nevada, droves of mine workers came from Yugoslavia, Germany, England, Scotland, Ireland, Scandinavia, Finland, and Italy, adding international flavors to the area's cuisine. Texas cowboys began to drive their cattle across the region, and chuck-wagon fare has been popular ever since. The French and Spanish Basque introduced sheep ranching, and their lamb dishes are still prominent. Other influences come from the Mexicans — as seen by the chilies, blue corn, cilantro, salsas, and tortillas found in local dishes.

Spinach Salad with Gorgonzola Croutons and Bacon Twists

A ROUNDUP LUNCH

SPINACH SALAD WITH
GORGONZOLA CROUTONS
AND BACON TWISTS

★

MARINATED SKIRT
STEAK AND PEPPERS

★

YELLOW SQUASH
BAKED WITH TOMATOES
AND CHILI

★

COUNTRY POTATO AND
ONION GRATIN

★

HERBED COTTAGE
CHEESE BREAD

★

BLUEBERRY
GINGERBREAD

★

THE HOGUE VINEYARD
WASHINGTON STATE
MERLOT 1990

Serves 6

the mountain states
menu

Feeding hungry ranch hands is serious business, and our Roundup Lunch is appropriately hearty. We begin with a substantial spinach salad and move on to our succulent Marinated Skirt Steak and Peppers entrée. Be sure to marinate this economical cut of beef for *at least* six hours to fully tenderize and season it. The accompanying baked squash dish adds Southwestern flavor with a bit of *jalapeño* and coriander, while our potato gratin pairs russet potatoes and onions (Idaho's top crops) for simple, homey goodness. For a yummy finale we combine blueberries, a regional favorite, and gingerbread, an English and Scottish classic. Wild blueberries are always tastier than cultivated; pick them fresh mid-morning after the dew has evaporated off the berry.

SPINACH SALAD WITH GORGONZOLA CROUTONS AND BACON TWISTS

- 4 tablespoons crumbled Gorgonzola (about 1 ounce)
- 1 tablespoon unsalted butter, softened
- 4 1/2-inch-thick large slices of country bread, preferably sourdough
- 8 to 12 slices of bacon

For the dressing
- 1 garlic clove, minced and mashed to a paste with 1/4 teaspoon salt
- 4 to 6 teaspoons red-wine vinegar
- 2 teaspoons honey
- 4 tablespoons mayonnaise
- 2 tablespoons olive oil

- 1 pound spinach, coarse stems discarded and the leaves washed well and spun dry
- 2/3 red onion, sliced very thin into rings
- 2 hard-boiled large eggs, quartered

Preheat the oven to 375° F.
    On a cutting board mash the Gorgonzola and the butter together with a fork and spread half the mixture generously on one side of each slice of bread. Cut the slices into 1-inch pieces and arrange the pieces, cheese sides up, on a baking sheet. Twist each bacon slice into a tight spiral and arrange the bacon twists on the rack of a broiler pan, pressing the ends of each twist onto the pan (the twists will unravel somewhat as they bake). Bake the croutons in the upper third and the bacon in the middle of the oven for 15 minutes, or until the croutons are golden and the bacon is crisp. Transfer the bacon with a slotted spatula to paper towels to drain.
    Make the dressing: In a blender blend together the garlic paste, the vinegar, the honey, the mayonnaise, and the oil until the dressing is smooth.
    In a large bowl toss together the spinach, the croutons, and the onion, add the bacon twists and the eggs, and drizzle the dressing over the salad. **Serves 6.**
    Photo on page 115

MARINATED SKIRT STEAK AND PEPPERS

- 2 1/4 pounds skirt or flank steaks
- 1/3 cup fresh lemon juice
- 1/2 cup vegetable oil
- 4 1/2 tablespoons soy sauce
- 1 1/2 tablespoons Worcestershire sauce
- 3 large red or green bell peppers, cut lengthwise into sixths

In a shallow ceramic or glass dish just large enough to hold the steaks in one layer combine the lemon juice, the oil, the soy sauce, and the Worcestershire sauce, add the steaks and the peppers, turning them to coat them with the marinade, and let them marinate, covered and chilled, turning them occasionally, for at least 6 hours or overnight. Drain the steaks and the peppers over a small saucepan and boil the marinade for 1 minute. Grill the steaks and the peppers on an oiled rack set 5 to 6 inches over glowing coals, basting them with the boiled marinade, for 4 minutes on each side, or until the steaks are cooked to medium-rare and the peppers are softened and charred slightly. (Alternatively, the steaks and the peppers may be cooked on an oiled preheated ridged grill pan in the same manner.) Transfer the steaks to a cutting board, halve them crosswise, and arrange them with the peppers on a heated platter. **Serves 6.**

YELLOW SQUASH BAKED WITH TOMATOES AND CHILI

- 3 pounds yellow summer squash, quartered lengthwise and cut crosswise into 1/8-inch pieces
- 1 tablespoon salt
- 3 tomatoes, peeled, seeded, and chopped
- 1 fresh or bottled *jalapeño* chili, minced (wear rubber gloves)
- 1 1/2 tablespoons minced fresh coriander, plus additional for garnish

In a colander toss the squash with the salt, let it drain for 1 hour, and pat it dry.

Preheat the oven to 375° F. Oil a shallow 2-quart gratin dish.

In the prepared gratin dish combine the squash, the tomatoes, the *jalapeño*, 1½ tablespoons of the coriander, and black pepper to taste. Bake the mixture in the oven, stirring occasionally, for 1 hour to 1 hour and 10 minutes, or until the squash is tender and most of the liquid is evaporated, season it with salt, and garnish it with the additional coriander. Serve the dish warm or at room temperature. **Serves 6.**

the mountain states menu

Sunrise at Mount Moran, Snake River, Idaho

COUNTRY POTATO AND ONION GRATIN

- 2 pounds russet (baking) potatoes
- 2 medium onions, chopped
- 2 large garlic cloves, minced
- 1 large egg
- 2 cups milk
- 2 tablespoons cold unsalted butter, cut into bits

Preheat the oven to 375° F. Butter a 13- to 14-inch oval gratin dish (or 2-quart shallow baking dish, preferably ceramic).

Peel the potatoes, slice them thin using a *mandoline* or food processor fitted with an ⅛-inch slicing disk, and in the prepared gratin dish arrange them in 4 layers, overlapping them and sprinkling each layer with one fourth of the onions, one fourth of the garlic, and salt and pepper to taste. In a small bowl whisk the egg, add the milk, scalded, in a stream, whisking, and pour the custard slowly and evenly over the potato and onion mixture, allowing it to seep between the layers. Dot the top with the butter and bake the gratin in the middle of the oven for 45 minutes, or until it is golden and bubbling and the potatoes are tender. **Serves 6.**

HERBED COTTAGE CHEESE BREAD

- 1   1/4-ounce package (2 1/2 teaspoons) active dry yeast
- 2 1/2   cups all-purpose flour
- 1   cup small-curd cottage cheese
- 1   large egg, beaten lightly
- 1/3   cup finely chopped fresh chives or 2 tablespoons dried, crumbled
- 1   tablespoon sugar
- 1   teaspoon salt
- 1   tablespoon minced fresh thyme leaves or 1 teaspoon dried, crumbled
- 1   tablespoon minced fresh basil leaves or 1 teaspoon dried, crumbled
- 1   tablespoon minced fresh rosemary leaves or 1 teaspoon dried, crumbled
-     unsalted butter, melted, for brushing the loaf

In a large bowl proof the yeast in ½ cup lukewarm water for 15 minutes, or until it is foamy. Add 1 cup of the flour, the cottage cheese, the egg, the chives, the sugar, the salt, the thyme, the basil, and the rosemary and beat the mixture until it is combined well. Stir in the remaining 1½ cups flour, ½ cup at a time, and beat the mixture with a wooden spoon until it is combined well (do not knead the dough). Transfer the dough to a buttered bowl and let it rise, covered loosely, in a warm place, for 1½ hours, or until it is double in bulk.

Preheat the oven to 350° F. Butter a loaf pan, 9 by 5 by 3 inches.

Stir down the dough, transfer it to the prepared pan, and let the loaf rise, covered loosely, for 30 minutes, or until it is nearly double in bulk. Bake the loaf in the middle of the oven for 10 minutes, brush the top with the butter, and bake the loaf for 30 to 35 minutes more, or until it sounds hollow when the bottom is tapped. Let the loaf cool in the pan on a rack for 5 minutes, turn it out onto the rack, and let it cool completely.

BLUEBERRY GINGERBREAD

- 1 3/4   cups all-purpose flour
- 1   teaspoon baking soda
- 1/4   teaspoon salt
- 1   teaspoon ground ginger
- 2   teaspoons cinnamon
- 1/4   teaspoon ground allspice
- 1/2   cup sour cream
- 1/2   cup unsulfured light molasses
- 1/2   stick (1/4 cup) unsalted butter, softened
- 1/2   cup granulated sugar
- 2   large eggs
- 1   cup blueberries, picked over and tossed with 1 tablespoon flour
- 1   tablespoon confectioners' sugar
-     whipped cream as an accompaniment

Preheat the oven to 350° F. Butter an 8-inch square baking pan.

In a bowl sift together the flour, the baking soda, the salt, the ginger, the cinnamon, and the allspice. In another bowl combine the sour cream and the molasses.

In a large bowl cream the butter, add the sugar, a little at a time, beating, and beat the mixture until it is light and fluffy. Beat in the eggs, 1 at a time, beating well after each addition, stir in the flour mixture alternately in batches with the sour cream mixture, and fold in the blueberries. Spread the batter in the prepared pan, bake it in the middle of the oven for 40 to 45 minutes, or until a tester inserted in the center comes out clean, and let the gingerbread cool in the pan on a rack for 10 minutes. Run a thin knife around the edge, invert the gingerbread onto the rack, and let it cool completely. Transfer the gingerbread to a serving plate, sift the confectioners' sugar decoratively over it, and serve the gingerbread with the whipped cream.

starters
the mountain states

Jim Moore's place at Campbell's Ferry, Idaho

HERBED SMOKED TROUT SPREAD

- 1 smoked trout (about 1/2 pound), skinned and boned
- 1/2 cup farmer cheese (about 4 ounces)
- 3 tablespoons mayonnaise
- 1 tablespoon fresh lemon juice, or to taste
- 1 tablespoon Dijon-style mustard
- 2 tablespoons minced fresh dill
- toast points or crackers as an accompaniment

In a food processor blend together until smooth the smoked trout, the cheese, the mayonnaise, the lemon juice, the mustard, the dill, and salt and pepper to taste, transfer the spread to a crock or ramekin, and chill it, covered, for at least 1 hour and up to 2 days. Serve the spread at room temperature with the toast points or the crackers. **Makes about 1 1/2 cups.**

FISH AND WHITE BEAN SALAD WITH FRIED ONIONS

- 1 cup dried pea beans or dried navy beans, rinsed, picked over, and soaked in 3 cups cold water overnight or quick-soaked (procedure on page 73)
- 1 1/2 teaspoons salt
- 5 tablespoons olive oil (preferably extra-virgin)
- 2 tablespoons red-wine vinegar
- 2 tablespoons minced fresh coriander, plus whole fresh coriander leaves for garnish
- vegetable oil for frying the onion
- 2 cups thinly sliced onion
- 1 pound freshwater trout, sea bass, or snapper fillets
- 1/4 cup fresh lemon juice
- 1 to 2 tablespoons fresh lime juice
- coarse salt for seasoning the salad

Drain the beans, transfer them to a saucepan, and add 5 cups water. Bring the liquid to a boil and simmer the beans, covered partially, for 30 minutes, or until they are just tender. Add 1 teaspoon of the salt and simmer the beans for 5 minutes more. Drain the beans and in a bowl toss them with 3 tablespoons of the olive oil, the vinegar, and the minced coriander. Season the bean mixture with salt and pepper and let it stand for 1 hour.

In a large skillet heat ¼ inch of the vegetable oil over moderately high heat until it is hot but not smoking, in it fry the onion in batches until it is golden and crisp, and transfer it to paper towels to drain. Sprinkle the onion with salt to taste.

In a stainless-steel or enameled skillet combine the fish, the lemon juice, and the remaining ½ teaspoon salt and add enough water to just cover the fish. Bring the liquid to a simmer over moderate heat and poach the fish, covered, at a bare simmer for 5 to 7 minutes, or until it just flakes when tested with a fork. Drain the fish, skin it if necessary, and flake it.

Divide the beans among 4 salad plates, mound the fish in the center, and drizzle the lime juice and the remaining 2 tablespoons olive oil over the fish. Arrange some of the onion on top of each salad, season the salads with the coarse salt and pepper, and garnish them with the whole coriander leaves. Serve the salad at room temperature. **Serves 4.**

LENTIL SOUP WITH CHORIZO

- 1 onion, chopped
- 1 rib of celery, chopped fine
- 2 garlic cloves, minced
- 1 tablespoon olive oil
- 1 pound lentils, picked over and rinsed
- 4 cups chicken broth
- 1 28- to 32-ounce can whole tomatoes, drained, reserving the juice, and chopped
- 3/4 teaspoon dried thyme, crumbled
- 1 bay leaf
- 1 pound cured *chorizo* (spicy pork sausage, available at Hispanic markets and many supermarkets), cut into 1/4-inch dice
- 3 carrots, halved lengthwise and sliced thin crosswise

In a heavy kettle cook the onion, the celery, and the garlic in the oil over moderate heat, stirring, until the vegetables are golden, add the lentils, the broth, 4 cups water, the chopped tomatoes and the reserved juice, the thyme, the bay leaf, the *chorizo*, and the carrots and simmer the mixture, covered, stirring occasionally, for 1¼ hours. Discard the bay leaf and season the soup with salt and pepper. **Makes about 16 cups, serving 6 to 8.**

CHICK-PEA NIBBLES

- 4 cups cooked chick-peas or two 20-ounce cans chick-peas, drained, rinsed, and patted dry
- 2 tablespoons vegetable oil
- 1 garlic clove, halved
- 1 teaspoon chili powder, or to taste

Preheat the oven to 350° F.

In a jelly-roll pan just large enough to hold the chick-peas in one layer heat the oil in the oven for 5 minutes. Add the garlic, bake it, turning it, until it is golden on all sides, and discard it. Arrange the chick-peas in one layer in the pan and bake them, stirring occasionally, for 30 to 35 minutes, or until they are browned lightly. Sprinkle the chick-peas with the chili powder and bake them for 5 minutes more. Transfer the chick-peas to a bowl, season them with salt to taste, and serve them warm as an hors d'oeuvre. **Makes 4 cups.**

LETTUCE ROLLS WITH BULGUR AND VEGETABLES

- 1 head of iceberg lettuce (about 1 1/2 pounds)
- 1 cup fine *bulgur* (available at natural foods stores)
- 1 teaspoon cuminseed
- 1/3 cup olive oil
- 1/4 cup fresh lemon juice, or to taste
- 2 garlic cloves, minced, or to taste
- 1 teaspoon salt
- 4 tomatoes, peeled, seeded, and chopped
- 1 cup chopped green bell pepper
- 1 cup minced scallion
- 1/2 cup minced fresh parsley leaves
- 1/2 cup minced fresh mint leaves

Separate the lettuce leaves, rinse them under running cold water, and pat them dry. Chill the leaves, wrapped in paper towels.

In a large ceramic or glass bowl let the *bulgur* soak in 2 cups water, covered loosely, overnight, or until it is just tender, and drain it.

In a dry small skillet toast the cuminseed until it is browned and grind it in a coffee or spice grinder. In a large bowl combine the cumin, the oil, the lemon juice, the garlic, the salt, and pepper to taste. Add the *bulgur*, the tomatoes, the bell pepper, the scallion, the parsley, and the mint, toss the mixture well, and chill it, covered, for at least 2 hours. Transfer the mixture to a platter and surround it with the lettuce leaves. To serve, divide the mixture along the leaves and roll up the leaves, enclosing the filling. Serves 6.

DEVILED POTATO SKINS

- 2 tablespoons unsalted butter
- 1 teaspoon Worcestershire sauce
- 1 1/2 teaspoons Dijon-style mustard
  cayenne to taste
  the skins, with about 1/8 inch potato flesh, from 4 baked russet (baking) potatoes, cut lengthwise into 1-inch-wide strips
  sour cream dipping sauce (recipe follows) as an accompaniment

Preheat the oven to 450° F. Butter a baking sheet.

In a small heavy skillet melt the butter with the Worcestershire sauce over low heat, remove the skillet from the heat, and stir in the mustard and the cayenne. Brush the insides of the potato skins with the mustard mixture, arrange the skins, brushed sides up, on the prepared baking sheet, and sprinkle them with salt and pepper. Bake the skins in the oven for 5 to 10 minutes, or until they are golden and crisp, and serve them with the dipping sauce. **Serves 4 as an hors d'oeuvre.**

SOUR CREAM DIPPING SAUCE

- 1 cup sour cream
- 2 teaspoons Dijon-style mustard
- 2 scallions, minced
- 1/2 teaspoon Worcestershire sauce

In a small serving bowl combine the sour cream, the mustard, the scallions, and the Worcestershire sauce. **Makes about 1 cup.**

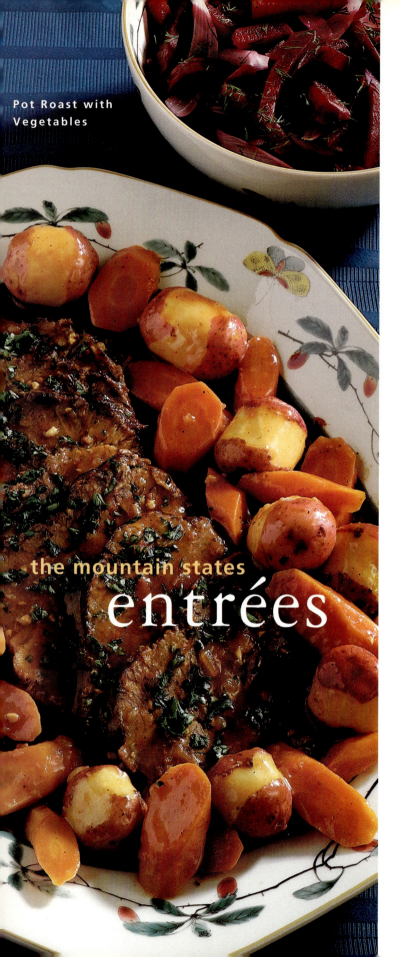

Pot Roast with Vegetables

the mountain states
entrées

POT ROAST WITH VEGETABLES

- 1 tablespoon vegetable oil
- 1 3 1/2- to 4-pound boneless chuck roast, rolled and tied
- 2 onions, chopped fine
- 4 garlic cloves, chopped fine
- 3/4 cup canned crushed tomatoes
- 1/4 cup red-wine vinegar
- 1 tablespoon firmly packed brown sugar
- 1 bay leaf
- 1 pound carrots, cut diagonally into 1-inch-thick slices
- 1 1/2 pounds small red potatoes, peeled and kept in a bowl of cold water if desired
- 1 1/2 tablespoons cornstarch dissolved in 1 1/2 tablespoons cold water
  minced fresh parsley leaves for garnish
  roasted beet and onion salad (page 130) as an accompaniment if desired

Preheat the oven to 350° F.

In a large heavy flameproof casserole heat the oil over moderately high heat until it is hot but not smoking and in it brown the beef, patted dry and seasoned with salt and pepper, on all sides. Transfer the beef to a plate, add the onions and the garlic to the casserole, and cook the mixture over moderate heat, stirring, until the onions are golden. Stir in the tomatoes, the vinegar, the sugar, the bay leaf, and 2½ cups water, bring the mixture to a boil, and add the beef. Braise the beef, covered, in the oven for 1 hour, add the carrots, and braise the mixture, covered, for 30 minutes. Add the potatoes, drained if necessary, and braise the mixture, covered, for 30 minutes, or until the beef and the vegetables are tender. *The pot roast may be prepared up to this point 2 days in advance, cooled, uncovered, and chilled, covered. Discard any solidified fat before reheating the pot roast.*

Transfer the beef with slotted spoons to a cutting board and let it stand for 10 minutes. Skim the fat from the top of the cooking mixture and bring the mixture to a boil. Stir the cornstarch mixture and add enough of it to the boiling cooking mixture, stirring, to thicken the gravy to the desired consistency. Simmer the gravy mixture, stirring occasionally, for 2 minutes, season it with salt and pepper, and discard the bay leaf. Slice the beef, arrange it on a heated platter, and transfer the vegetables with a slotted spoon to the platter. Spoon some of the gravy over the beef and serve the remaining gravy on the side. Garnish the beef with the parsley and serve it with the salad. **Serves 6**.

GRILLED BEER-MARINATED BUTTERFLIED LEG OF LAMB WITH ONIONS

- 12 ounces beer (not dark)
- 1/2 cup olive oil
- 6 tablespoons balsamic vinegar
- 2 tablespoons Worcestershire sauce
- 1 teaspoon dried thyme, crumbled
- 2 tablespoons Dijon-style mustard
- 4 large garlic cloves, minced
- 1 1/2 teaspoons salt
- 1 teaspoon freshly ground black pepper
- 1 3 1/2- to 4-pound butterflied leg of lamb
- 6 1/2-inch-thick slices of yellow or red onion, secured horizontally with wooden picks

In a large shallow dish whisk together the beer, the oil, the vinegar, the Worcestershire sauce, the thyme, the mustard, the garlic, the salt, and the pepper and add the lamb and the onion slices, coating them thoroughly with the marinade. Let the lamb marinate, covered and chilled, turning it once, overnight.

Let the mixture stand at room temperature for 1 hour and grill the lamb with the onions, discarding the marinade, on an oiled rack set 5 to 6 inches over glowing coals for 12 to 14 minutes on each side, or until a meat thermometer inserted in the thickest part registers 140° F. for medium-rare meat. Transfer the lamb to a carving board and the onions to a platter, discarding the wooden picks. Let the lamb stand for 5 minutes and, holding a carving knife at a 45° angle, cut the lamb across the grain into thin slices. Transfer the lamb to the platter. **Serves 6**.

PENNE WITH ROASTED SHIITAKE MUSHROOMS AND BELL PEPPERS

- 3/4 pound fresh *shiitake* mushrooms, stems discarded and the caps sliced thin
- 3 red and/or yellow bell peppers, sliced thin
- 1 large onion, sliced thin
- 2 tablespoons olive oil
- 3/4 cup heavy cream
- 1/4 teaspoon dried hot red pepper flakes
- 1 pound *penne* (quill-shaped pasta)
- 1/3 cup loosely packed fresh coriander, chopped fine
- 1/2 cup freshly grated Parmesan

Preheat the oven to 450° F.

Arrange the *shiitake*, the bell peppers, and the onion in a jelly-roll pan, drizzle the vegetables with the oil, and roast them in the middle of the oven, stirring occasionally, for 25 to 30 minutes, or until they are golden. In a saucepan bring the cream to a boil with the red pepper flakes and stir in the vegetables and salt and black pepper to taste. In a kettle of boiling salted water boil the *penne* until it is *al dente*, drain it well, and toss it with the sauce, the coriander, and the Parmesan. **Serves 4 to 6.**

VENISON AND ZUCCHINI KEBABS WITH CITRUS PEPPER MARINADE

- 1 cup vegetable oil
- 1/3 cup fresh lemon juice
- 3 tablespoons frozen orange juice concentrate
- 3 scallions including the green tops, sliced thin
- 1 tablespoon tarragon mustard (available at specialty foods shops) or Dijon-style mustard
- 6 juniper berries (available in the spice section of supermarkets), crushed lightly
- 1 teaspoon coarsely ground black pepper
- 1 teaspoon salt
- 1 1/2 pounds boneless tenderloin of venison*, trimmed and cut into 1 1/2-inch pieces
- 3 zucchini, scrubbed and cut crosswise into 1/2-inch pieces

* To locate venison in your area, call The North American Deer Farmers Association, tel. (301) 459-7708. Domestic venison is available by mail order from Millbrook Venison Products, tel. (800) 774-3337; venison from New Zealand and Scotland is available from D'Artagnan, tel. (800) 327-8246.

In a shallow ceramic or glass dish combine the oil, the lemon juice, the orange juice concentrate, the scallions, the mustard, the juniper berries, the pepper, and the salt, add the venison, tossing it to coat it with the marinade, and let it marinate, covered and chilled, tossing it occasionally, for at least 6 hours or overnight. Drain the venison and thread it alternately with the zucchini pieces (crosswise through the skin) on skewers. Grill the kebabs on an oiled rack set about 6 inches over glowing coals, turning them, for 15 minutes, or until the venison is cooked to medium-rare. **Serves 6.**

CRISPY BRAISED DUCK WITH TURNIPS AND OLIVES

- 1   4 1/2- to 5-pound duck, cut into serving pieces (2 breasts, 2 whole legs, and 2 wings), trimmed of as much fat as possible, and the skin pricked well with the point of a sharp knife
- 1   tablespoon vegetable oil
- 1   onion, chopped
- 3   garlic cloves, minced
- 1/4 teaspoon dried thyme, crumbled
- 3/4 cup dry white wine or dry vermouth
- 3/4 cup chicken broth
- 3/4 pound turnips, peeled and cut into 1-inch-thick wedges
- 1   teaspoon cornstarch dissolved in 1 tablespoon cold water
- 1/2 cup Kalamata or other brine-cured black olives
- 2   teaspoons fresh lemon juice, or to taste
- 3   tablespoons minced fresh parsley leaves

Preheat the oven to 350° F.

Pat the duck dry and season it with salt and pepper. In a wide heavy flameproof casserole heat the oil over moderately high heat until it is hot but not smoking and in it brown the duck well, in batches if necessary, transferring it as it is browned with tongs to a plate. Pour off all but ½ tablespoon of the fat, add the onion, and cook it over moderately low heat, stirring, until it is softened. Add the garlic and the thyme and cook the mixture, stirring, for 1 minute. Add the wine or the vermouth and the broth and bring the mixture to a boil. Return the duck to the casserole, skin sides up, in one layer and braise it, covered, in the middle of the oven for 15 minutes. Stir in the turnips and braise the mixture, covered, for 45 minutes, or until the duck and the turnips are tender. Transfer the duck, skin sides up, to a flameproof platter, skim any fat from the cooking liquid, and bring the liquid to a boil over moderately high heat. Stir the cornstarch mixture, add it to the sauce and turnip mixture, stirring, and stir in the olives and the lemon juice. Simmer the sauce and turnip mixture for 2 minutes, season it with salt and pepper, and keep it warm. Broil the duck under a preheated broiler about 4 inches from the heat for 1 to 2 minutes, or until the skin is crisp. Spoon the sauce and turnips around the duck and sprinkle the dish with the parsley. **Serves 4.**

side dishes

the mountain states

Sautéed Potatoes Provençale;
Potato Rosemary Focaccia

SAUTÉED POTATOES PROVENÇALE

- 3 tablespoons red-wine vinegar
- 2 garlic cloves, minced
- 2 teaspoons freshly grated lemon zest
- 1/2 cup olive oil
- 3 pounds large boiling potatoes (about 6), peeled, sliced 1/4 inch thick, and patted dry
- 1/3 cup minced fresh parsley leaves (preferably flat-leafed)

In a small saucepan combine the vinegar, the garlic, the zest, and salt and pepper to taste, bring the mixture to a boil, and simmer it for 2 minutes. Remove the pan from the heat and whisk in ¼ cup of the oil. In each of 2 large skillets heat 2 tablespoons of the remaining oil over moderately high heat until it is hot but not smoking and in it cook the potatoes in one layer in batches over moderate heat, turning them, for 10 to 15 minutes, or until they are golden brown on the outside and tender within. Transfer the potatoes to a serving dish, pour the garlic mixture over them, and toss the potatoes with the parsley. **Serves 6.**

POTATO ROSEMARY FOCACCIA

- 2 1/2 teaspoons (a 1/4-ounce package) active dry yeast
- 4 1/2 cups all-purpose flour
- 2 cups mashed cooked russet (baking) potatoes (about 1 1/4 pounds)
- 1 tablespoon salt
- 2 garlic cloves, sliced thin
- 1 teaspoon dried rosemary, crumbled
- 1/3 cup olive oil
- 1 1/2 pounds small red potatoes

In a small bowl sprinkle the yeast over 1 cup warm water and let it proof for 5 minutes, or until it is foamy. In a large bowl combine well 4 cups of the flour, the mashed potatoes, and the salt until the mixture resembles coarse meal, add the yeast mixture, and stir the dough until it is combined well. Turn the dough out onto a floured surface and knead it, incorporating as much of the remaining ½ cup flour as necessary to prevent it from sticking, for 8 to 10 minutes, or until it is smooth and elastic. Form the dough into a ball, put it in an oiled bowl, and turn it to coat it with the oil. Let the dough rise, covered with plastic wrap, in a warm place for 1½ hours, or until it is double in bulk. While the dough is rising, in a small bowl stir together the garlic, the rosemary, and the oil and let the mixture stand, covered. Turn the dough out into a well-oiled 15½- by 10½-inch jelly-roll pan, press it evenly into the pan, and let it rise, covered loosely, in a warm place for 45 minutes, or until it is almost double in bulk.

Preheat the oven to 400° F.

Using a *mandoline* or other hand-held slicer cut the red potatoes into paper-thin slices, arrange the slices on the dough, overlapping them, and brush them with the oil mixture, discarding the garlic. Sprinkle the *focaccia* with salt and pepper to taste and bake it in the bottom third of the oven for 40 to 50 minutes, or until it is golden. Let the *focaccia* cool in the pan on a rack and serve it warm or at room temperature.

Roasted Beet and Onion Salad

SAUTÉED GREEN BEANS WITH CHILI CRUMBS

- 2 tablespoons unsalted butter
- 1/2 teaspoon dried oregano, crumbled
- 1 1/2 teaspoons chili powder
- 1/8 teaspoon cayenne
- 1 cup coarse fresh whole-grain or rye bread crumbs, toasted lightly
- 2 tablespoons vegetable oil
- 1 pound green beans, trimmed and cut into 1/2-inch pieces
- fresh lemon juice to taste

ROASTED BEET AND ONION SALAD

- 2 1/4 pounds beets, scrubbed, leaving 1 inch of the stems attached
- 1 1/2 pounds onions, unpeeled
- 3 tablespoons balsamic vinegar, or to taste
- 3 tablespoons finely chopped fresh dill, or to taste

Preheat the oven to 350° F.

Divide the beets and the onions into small groups, separating the vegetables by size, wrap the groups tightly in foil, and roast the vegetables in the oven for 1½ to 2 hours, or until they are tender. *The beets and the onions may be roasted 2 days in advance and kept covered and chilled.* Unwrap the beets and the onions carefully and let them cool until they can be handled. Peel the beets and cut them into ⅓-inch-thick sticks. Peel the onions and cut them lengthwise into ⅓-inch-wide strips.

In a bowl toss the beets with the vinegar and salt and pepper to taste, add the onions and 2 tablespoons of the dill, and toss the mixture gently. Transfer the salad to a serving bowl, sprinkle it with the remaining 1 tablespoon dill, and serve the salad warm or chilled. **Serves 6.**

In a large heavy skillet melt the butter over moderate heat, stir in the oregano, the chili powder, and the cayenne, and add the bread crumbs. Cook the mixture, stirring occasionally, until the crumbs are toasted lightly and transfer it to a bowl. In the skillet, cleaned, heat the oil over moderately high heat until it is hot and almost smoking and in it sauté the beans, stirring, for 6 to 8 minutes, or until they are crisp-tender and browned lightly. Stir in the lemon juice and salt and black pepper to taste, add the crumb mixture, and toss the mixture well. **Serves 4.**

CELERY PINE NUT SLAW

For the dressing

- 3 tablespoons Dijon-style mustard
- 1/4 cup half-and-half
- 1 large egg plus 1 large egg yolk
- 3 tablespoons white-wine vinegar
- 1/4 cup olive oil

- 1 pound celery, shredded (preferably in a food processor)
- 8 cups finely shredded red cabbage
- 1 onion, minced
- 1/3 cup minced fresh parsley leaves
- 1/3 cup pine nuts, toasted lightly

Make the dressing: In a stainless-steel or enameled saucepan combine the mustard, the half-and-half, the whole egg, the egg yolk, the vinegar, and salt and pepper to taste and cook the mixture over moderately low heat, whisking, until it is thickened and a candy thermometer registers 160° F. Remove the pan from the heat and add the oil in a stream, whisking.

In a salad bowl combine the celery, the cabbage, the onion, the parsley, and the pine nuts, toss the slaw with the dressing and salt and pepper to taste, and serve it at room temperature or chilled. Serves 6 to 8.

BAKED LENTILS IN BARBECUE SAUCE

- 1 1/2 cups lentils, picked over and rinsed
- 1 1/3 cups cider vinegar
- 2 onions, 1 halved and each half stuck with a clove, and the other sliced
- 1 cup canned tomato purée
- 1/3 cup unsulfured molasses
- 1/4 cup plus 2 tablespoons firmly packed light brown sugar
- 4 teaspoons dry mustard
- 2 teaspoons ground ginger
- 2 teaspoons Worcestershire sauce
- 1/4 teaspoon Tabasco, or to taste
- 1 1/4-pound piece of lean salt pork

In a large stainless-steel or enameled saucepan cover the lentils with 5 cups water and ½ cup of the vinegar, bring the liquid to a boil, and boil the lentils for 2 minutes. Remove the pan from the heat and let the lentils soak for 1 hour. Drain the lentils, return them to the saucepan, and add 5 cups water, ½ cup of the remaining vinegar, and the cloved onion. Bring the liquid to a boil and simmer the mixture, covered partially, for 30 to 35 minutes, or until the lentils are tender. Discard the onion and drain the lentils in a colander set over a bowl, reserving the liquid.

Preheat the oven to 325° F.

In a large ceramic or glass bowl combine well 1½ cups of the reserved cooking liquid, the tomato purée, the remaining ⅓ cup vinegar, the molasses, ¼ cup of the sugar, the mustard, the ginger, the Worcestershire sauce, and the Tabasco. Arrange half the sliced onion in the bottom of a stainless-steel or enameled casserole, top it with half the lentils, and arrange the remaining sliced onion over the lentils. Top the onion with the remaining lentils and pour the barbecue sauce over the mixture. Score the rind of the salt pork and in a saucepan of boiling water blanch the salt pork for 1 minute. Drain the salt pork and cut it into 6 pieces. Push the pieces rind sides down into the lentils, add enough of the remaining cooking liquid to just cover the mixture, and bring the liquid to a simmer over moderate heat. Bake the mixture, covered with foil and the lid, in the oven, adding more of the cooking liquid as necessary to keep it moist, for 3 to 3½ hours, or until the lentils are very tender. Season the mixture with salt and pepper, force the remaining 2 tablespoons sugar through a coarse sieve over the top, and bake the mixture, uncovered, in the oven for 15 to 20 minutes, or until a thin crust has formed. Serves 4 to 6.

the mountain states side dishes

the mountain states
desserts

SWEET CARROT PUDDING

- 1/2 stick (1/4 cup) unsalted butter, softened
- 1/4 cup vegetable shortening
- 1 1/2 cups firmly packed light brown sugar
- 3 large eggs
- 3 tablespoons fresh lemon juice
- 1 1/2 teaspoons freshly grated lemon zest
- 1 cup all-purpose flour
- 1/2 teaspoon baking soda
- 1/2 teaspoon baking powder
- 1/2 teaspoon salt
- 1/2 teaspoon ground allspice
- 1 1/2 cups grated carrot (about 1/2 pound)
- lightly sweetened whipped cream spiced with ground ginger to taste as an accompaniment

Preheat the oven to 350° F. Butter generously a 6-cup ring mold.

    In a large bowl cream together the butter and the shortening, add the sugar, a little at a time, beating, and beat the mixture until it is light and fluffy. Beat in the eggs, 1 at a time, and add the lemon juice and the zest. Into a bowl sift together the flour, the baking soda, the baking powder, the salt, and the allspice and stir the mixture into the butter mixture. Stir in the grated carrot, transfer the batter to the prepared mold, and cover the mold with a buttered round of foil.

    Set the mold in a baking pan, add enough hot water to the pan to reach two thirds of the way up the side of the mold, and bake the pudding in the middle of the oven for 30 minutes. Remove the foil and bake the pudding for 30 minutes more, or until a tester inserted halfway between the center and the edge comes out clean. Let the pudding cool in the mold on a rack for 10 minutes. Invert a platter over the mold and invert the pudding onto it. Serve the pudding warm with the gingered whipped cream.

ZUCCHINI RAISIN WHISKEY CAKE

For the cake
- 1/2 cup raisins
- 1/3 cup rye whiskey
- 2 1/2 cups all-purpose flour
- 2 teaspoons baking powder
- 1 teaspoon baking soda
- 1/2 teaspoon salt
- 1/2 teaspoon cinnamon
- 2 large eggs
- 1/2 cup flavorless vegetable oil
- 1 1/4 cups granulated sugar
- 2 cups coarsely grated zucchini (about 1/2 pound)
- 1 cup chopped walnuts
- 2 teaspoons freshly grated lemon zest

For the icing
- 4 ounces cream cheese, softened
- 1/2 stick (1/4 cup) unsalted butter, softened
- 2/3 cup confectioners' sugar
- 1 1/2 teaspoons freshly grated lemon zest

Preheat the oven to 350° F. Line the bottom of a buttered 10-inch springform pan or deep cake pan with a round of wax paper and butter the paper.

    Make the cake: In a cup let the raisins macerate in the whiskey for 10 minutes. Into a bowl sift together the flour, the baking powder, the baking soda, the salt, and the cinnamon. In a large bowl whisk together the eggs, the oil, and the granulated sugar, stir in the flour mixture, the zucchini, the raisin mixture, the walnuts, and the zest, and stir the batter until it is combined well. Pour the batter into the prepared pan, smoothing the top, and bake the cake in the middle of the oven for 45 to 55 minutes, or until a tester comes out clean. Let the cake cool in the pan on a rack for 10 minutes, turn it out onto the rack, discarding the wax paper, and let it cool completely.

    Make the icing: In a bowl with an electric mixer cream the cream cheese and the butter with the confectioners' sugar and the zest.

    Spread the icing over the top and side of the cake.

Paradise Valley in the Montana Rockies

Roll out half the dough ½ inch thick on a well-floured surface and with a 3- to 3½-inch doughnut cutter cut out doughnuts, reserving the center pieces. With the other half of the dough either cut out more round doughnuts in the same manner or shape the dough into crullers. For the crullers, roll the dough into a ½-inch-thick rectangle about 14 by 5 inches and cut it into 5- by ½-inch strips. To form each cruller twist 2 strips of dough together and pinch the ends to secure them. In a deep skillet heat 2 inches of the oil until it registers 375° F. on a deep-fat thermometer and in it fry the round doughnuts, the reserved doughnut centers, and the crullers in batches, turning them once, for 2 to 3 minutes, or until they are golden, transferring them as they are fried to paper towels to drain. (Make sure the oil returns to 375° F. before adding each new batch.)

In a shallow bowl stir together the remaining ½ cup sugar and the remaining ½ teaspoon cinnamon. While the doughnuts are still warm roll them, 1 at a time, in the sugar mixture, coating them well. *The doughnuts keep, wrapped in plastic wrap, for 1 day.* **Makes about 20 doughnuts.**

SPICED POTATO DOUGHNUTS

- 3 1/2 cups all-purpose flour
- 4 teaspoons baking powder
- 1 teaspoon salt
- 2 1/2 teaspoons cinnamon
- 1 teaspoon freshly grated nutmeg
- 2 large eggs
- 3 tablespoons unsalted butter, melted
- 1 1/4 cups sugar
- 1 1/2 cups mashed cooked russet (baking) potatoes (about 1 pound)
- 1/2 cup milk
- 2 teaspoons freshly grated orange zest if desired
- 1 teaspoon vanilla
- vegetable oil for deep-frying the doughnuts

Into a bowl sift together the flour, the baking powder, the salt, 2 teaspoons of the cinnamon, and the nutmeg. In a small bowl whisk together the eggs, the butter, ¾ cup of the sugar, the potatoes, the milk, the zest, and the vanilla until the mixture is combined well, add the potato mixture to the flour mixture, and stir the dough until it is just combined. Chill the dough, covered, for 1 hour, or until it is cold and can be handled easily.

BUTTERSCOTCH PUDDING

- 1 cup firmly packed dark brown sugar
- 1/3 cup cornstarch
- 1/2 teaspoon salt
- 2 1/2 cups milk
- 1 cup heavy cream
- 3 large egg yolks, beaten lightly
- 1/2 stick (1/4 cup) unsalted butter, cut into bits
- 2 teaspoons vanilla
- whipped cream as an accompaniment
- shaved semisweet chocolate for garnish

In a heavy saucepan whisk together the sugar, the cornstarch, and the salt and add the milk in a stream, whisking until the mixture is combined well. Whisk in the heavy cream and the egg yolks, bring the mixture to a boil over moderate heat, whisking constantly, and boil it, whisking, for 1 minute. Remove the pan from the heat, stir in the butter and the vanilla, and pour the pudding through a fine sieve into a bowl. Divide the pudding among six 6- to 8-ounce dessert cups and let it cool. Chill the puddings, covered, for 2 hours, or until they are set. Serve the puddings topped with the whipped cream and garnished with the shaved chocolate. **Serves 6.**

TRAIL MIX COOKIES

- 1 cup vegetable shortening
- 1 1/2 cups firmly packed dark brown sugar
- 2 large eggs
- 1/2 cup buttermilk
- 1 1/2 cups all-purpose flour
- 1 teaspoon baking soda
- 1 teaspoon baking powder
- 1 teaspoon salt
- 1 teaspoon cinnamon
- 3 cups quick-cooking rolled oats
- 1 12-ounce package semisweet chocolate chips
- 2/3 cup dry-roasted peanuts, chopped coarse
- 1 cup raisins
- 1/2 cup roasted sunflower seeds

Preheat the oven to 375° F. Grease baking sheets.

In a bowl cream together the shortening and the sugar until the mixture is light and fluffy, add the eggs, 1 at a time, beating well after each addition, and stir in the buttermilk. Into another bowl sift together the flour, the baking soda, the baking powder, the salt, and the cinnamon and stir the flour mixture into the sugar mixture. Add the oats, the chocolate chips, the peanuts, the raisins, and the sunflower seeds and combine the mixture well.

Drop rounded tablespoons of the dough 2 inches apart onto the prepared baking sheets and bake the cookies in the oven for 10 to 12 minutes, or until they begin to color around the edges. Transfer the cookies with a metal spatula to racks to cool. **Makes about 56 cookies.**

INDIAN PUDDING WITH BULGUR

- 4 cups milk
- 1/4 cup *bulgur* (available at natural foods stores)
- 1/4 cup yellow cornmeal
- 2 tablespoons unsalted butter
- 3 large eggs, beaten lightly
- 1/2 cup unsulfured molasses
- 3 tablespoons honey
- 1/2 teaspoon cinnamon
- 1/2 teaspoon ground ginger
- heavy cream as an accompaniment

Preheat the oven to 300° F. Butter a 1½-quart baking dish.

In a heavy saucepan scald the milk over moderate heat, add gradually the *bulgur*, the cornmeal, and the butter, stirring, and simmer the mixture, stirring, for 15 minutes. Let the mixture cool for 10 minutes. In a bowl beat together the eggs, the molasses, the honey, the cinnamon, the ginger, and a pinch of salt, add the milk mixture in a stream, stirring, and combine the mixture well. Transfer the pudding to the prepared baking dish and bake it in the middle of the oven for 2 hours, or until a knife inserted in the center comes out clean. Let the pudding cool in the dish on a rack for 30 minutes and serve it with the cream. **Serves 4 to 6.**

BUTTERMILK LAYER CAKE WITH CHOCOLATE SOUR CREAM FROSTING

For the cake layers
- 2 sticks (1 cup) unsalted butter, softened
- 2 cups sugar
- 3 large eggs
- 1 teaspoon vanilla
- 1/2 teaspoon almond extract
- 2 1/2 cups cake flour (not self-rising)
- 2 1/2 teaspoons baking powder
- 1/2 teaspoon salt
- 1 cup buttermilk

For the frosting
- 18 ounces semisweet chocolate, melted and cooled
- 1 1/2 cups sour cream at room temperature
- 3/4 teaspoon vanilla
- 1/4 teaspoon salt

Preheat the oven to 350° F. Butter and flour two 9-inch round cake pans.

Make the cake layers: In a large bowl with an electric mixer cream together the butter and the sugar until the mixture is light and fluffy and beat in the eggs, 1 at a time, beating well after each addition, the vanilla, and the almond extract. Into a bowl sift together the flour, the baking powder, and the salt and stir the flour mixture into the butter mixture alternately with the buttermilk. Divide the batter between the prepared pans and smooth the tops. Bake the cake layers in the middle of the oven for 25 to 30 minutes, or until a tester inserted in the centers comes out clean, and let them cool in the pans on racks for 5 minutes. Turn the cake layers out onto the racks and let them cool completely.

Make the frosting: In a bowl with an electric mixer beat together the chocolate, the sour cream, the vanilla, and the salt until the mixture is smooth and glossy.

On a cake plate arrange 1 layer of the cake, spread it with some of the frosting, and top the frosting with the second cake layer. Spread the side and top of the cake with the remaining frosting.

On this page, Sabino Canyon, Tucson, Arizona and right, the Museum of International Folk Art in Santa Fe, New Mexico

Texas, New Mexico, Arizona

the

southwest

the southwest

Vast open wilderness appears in a mix of dramatic landscapes — fertile valleys, jagged mountain ranges, plateaus and mesas, and desolate deserts — that stretch from the plains of west Texas to California, and from the Mexican border north to the Grand Canyon and Colorado. Remarkably deep-blue skies, bright sunlight, and pure, refreshing air distinguish the region.

The traditional dishes of the Southwest are based on corn, beans, and squash — crops that were grown and enjoyed by early natives. But it was the Spanish who took a bland cuisine and transformed it into an unforgettable one. In 1540 they traveled north from Mexico in search of gold and discovered the fertile valleys of the upper Rio Grande instead. Soon thereafter Spanish missionaries and Mexican settlers moved to the area with vegetable seeds and fruit seedlings for tomatoes and sweet potatoes, avocados, peaches, apricots, oranges, and lemons, grape cuttings for wine, and Mexican foods, including chilies, tortillas, *tomatillos* (a cherry resembling a small tomato), and chocolate. They set up ranches with their longhorn cattle and sheep, adding beef, lamb, and cheese to the cuisine, and introduced wheat. Spanish olives, garlic, *chorizo* (spicy pork sausage), and rice were all readily assimilated into this flavorful mix.

After the Mexican-American War in 1848, American settlers — primarily of English, Scottish, and Irish descent — came from the east with their own diverse food specialties. The English brought their shorthorn and Hereford cattle, the precursor to todays tender "western" beef, and chuck wagon fare became popular. Beef barbecue and chili con carne are Texan passions.

Sopa de Lima

A SOUTHWESTERN SUNSET DINNER

SOPA DE LIMA

★

LAYERED MEXICAN
SALAD WITH CORIANDER
CHILI DRESSING

★

CANTALOUPE SHERBET

★

BROWN SUGAR
PECAN COOKIES

★

LLANO ESTACADO
TEXAS SAUVIGNON
BLANC 1992

Serves 4

photo © Corren Alston

the southwest
menu

Southwestern sunsets are breathtaking, and our colorful, light menu offers the perfect complement to such beautiful surroundings. We begin with our *Sopa de Lima* (Lime Soup), which is sure to tingle your taste buds with bell pepper, onion, garlic, tomato, lime juice, and hot green chilies. As a special accompaniment, corn tortillas are cut into strips and fried. (Both corn and wheat tortillas are enjoyed throughout the Southwest; Arizonans, influenced by the Mexican state of Sonora to the south, more often prefer the wheat variety.) More local favorites follow in our entrée salad — lettuce, black beans, coriander, corn, Monterey Jack, and avocado. Be sure to use a deep 2-quart glass dish to show off this salad's pretty layers. Both desserts can be made well in advance.

**Taos Pueblo,
New Mexico**

SOPA DE LIMA
Lime Soup

- 1 large red bell pepper, chopped
- 1 onion, minced
- 1 large garlic clove, minced
- 5 tablespoons vegetable oil
- 1 pound tomatoes, peeled, seeded, and chopped
- 3 3-inch fresh green hot chilies, seeded and minced (wear rubber gloves)
- 6 cups chicken broth
- 1 lime, halved crosswise and juiced, reserving the juice and the shell, plus lime wedges as an accompaniment
- 6 6 to 6 1/2-inch corn tortillas (recipe follows or store-bought*), halved and cut crosswise into 1/2-inch strips
- 2 pounds chicken breasts, cooked, skinned, boned, and the meat shredded

* available at Hispanic markets and some specialty foods shops and supermarkets

Preheat the oven to 250° F.

In a saucepan cook the bell pepper, the onion, and the garlic in 2 tablespoons of the oil over moderately low heat, stirring, until the pepper is softened, add the tomatoes, and cook the mixture, stirring, for 2 minutes. Add the chilies, the broth, and the juice and shell of the lime, bring the liquid to a boil, and simmer the mixture for 5 minutes. Discard the lime shell.

In a large heavy skillet heat the remaining 3 tablespoons oil over moderate heat until it is hot but not smoking and in it cook the tortilla strips in batches, stirring, for 30 seconds to 1 minute, or until they are golden and crisp, transferring them with a slotted spatula as they are fried to paper towels to drain. Keep the tortilla strips warm on a baking sheet in the oven.

Add the chicken to the broth mixture and simmer the mixture until the chicken is heated through. Season the soup with salt and pepper and serve it with the tortilla strips and the lime wedges. **Makes about 8 cups, serving 4.**

Photo on page 139

CORN TORTILLAS

- 2 cups *masa* flour (corn flour)

In a bowl combine the *masa* flour and 1¼ cups warm water and blend the mixture until it forms a smooth ball. Divide the dough into 12 pieces, form each piece into a ball, and cover the balls with an inverted bowl.

Cut wax paper into twenty-four 7-inch squares. Put 1 square of the wax paper on the bottom half of a tortilla press (available at kitchenware shops) and arrange a dough ball on it, slightly off center toward the edge opposite the handle. Flatten the ball slightly and cover it with another square of the wax paper. Lower the top of the press and press down firmly on the lever. The tortilla will measure about 6 to 6½ inches in diameter. Remove the tortilla, keeping it between the wax paper squares. Continue to make tortillas in the same manner with the remaining dough and the remaining wax paper.

Heat a griddle over high heat until it is hot. Peel off the top wax paper square from a tortilla carefully and invert the tortilla onto the griddle. After 5 seconds peel off the remaining wax paper, cook the tortilla, turning it, for 1 to 2 minutes, or until it looks dry and is flecked with golden brown spots, and transfer it with a spatula or tongs to a plate or a kitchen towel. Cook the remaining tortillas in the same manner. Let the tortillas cool, stack them between sheets of wax paper, and, if they are not to be used immediately, wrap them in plastic wrap. *The tortillas may be made 1 day in advance and kept chilled in a plastic bag.* Makes 12 tortillas.

the southwest menu

LAYERED MEXICAN SALAD WITH CORIANDER CHILI DRESSING

- 2/3 cup dried black beans, picked over and rinsed
- 1 tablespoon vegetable oil
- 1 tablespoon white-wine vinegar
- 1/2 teaspoon salt

For the dressing
- 2 1/2 tablespoons white-wine vinegar
- 1/2 teaspoon chili powder
- 1/2 cup vegetable oil
- 1/3 cup packed fresh coriander

- 1/2 cup chopped scallion
- 2 cups thinly sliced iceberg lettuce
- 2 cups fresh corn, boiled for 2 minutes, refreshed under cold water, and drained well, or thawed frozen
- 1 small red bell pepper, finely chopped
- 1 cup coarsely grated Monterey Jack
- 1 avocado (preferably California)
- 1 coriander sprig for garnish

In a large saucepan cover the beans with 2 inches cold water, bring the water to a boil, and boil the beans for 3 minutes. Remove the pan from the heat, let the beans soak for 10 minutes, and drain them. In the pan cover the beans with 2 inches cold water, bring the water to a boil, and simmer the beans for 45 minutes, or until they are just tender. Drain the beans in a sieve, refresh them under cold water, and transfer them to a bowl. Add the oil, the vinegar, and the salt, combine the mixture well, and chill it, covered, for at least 2 hours and up to 24 hours.

Make the dressing while the bean mixture is chilling: In a blender combine the vinegar, the chili powder, and salt and pepper to taste, with the motor running add the oil in a stream, and blend the mixture until it is emulsified. Add the coriander and blend the dressing until the coriander is chopped fine.

Add the scallion to the bean mixture and toss the mixture to combine it. In the bottom of a 2-quart glass soufflé dish or bowl arrange the lettuce and top it with the bean mixture. In a small bowl toss together the corn and the bell pepper, top the bean layer with the corn mixture, and top the corn layer with the Monterey Jack. *The salad may be prepared up to this point 8 hours in advance and kept covered and chilled.* Halve, pit, and chop the avocado and sprinkle it over the cheese. Garnish the salad with the coriander sprig and serve it with the dressing. **Serves 4.**

CANTALOUPE SHERBET

- 1/2 cup sugar
- 2 tablespoons triple sec
- 2 3-inch strips of orange zest
- 1 tablespoon fresh lemon juice
- 1 cantaloupe (about 2 1/2 pounds), seeds and rind discarded and the flesh chopped (about 3 1/2 cups)
- 1/4 cup heavy cream

In a saucepan stir together ½ cup water, the sugar, the triple sec, and the zest, boil the mixture, stirring, until the sugar is dissolved, and simmer it for 5 minutes. Stir in the lemon juice and transfer the syrup to a bowl. Chill the syrup, covered, until it is cold and discard the zest. In a blender or food processor purée the cantaloupe, scraping down the sides with a rubber spatula, until it is smooth, blend in the cream and the syrup, and force the mixture through a coarse sieve set over a bowl, pressing hard on the solids. Freeze the mixture in an ice-cream freezer according to the manufacturer's instructions. **Makes about 3 cups, serving 4.**

BROWN SUGAR PECAN COOKIES

- 2 sticks (1 cup) unsalted butter at room temperature
- 1 cup firmly packed light brown sugar
- 1 large egg yolk
- 1 teaspoon vanilla
- 1/2 cup pecans, toasted lightly and chopped
- 3/4 teaspoon cinnamon
- 1 1/2 cups all-purpose flour
- 3/4 teaspoon baking powder
- 1/2 teaspoon salt

Preheat the oven to 350° F.

In a bowl cream together the butter and the sugar and beat in the egg yolk, the vanilla, the pecans, and the cinnamon. Into the bowl sift together the flour, the baking powder, and the salt and combine the batter well. Drop the batter by tablespoons 3 inches apart onto ungreased baking sheets and bake the cookies in the middle of the oven for 12 to 15 minutes, or until they are golden. Let the cookies cool on the baking sheets for 5 minutes, transfer them with a metal spatula to racks, and let them cool completely. *The cookies may be made 1 month in advance and kept frozen in an airtight container.* **Makes about 32 cookies.**

the southwest menu

starters
the southwest

Chiles Rellenos

CHILES RELLENOS
Cheese-and-Chorizo-Stuffed Peppers with Tomatillo Sauce

- 6 4-inch fresh *poblano* chilies*
  vegetable oil for brushing the peppers
- 1/4 pound *chorizo* (spicy Spanish sausage)*, casings discarded and the meat chopped fine
- 1 1/2 cups grated Monterey Jack (about 5 ounces)

For the sauce
- 1 1/2 pounds fresh *tomatillos**, husked and rinsed, or three 11-ounce cans, drained
- 1/2 cup chopped onion
- 2 garlic cloves, chopped coarse
- 1/3 cup fresh coriander sprigs
- 1 tablespoon vegetable oil

For the batter
- 3 large eggs, separated
- 1/2 teaspoon salt
- 1 tablespoon all-purpose flour

vegetable oil for frying the stuffed peppers
flour for dredging the stuffed peppers
fresh coriander sprigs for garnish

* available at Hispanic or specialty produce markets

Brush the peppers with the oil and on a rack set on an electric burner at high heat, or using a long-handled fork over an open flame, roast them, turning them, for 5 minutes, or until they are evenly blistered and charred. Transfer the peppers to a bowl and cover the bowl tightly with plastic wrap. Let the peppers steam for 5 minutes, or until they are cool enough to handle, and, wearing rubber gloves, peel them, being careful not to tear the flesh. Make a lengthwise slit in the side of each pepper from the stem almost to the tip and remove the ribs and seeds carefully, leaving the stems intact. Rinse the peppers under gently running water and put them on paper towels to drain.

In a skillet cook the *chorizo* over moderate heat, stirring, for 5 to 10 minutes, or until it is cooked through, transfer it to paper towels to drain, and let it cool. In a bowl stir together the *chorizo* and the Monterey Jack. Pat the insides of the peppers dry and fill them with the *chorizo* mixture. (Be careful not to stuff the peppers too full; the slits should close when a stuffed pepper is held by the stem.)

Make the sauce: If using fresh *tomatillos,* in a large saucepan of boiling salted water boil the *tomatillos* for 10 minutes, or until they are tender, and drain them. In a blender or food processor blend the fresh or canned *tomatillos,* the onion, the garlic, and the coriander until the mixture is a slightly coarse purée. In a large skillet heat the oil over moderately high heat until it is hot but not smoking and in it cook the purée, stirring, for 5 minutes, or until it is thickened slightly. Add 1 cup water and simmer the sauce, stirring occasionally, for 15 to 20 minutes, or until it is thickened and reduced to about 2 ½ cups. Season the sauce with salt and black pepper and keep it warm, covered.

Make the batter: In a bowl with an electric mixer beat the egg whites with the salt until they barely hold stiff peaks, beat in the egg yolks, 1 at a time, and the flour, and beat the batter until it is just combined.

In a deep heavy skillet heat ¾ inch of the oil over high heat to 375° F. While the oil is heating, pat the stuffed peppers dry, dredge them in the flour, shaking off the excess, and dip them in the batter. Fry the peppers in the oil, in batches, turning them once, for 1 to 2 minutes, or until they are golden, and transfer them as they are done to paper towels to drain. (Make sure the oil returns to 375° F. before adding each new batch.) Divide the sauce and the peppers among 6 plates and garnish the peppers with the coriander sprigs. **Serves 6.**

AVOCADO AND GRAPEFRUIT SALAD WITH PINE NUT DRESSING

For the dressing
- 3 tablespoons fresh grapefruit juice
- 1/4 cup pine nuts, toasted lightly
- 2 teaspoons white-wine vinegar
- 1/3 cup olive oil, or to taste

- 3 ripe avocados (preferably California)
- 6 cups loosely packed spinach leaves removed from the stems (about 1 pound with the stems), washed well and spun dry
- 3 grapefruits, rind and pith cut away with a serrated knife and the grapefruits cut into sections
- 4 slices of lean bacon, cooked until crisp

Make the dressing: In a blender blend together the grapefruit juice, the pine nuts, the vinegar, and salt and pepper to taste until the mixture is smooth, with the motor running add the oil in a stream, and blend the dressing until it is emulsified.

Peel and pit the avocados and cut them into wedges. Divide the spinach among 6 salad plates, arrange the avocado wedges and the grapefruit sections decoratively on top, and drizzle each salad with some of the dressing. Crumble the bacon on top of the salads. **Serves 6.**

HAM AND VEGETABLE FRITTATA

- 1/3 cup chopped onion
- 1 green bell pepper, seeded and chopped
- 1 tablespoon unsalted butter
- 1/4 cup olive oil
- 2 small zucchini, scrubbed, trimmed, and chopped
- 1/4 cup peeled, seeded, and chopped tomato
- 1 small garlic clove, minced
- 1/2 teaspoon salt
- 1/4 pound cooked ham, chopped
- 6 large eggs, beaten lightly

Preheat the oven to 400° F.

In a stainless-steel or enameled skillet cook the onion and the bell pepper in the butter and 2 tablespoons of the oil over moderate heat, stirring, for 5 minutes, or until the onion is golden, add the zucchini, and cook the vegetables, covered, for 4 minutes. Add the tomato, the garlic, and the salt and cook the mixture, stirring occasionally, for 5 minutes, or until the bell pepper is tender. Transfer the mixture to a bowl and add the ham. Let the mixture cool and stir in the eggs.

Heat a 10-inch ovenproof omelet pan or nonstick skillet over moderately high heat until it is hot, add the remaining 2 tablespoons oil, and heat it, tilting and rotating the pan to coat it with the oil, until it is hot. Add the egg mixture, cook it over moderate heat for 3 to 5 minutes, or until the underside is set but the top is still runny, and bake it in the oven for 1 to 2 minutes, or until it is puffed and golden. Slide the *frittata* onto a heated serving dish and cut it into wedges. **Serves 4.**

GRILLED CHIPOTLE SHRIMP

- 4 canned whole *chipotle* chilies in *adobo* sauce* including 1 tablespoon of the sauce
- 2 garlic cloves, chopped
- 1 teaspoon salt
- 1/4 cup vegetable oil
- 1/4 cup fresh lime juice, plus lime wedges as an accompaniment
- 48 small shrimp (about 1 pound), shelled, deveined, rinsed, and drained well

*available at Hispanic markets, some specialty foods shops, and some supermarkets or by mail order from Adriana's Bazaar, New York City, tel. (212) 877-5757

In a shallow dish let forty-eight 8-inch wooden skewers soak in water to cover for 30 minutes. In a blender purée the chilies with the *adobo* sauce, the garlic, the salt, the oil, and the lime juice and transfer the mixture to a bowl. Add the shrimp, toss them until they are coated with the marinade, and let them marinate, covered and chilled, for 1 hour.

Wearing rubber gloves, remove the excess marinade from each shrimp, scraping the shrimp on the edge of the bowl, and thread the shrimp onto a skewer. Grill the shrimp on a rack set about 4 inches over glowing coals, turning them once, for 2 to 3 minutes, or until they are pink and just firm. (Alternatively, the shrimp can be broiled on racks set in jelly-roll pans under a preheated broiler about 4 inches from the heat, turning them once, for 2 to 3 minutes, or until the shrimp are pink and just firm.) Serve the shrimp with the lime wedges. **Makes 48 hors d'oeuvres.**

the southwest starters

◉ CHEESE AND SMOKED TURKEY QUESADILLAS

- 8 7-inch flour tortillas (page 149 or store-bought*)
- 3 tablespoons vegetable oil
- 1 cup grated Monterey Jack
- 1 cup grated sharp Cheddar
- 1 cup minced smoked turkey
- 2 fresh or pickled *jalapeño* chilies, or to taste, seeded and minced (wear rubber gloves)
- 1 1/2 tablespoons minced fresh coriander

    sour cream, *guacamole* and tomato *salsa* (both on page 155) as accompaniments

    * available at Hispanic markets and some specialty foods shops and supermarkets

Arrange half the tortillas in one layer on a large baking sheet and brush them lightly with some of the oil. Turn the tortillas over, divide the Monterey Jack, the Cheddar, the turkey, the chilies, and the coriander evenly among them, and top the mixture with the remaining tortillas. Brush the tops lightly with some of the remaining oil and broil the *quesadillas* under a preheated broiler about 3 inches from the heat for 1 minute, or until the tops are golden and crisp. Turn the *quesadillas* carefully with a spatula, brush the tops lightly with the remaining oil, and broil the *quesadillas* for 1 minute more, or until the tops are golden and crisp. Serve the *quesadillas,* cut into wedges, with the sour cream, the *guacamole,* and the *salsa.* **Serves 4 as a first course or 6 as an hors d'oeuvre.**

◉ SPICED RED PEPPER DIP

- 1/2 teaspoon anise seeds
- 2 roasted red bell peppers (procedure follows)
- 1 large garlic clove, chopped
- 1/2 cup firmly packed fresh coriander
- 1 cup mayonnaise
- 1/2 cup sour cream
- 1 teaspoon chili powder
- 1 teaspoon unsweetened cocoa powder
- 1/4 teaspoon cayenne

    cut up raw vegetables such as *jícama**, carrots, and cauliflower as accompaniments

    * available at specialty produce markets and many supermarkets

In a blender pulverize the anise seeds, add the roasted peppers, the garlic, and the coriander, and blend the mixture until the coriander is minced. Add the mayonnaise, the sour cream, the chili powder, the cocoa, the cayenne, and salt to taste and blend the mixture well. Serve the dip with the raw vegetables. **Makes about 2 1/4 cups.**

◉ to *roast peppers*

Using a long-handled fork char the peppers over an open flame, turning them, for 2 to 3 minutes, or until the skins are blackened. (Or broil the peppers on the rack of a broiler pan under a preheated broiler about 2 inches from the heat, turning them every 5 minutes, for 15 to 25 minutes, or until the skins are blistered and charred.) Transfer the peppers to a bowl and let them steam, covered, until they are cool enough to handle. Keeping the peppers whole, peel them, starting at the blossom end, cut off the tops, and discard the seeds and ribs.

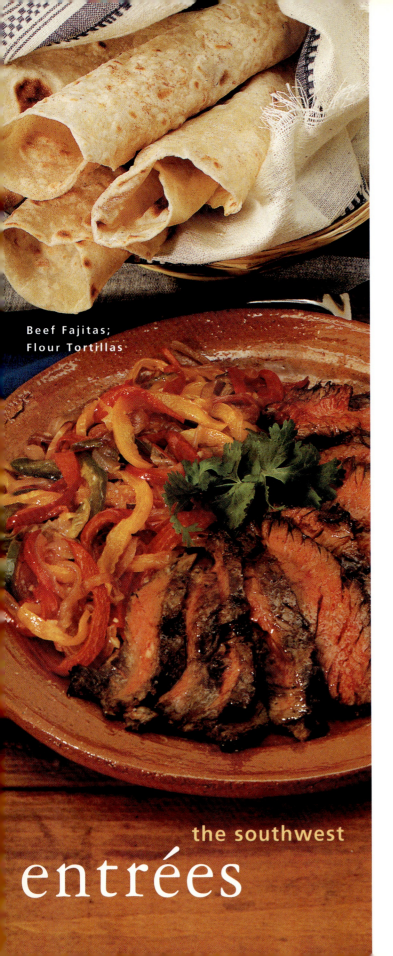

Beef Fajitas;
Flour Tortillas

the southwest
entrées

BEEF FAJITAS
*Grilled Marinated Skirt Steak with
Bell Peppers, Onions, and Flour Tortillas*

For the marinade

- 4 garlic cloves, minced and mashed to a paste with 1 teaspoon salt
- 1/4 cup fresh lime juice
- 1 1/2 teaspoons ground cumin
- 2 tablespoons olive oil

- 2 pounds skirt steak, trimmed and cut into large pieces to fit on a grill or broiler pan or in a ridged grill pan
- 2 tablespoons vegetable oil
- 3 assorted colored bell peppers, sliced thin
- 1 large red onion, sliced thin
- 2 garlic cloves, minced
- 12 7-inch flour tortillas (recipe follows or store-bought*), warmed (procedure follows)
- *guacamole* and tomato *salsa* (both on page 155) as accompaniments

* available at Hispanic markets and some specialty foods shops and supermarkets

Make the marinade: In a large bowl whisk together the garlic paste, the lime juice, the cumin, and the oil.
    Add the steak to the marinade, turning it to coat it well, and let it marinate, covered and chilled, for at least 1 hour or overnight. Grill the steak, drained, on a well-oiled rack set about 5 inches over glowing coals or in a hot well-seasoned ridged grill pan over moderately high heat for 3 to 4 minutes on each side, or until it is just springy to the touch, for medium-rare meat. (Alternatively, the steak may be

broiled on the rack of a broiler pan under a preheated broiler about 4 inches from the heat for 3 to 4 minutes on each side for medium-rare meat.) Transfer the steak to a cutting board and let it stand for 10 minutes.

While the steak is standing, in a large skillet heat the oil over moderately high heat until it is hot but not smoking, add the bell peppers, the onion, and the garlic, and sauté the mixture, stirring, for 5 minutes, or until the bell peppers are softened. Slice the steak thin across the grain on the diagonal and arrange the slices on a platter with the bell pepper mixture. Drizzle any steak juices over the steak and the bell pepper mixture and serve the steak and the bell pepper mixture with the tortillas, the *guacamole,* and the *salsa.*

To assemble a *fajita:* Spread some of the *guacamole* on a tortilla, top it with a few slices of the steak, some of the bell pepper mixture, and some of the *salsa,* and roll up the tortilla to enclose the filling. Makes 12 *fajitas,* serving 6.

FLOUR TORTILLAS

- 2 cups all-purpose flour
- 1/4 cup cold vegetable shortening, cut into pieces
- 1 teaspoon salt

In a bowl blend the flour and the shortening until the mixture resembles fine meal. In a small bowl stir together the salt and ⅔ cup warm water, add the salted water to the flour mixture, and toss the mixture until the liquid is incorporated. Form the dough into a ball and knead it on a lightly floured surface for 2 to 3 minutes, or until it is smooth. Divide the dough into 12 equal pieces, form each piece into a ball, and let the dough stand, covered with plastic wrap, for at least 30 minutes and up to 1 hour.

Heat a griddle over moderately high heat until it is hot, on a lightly floured surface roll 1 of the balls of dough into a 7-inch round, and on the griddle cook the tortilla, turning it once, for 1 to 1½ minutes, or until it is puffy and golden on both sides. Wrap the tortilla in a kitchen towel and make more tortillas with the remaining dough in the same manner, stacking and enclosing them in the towel as they are done. *The tortillas may be made 1 day in advance and kept chilled in a plastic bag.* Makes twelve 7-inch tortillas.

 to warm tortillas

Preheat the oven to 325° F.

Stack 6 tortillas at a time, wrap each stack in foil, and heat the tortillas in the middle of the oven for 15 minutes. (If the tortillas are very dry to begin with, pat each tortilla between dampened hands before stacking them.)

PICADILLO-STUFFED ONIONS
Onions Stuffed with Ground Meat, Tomatoes, and Peppers

- 4 3/4-pound onions
- 2 tablespoons olive oil
- 1/2 pound lean ground beef
- 1/2 pound lean ground pork
- 1 16-ounce can plum tomatoes, drained and chopped
- 1 4-ounce can mild green chilies, drained and chopped
- 1/4 cup raisins
- 2 tablespoons tomato paste
- 2 garlic cloves, minced
- 1 tablespoon cider vinegar, or to taste
- 1/4 teaspoon cinnamon
- 1/8 teaspoon ground cloves
- 1/2 cup coarsely chopped pimiento-stuffed olives
- 1/4 cup drained and chopped pimiento
- 2 cups beef broth, plus additional if necessary
- minced fresh parsley leaves for garnish

Preheat the oven to 350° F.

With a melon-ball cutter scoop out the centers of the onions, leaving a ¼-inch shell. Chop enough of the centers to measure 1 cup. In a large saucepan of boiling salted water cook the onion shells over moderately high heat for 5 minutes. Drain the shells and invert them on a rack.

In a stainless-steel or enameled skillet cook the chopped onion in the oil over moderate heat, stirring, until it is softened, add the beef and the pork, and cook the mixture, stirring, until the meat is no longer pink. Add the tomatoes, the chilies, the raisins, the tomato paste, the garlic, the vinegar, the cinnamon, the cloves, and salt and pepper to taste and cook the mixture, stirring, for 10 minutes, or until the excess liquid is evaporated but the mixture is still moist. Stir in the olives and the pimiento.

Sprinkle the onion shells with salt and pepper and divide the stuffing among them, mounding it. Arrange the onions in a flameproof casserole just large enough to hold them and add enough of the broth to the casserole to reach 1 inch up the sides of the onions. Bring the broth to a boil over moderate heat and bake the onions, covered, in the oven for 45 minutes, or until they are tender. Transfer the onions with a slotted spoon to a heated serving dish and garnish them with the parsley. **Serves 4.**

BAKED RED SNAPPER WITH TOMATOES AND OLIVES

- 6 6-ounce red snapper or tilapia fillets
- 1/4 cup extra-virgin olive oil
- 4 sprigs of fresh thyme
- 3 tomatoes, peeled, seeded, and chopped
- 1/2 cup coarsely chopped green olives
- 1/4 teaspoon dried hot red pepper flakes
- 2 garlic cloves, minced
- 1/2 cup finely chopped red onion
- 1 tablespoon fresh lime juice

Preheat the oven to 400° F. Oil lightly a shallow baking dish large enough to hold the fillets in one layer.

In a bowl stir together the oil, the thyme, the tomatoes, the olives, the red pepper flakes, the garlic, the onion, and the lime juice. In the prepared baking dish arrange the fillets, skin sides down, season them with salt, and spoon the tomato mixture over them. Bake the fish, uncovered, in the middle of the oven for 15 to 20 minutes, or until it just flakes. **Serves 6.**

HUEVOS RANCHEROS
Eggs with Tomato and Pepper Sauce on Tortillas

For the sauce
- 1 cup chopped onion
- 2 green bell peppers, seeded and chopped
- 2 garlic cloves, minced
- 3 tablespoons lard
- 2 28- to 32-ounce cans plum tomatoes, drained and chopped
- 1 pickled *jalapeño* chili, seeded and minced (wear rubber gloves)
- 1 teaspoon sugar
- 1 tablespoon minced fresh coriander
- 1/2 teaspoon salt

- 8 large eggs
- 1/4 cup lard for frying the tortillas
- 8 corn tortillas (page 141 or store-bought*) coriander sprigs for garnish

* available at Hispanic markets and some specialty foods shops and supermarkets

Make the sauce: In a large stainless-steel or enameled skillet cook the onion, the bell peppers, and the garlic in the lard over moderate heat, stirring occasionally, for 5 minutes, or until the onion is softened. Add the tomatoes, the *jalapeño,* the sugar, the coriander, the salt, and black pepper to taste and simmer the sauce, stirring occasionally, for 25 to 30 minutes, or until it is thickened slightly.

Make 8 indentations in the sauce with the back of a spoon, break an egg into each indentation, and cook the eggs, covered, over moderate heat for 1 minute. Spoon a little of the sauce over the egg whites and cook the eggs, covered, spooning the sauce over the whites 2 or 3 times, for 4 minutes, or until they are set.

While the eggs are cooking, in a large skillet heat the lard over moderately high heat until it is hot and in it fry the tortillas, 2 at a time, turning them, for 30 seconds, transferring them with tongs as they are fried to paper towels to drain. Arrange 2 overlapping tortillas on each of 4 heated plates and arrange 1 egg on each tortilla, transferring it with a slotted spoon. Spoon the sauce around the egg yolks and garnish the plates with the coriander. **Serves 4.**

Fettuccine with Pine Nuts, Prosciutto, and Brown Butter

the southwest entrées

FETTUCCINE WITH PINE NUTS, PROSCIUTTO, AND BROWN BUTTER

- 3/4 pound fresh or dried fettuccine
- 1 stick (1/2 cup) unsalted butter
- 2 teaspoons fresh lemon juice, or to taste
- 2 ounces thinly sliced prosciutto, torn into 2-inch-long strips
- 1 cup finely chopped fresh parsley leaves
- 1/3 cup pine nuts, toasted lightly
  thin lemon wedges as an accompaniment

In a kettle of boiling salted water cook the fettuccine until it is *al dente* and drain it. While the fettuccine is cooking, in a skillet heat the butter over moderately high heat, swirling it, until it is golden brown, remove the skillet from the heat, and stir in the lemon juice, the prosciutto, the parsley, and the pine nuts. In a bowl toss the fettuccine with the sauce and salt and pepper to taste and serve it with the lemon wedges. **Serves 2 to 3.**

BARBECUED CHILI-MARINATED PORK SPARERIBS

- 2 racks of pork spareribs (about 6 pounds)
- 8 dried New Mexican red chilies* (about 2 ounces), the seeds and stems discarded and the chilies rinsed well (use rubber gloves)
- 1/2 cup ketchup
- 2 garlic cloves
- 1/2 cup cider vinegar
- 3 tablespoons firmly packed brown sugar
- 2 teaspoons salt
- 3 tablespoons Tequila
- 1/2 cup vegetable oil
- 1/2 teaspoon ground cumin
- 1/8 teaspoon ground allspice

*available at specialty foods shops and some supermarkets and by mail order from The Chile Shop, Santa Fe, NM, tel. (505) 983-6080

In a large kettle combine the spareribs with water to cover, bring the water to a boil, and simmer the spareribs, skimming the froth as necessary, for 50 minutes. Drain the spareribs well and pat them dry.

While the spareribs are simmering, in a blender purée the chilies, ¾ cup hot water, the ketchup, the garlic, the vinegar, the sugar, the salt, the Tequila, the oil, the cumin, and the allspice. In a jelly-roll pan or on a tray coat the spareribs generously with some of the chili sauce, reserving the remaining sauce in a small bowl, covered and chilled, and let the spareribs marinate, covered with plastic wrap and chilled, for at least 8 hours or overnight.

Let the spareribs stand at room temperature for 1 hour and grill them on an oiled rack set 5 to 6 inches over glowing coals for 6 minutes on each side. In a small saucepan simmer the reserved chili sauce for 3 minutes and serve it with the ribs. **Serves 6.**

SPICED ROAST CHICKEN WITH RICE, CHORIZO, AND PEPPER STUFFING

For the stuffing
- 1 garlic clove, minced
- 1 onion, chopped
- 2 tablespoons unsalted butter
- 1 green bell pepper, chopped
- 1 cup chopped celery
- 6 ounces *chorizo* (spicy Spanish sausage, available at Hispanic or specialty produce markets), cut into 1/4-inch dice
- 1 roasted red bell pepper (procedure on page 147), chopped
- 1 pickled *jalapeño* chili, seeded and chopped (wear rubber gloves)
- 3 cups steamed rice (page 71)

- 1 6-pound roasting chicken
- 1 slice of bread
- 1/2 teaspoon ground cumin
- 1/2 teaspoon chili powder
- 1/4 teaspoon dried oregano, crumbled

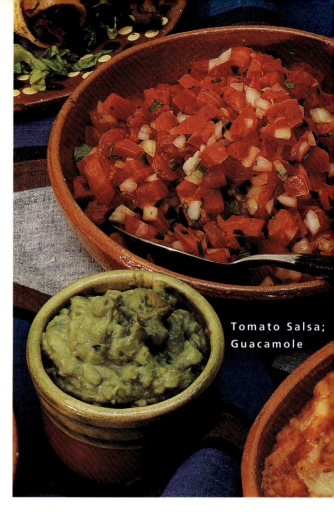

Tomato Salsa; Guacamole

Make the stuffing: In a skillet cook the garlic and the onion in the butter over moderately low heat, stirring, until the onion is softened, add the green bell pepper, the celery, and the *chorizo,* and cook the mixture, stirring, for 3 to 5 minutes, or until the vegetables are softened. Transfer the mixture to a bowl, stir in the roasted bell pepper, the *jalapeño,* the rice, and salt and pepper to taste, and let the stuffing cool completely.

Preheat the oven to 325° F.

Rinse the chicken, pat it dry, and trim the excess fat from the cavity. Stuff the chicken loosely with some of the stuffing, cover the stuffing with the bread, and truss the chicken. Put the chicken on a rack in a roasting pan and sprinkle it with the cumin, the chili powder, the oregano, and salt and pepper to taste. Transfer the remaining stuffing to a small baking dish and reserve it, covered with foil and chilled. Roast the chicken in the oven, basting it occasionally, for 2 hours, or until the juices run clear when the fleshy part of a thigh is pricked with a skewer. During the last 30 to 45 minutes of roasting, bake the remaining stuffing in the baking dish, covered, in the oven until it is heated through and moisten it with some of the pan juices before serving. **Serves 6 to 8.**

the southwest side dishes

GUACAMOLE

- 2 ripe avocados (preferably California)
- 1 small onion, minced
- 1 garlic clove, minced and mashed to a paste with 1/2 teaspoon salt
- 4 teaspoons fresh lime juice, or to taste
- 1/2 teaspoon ground cumin
- 1 fresh or pickled *jalapeño* chili if desired, seeded and minced (wear rubber gloves)
- 3 tablespoons chopped fresh coriander if desired

Halve and pit the avocados and scoop the flesh into a bowl. Mash the avocados coarse with a fork and stir in the onion, the garlic paste, the lime juice, the cumin, the chili, and the coriander. *The guacamole may be made 2 hours in advance and kept chilled, its surface covered with plastic wrap.* Makes about 2 cups.

TOMATO SALSA

- 1 pound tomatoes, peeled if desired, seeded, and chopped
- 1 small onion, minced
- 1 fresh or pickled *jalapeño* chili, or to taste, seeded and minced (wear rubber gloves)
- 1 tablespoon fresh lime juice
- 2 tablespoons chopped fresh coriander if desired

In a bowl toss together the tomatoes, the onion, the chili, the lime juice, the coriander, and salt to taste and let the *salsa* stand for 30 minutes. *The salsa may be made 4 hours in advance and kept covered and chilled.* Let the *salsa* come to room temperature before serving. Makes about 2 cups.

MACARONI AND CHEESE WITH PEPPERS

- 1 large onion, chopped
- 1 red bell pepper, chopped
- 1/2 stick (1/4 cup) unsalted butter
- 1/4 cup all-purpose flour
- 3 cups milk
- 1 1/2 teaspoons ground cumin
- 1/2 teaspoon ground coriander seed
- 1 pound elbow macaroni
- 2 tomatoes, peeled, seeded, and chopped
- 3/4 pound Monterey Jack with hot peppers, grated coarse

For the topping
- 2 tablespoons unsalted butter
- 1 1/2 cups fine fresh bread crumbs
- 1/4 cup yellow cornmeal

Preheat the oven to 350° F. Butter generously a large shallow baking dish (at least 4 quarts).

In a large skillet cook the onion and the bell pepper in the butter over moderately low heat, stirring, until they are softened, stir in the flour, and cook the *roux,* stirring, for 3 minutes. Stir in the milk, bring the mixture to a boil, stirring, and simmer it for 5 minutes. Stir in the cumin and the coriander seed and remove the sauce from the heat. In a kettle of boiling salted water cook the macaroni for 8 to 10 minutes, or until it is *al dente,* drain it well, and transfer it to a large bowl. Add the sauce, the tomatoes, the Monterey Jack, and salt and pepper to taste and combine the mixture well. Transfer the macaroni mixture to the prepared baking dish and smooth the top.

Make the topping: In a large skillet melt the butter over moderate heat, add the bread crumbs, the cornmeal, and salt and pepper to taste, and cook the mixture, stirring, until it is golden.

Sprinkle the topping over the macaroni mixture and bake the macaroni and cheese in the oven for 1 hour. Serves 8 to 10.

MEXICALI POTATO PIE
Potato Pie with Cheese, Chilies, and Olives

- 1 1/2 pounds round white potatoes, scrubbed
- 1 onion, minced
- 1/4 teaspoon dried hot red pepper flakes
- 5 tablespoons olive oil
- 2 large eggs, beaten lightly
- 1/4 pound Monterey Jack or Münster, grated
- 1 4-ounce can green chilies, drained and chopped
- 1/2 cup black olives, chopped
- 1 tablespoon fresh lemon juice, or to taste
- 6 tablespoons dry bread crumbs

Preheat the oven to 350° F.

In a large heavy saucepan cover the potatoes with 2 inches salted water, bring the water to a boil, and simmer the potatoes, covered, for 30 to 40 minutes, or until they are tender. Drain the potatoes and let them cool until they can be handled. Peel the potatoes and force them through a ricer or food mill into a large bowl. In a small skillet cook the onion with the red pepper flakes in 2 tablespoons of the oil over moderate heat, stirring, until it is softened, add the mixture to the potato with the eggs, the cheese, the chilies, the olives, the lemon juice, and salt and pepper, and combine the mixture well.

Coat the bottom and side of a 9-inch pie plate with 1 tablespoon of the remaining oil and coat the pie plate with 3 tablespoons of the bread crumbs. Spread the potato mixture in the pie plate, sprinkle it with the remaining 3 tablespoons crumbs, and drizzle the remaining 2 tablespoons oil over the top. Bake the pie in the middle of the oven for 1 hour, let it cool on a rack for 5 minutes, and cut it into wedges. Serve the pie warm or at room temperature. **Serves 6.**

YAM CORNMEAL MUFFINS

- 1 pound yams
- 3/4 cup all-purpose flour
- 1 cup yellow cornmeal
- 2 1/2 teaspoons baking powder
- 1/2 teaspoon baking soda
- 3/4 teaspoon salt
- 1 cup buttermilk
- 2 large eggs, beaten lightly
- 2 tablespoons unsalted butter, melted and cooled, plus softened butter as an accompaniment

Preheat the oven to 400° F. Butter twelve ¼-cup muffin tins.

In a saucepan cover the yams with cold water, bring the water to a boil, and simmer the yams, covered, for 35 to 40 minutes, or until they are tender. Drain the yams and let them cool until they can be handled. Peel the yams and force them through a ricer or food mill into a small bowl.

Into a bowl sift together the flour, the cornmeal, the baking powder, the baking soda, and the salt. In another bowl combine the buttermilk, the eggs, the melted butter, and the yams. Make a well in the center of the flour mixture, add the buttermilk mixture, and stir the batter until it is just combined. (The batter should be lumpy.) Spoon the batter into the prepared muffin tins, filling them three-fourths full, and bake the muffins in the middle of the oven for 20 to 25 minutes, or until a tester comes out clean. Serve the muffins with the softened butter. **Makes 12 muffins.**

the southwest side dishes

THREE-CORN PUDDING

- 1/2 cup hominy grits (not quick-cooking or instant)
- 1 teaspoon salt
- 2 tablespoons unsalted butter
- 1 17-ounce can cream-style corn
- 1/2 cup yellow cornmeal (preferably stone-ground)
- 3 large eggs, beaten lightly
- 1/4 cup milk
- 1/4 pound Monterey Jack, grated
- 1 4-ounce can green chilies, drained and minced
- cayenne to taste

Preheat the oven to 350° F. Butter a 1½-quart baking dish.

In a heavy saucepan bring 2 cups water to a boil, add the grits gradually, stirring constantly, and the salt, and simmer the mixture, covered, stirring occasionally, for 25 minutes, or until it is thick and the grits have absorbed the water. Add the butter, stirring until it is melted, and let the mixture stand, covered, for 10 minutes. Transfer the grits mixture to a large bowl, add the corn and the cornmeal, and combine the mixture well. In a small bowl beat together the eggs and the milk, add the egg mixture to the corn mixture, and combine the mixture well. Stir in the Monterey Jack, the chilies, the cayenne, and salt to taste, transfer the mixture to the prepared baking dish, and bake it in the middle of the oven for 1 hour and 10 minutes, or until it is set and a skewer inserted in the center comes out clean. Let the pudding stand for 10 minutes before serving. **Serves 6.**

Red Rock country, Arizona

ROMAINE SALAD WITH CORIANDER GARLIC DRESSING

- 1 large garlic clove, chopped fine
- 1 tablespoon fresh lemon juice
- 2 teaspoons white-wine vinegar
- 1/4 cup packed fresh coriander
- 1/3 cup vegetable oil
- 1 large head of romaine, rinsed, spun dry, and torn into bite-size pieces (about 9 cups)

In a blender blend together the garlic, the lemon juice, the vinegar, the coriander, the oil, and salt and pepper to taste. In a large bowl toss the romaine with the dressing. **Serves 6.**

the southwest desserts

CAPIROTADA
New Mexican Bread-and-Butter Pudding with Longhorn Cheese and Raisins

- 1 cup sugar
- 1/2 teaspoon vanilla
- 1 teaspoon cinnamon
- 8 slices of homemade-type white bread, toasted and crusts removed
- 3 tablespoons unsalted butter, softened
- 1 cup raisins
- 1/2 pound Longhorn cheese or mild Cheddar, grated

Preheat the oven to 350° F. Butter an 8-inch square baking pan.

In a deep heavy saucepan melt the sugar over moderately high heat, stirring, for 4 minutes, or until it is a deep caramel, remove the pan from the heat, and add 1½ cups water carefully in a slow stream, stirring. (The sugar will harden initially but will dissolve as the mixture is stirred.) Cook the mixture over moderately low heat, stirring, until the sugar is dissolved, add the vanilla and the cinnamon, and simmer the syrup for 1 minute. Spread the bread with the butter and arrange it, buttered side down in two layers, in the prepared baking pan. Sprinkle the bread with the raisins, top the mixture with the cheese, and pour the syrup over the pudding, pressing down on the top and making sure that the cheese is moistened with the syrup. Bake the pudding in the middle of the oven for 30 minutes and serve it warm. **Serves 6.**

CHEESE DOME WITH PEACH SAUCE

- 1 cup heavy cream
- 1/3 cup confectioners' sugar
- 2 teaspoons vanilla
- 2 cups small-curd cottage cheese
- 1 1/2 cups peach sauce (recipe follows)

In a bowl beat the cream with the sugar and the vanilla until it holds soft peaks. Force the cottage cheese through the fine disk of a food mill into the bowl and fold it into the cream mixture gently but thoroughly. Line a 7½-inch sieve with a double thickness of rinsed and squeezed cheesecloth, fill it with the cheese mixture, and bring the cheesecloth corners over the top. Cover the top with plastic wrap, set the sieve over a bowl, and let the mixture drain, chilled, overnight.

Discard the plastic wrap, invert a platter over the sieve, and unmold the dessert onto it. Remove the cheesecloth and serve the dessert, cut into wedges, with the peach sauce. (The cheese dome will be soft.) **Serves 6.**

PEACH SAUCE

- 3 peaches (about 1 pound)
- 2 tablespoons sugar
- 1/2 teaspoon cornstarch
- 1 tablespoon Amaretto

In a kettle of boiling water blanch the peaches for 1 minute, plunge them into a bowl of ice and cold water to stop the cooking, and drain them. Peel and pit the peaches and cut them into ¼-inch pieces.

In a heavy saucepan combine the peaches, the sugar, and ½ cup water and simmer the mixture, covered, stirring occasionally, for 15 minutes, or until the peaches are softened. In a small bowl dissolve the cornstarch in the Amaretto, stir the mixture into the peach mixture, and simmer the sauce, stirring, for 2 minutes. Let the sauce cool completely and chill it, covered, until it is cold. **Makes about 1 1/2 cups.**

FARINA FLAN

- 3/4 cup sugar
- a pinch of cream of tartar
- 2 3/4 cups milk
- 1/3 cup quick-cooking farina
- 1/3 cup fresh orange juice
- 3 large whole eggs
- 2 large egg yolks
- 2 teaspoons freshly grated orange zest

In a small heavy saucepan combine ½ cup of the sugar, the cream of tartar, and 2 tablespoons water and cook the mixture over moderately low heat, stirring and washing down any sugar crystals clinging to the sides with a brush dipped in cold water, until the sugar is dissolved. Bring the syrup to a boil over moderately high heat and cook it, swirling the pan, until it is a deep caramel. Pour the caramel into a 1¼- to 1½-quart soufflé dish, tilting the dish to coat the bottom evenly, and chill it for 20 minutes, or until it is hard and cold.

Preheat the oven to 350° F.

In a heavy stainless-steel or enameled saucepan scald the milk over moderate heat, add the farina in a slow stream, stirring, and the remaining ¼ cup sugar, and simmer the mixture, covered, stirring occasionally, for 5 minutes. In a heatproof large bowl whisk together the orange juice, the whole eggs, the egg yolks, and the zest, add the farina mixture in a slow stream, whisking, and pour the custard into the soufflé dish. Put the dish in a baking pan, add enough hot water to the pan to reach halfway up the side of the dish, and bake the flan, covered with foil, in the oven for 1 hour to 1 hour and 15 minutes, or until it is just set and a knife inserted in the center comes out clean. Let the flan cool, run a thin knife around the edge, and invert a serving plate over the dish. Invert the flan onto the plate and serve it at room temperature. Serves 6.

CHOCOLATE KAHLÚA CREAM PIE

- 1 cup chocolate wafer crumbs
- 1/4 cup pecans, ground fine
- 1/2 stick (1/4 cup) unsalted butter, melted and cooled
- 2/3 cup plus 2 tablespoons sugar
- 1/4 teaspoon cinnamon
- 2 tablespoons cornstarch
- 4 large egg yolks
- 2 cups milk
- 3 tablespoons Kahlúa
- 2 ounces unsweetened chocolate, chopped

For the topping
- 2/3 cup well-chilled heavy cream
- 1 tablespoon sugar
- 1 tablespoon Kahlúa

cinnamon for garnish

Preheat the oven to 350° F.

In a bowl combine well the wafer crumbs, the pecans, the butter, 2 tablespoons of the sugar, and the cinnamon, pat the mixture into a 9-inch (1-quart) glass pie plate, and bake the shell in the middle of the oven for 10 to 12 minutes, or until it is just set. Let the shell cool on a rack.

In a bowl whisk together the remaining ⅔ cup sugar, the cornstarch, and the egg yolks and whisk in the milk, scalded. In a heavy saucepan bring the custard to a boil over moderate heat, whisking, and simmer it, whisking, for 2 minutes. Whisk in the Kahlúa and the chocolate until the mixture is smooth and pour the mixture into the shell, smoothing the top. Chill the pie, its surface covered with plastic wrap, for at least 6 hours.

Make the topping: In a chilled bowl with chilled beaters beat the cream until it holds soft peaks, beat in the sugar and the Kahlúa, and beat the topping until it holds stiff peaks.

Spread the topping over the pie. *The pie may be made 1 day in advance and kept covered and chilled.* Sprinkle the pie with the cinnamon.

MANGO STRAWBERRY SHORTCAKES

- 2 pints strawberries, hulled and sliced
- 2 ripe mangoes, peeled and the flesh cut from the pit and chopped
- 1/3 cup granulated sugar
- 2 teaspoons triple sec or other orange-flavored liqueur

For the biscuits
- 2 cups all-purpose flour
- 1 tablespoon baking powder
- 1 1/2 teaspoons cinnamon
- 1/2 teaspoon salt
- 3 tablespoons firmly packed brown sugar
- 1 stick (1/2 cup) cold unsalted butter, cut into bits
- 1 cup milk
- 2 teaspoons granulated sugar

- 1 cup well-chilled heavy cream
- 2 tablespoons confectioners' sugar
- 3 tablespoons sour cream

In a bowl combine the strawberries and the mangoes with the granulated sugar and the liqueur, mash the fruit lightly with a fork, and let it macerate, covered and chilled, stirring occasionally, for 1 hour.

Preheat the oven to 425° F. Butter a baking sheet.

Make the biscuits: Into a bowl sift together the flour, the baking powder, 1 teaspoon of the cinnamon, and the salt, add the brown sugar and the butter, and blend the mixture until it resembles coarse meal. Add the milk and stir the mixture until it just forms a dough. In a small bowl stir together the granulated sugar and the remaining ½ teaspoon cinnamon. Drop the dough in 8 mounds onto the prepared baking sheet, sprinkle the mounds with the cinnamon sugar, and bake the biscuits in the middle of the oven for 20 to 25 minutes, or until they are golden. Transfer the biscuits to a rack and let them cool. *The biscuits may be made 1 day in advance and kept, wrapped well, at room temperature.*

Halve the biscuits with a fork, transfer the bottoms to a platter, and spoon the fruit with its liquid over them. In a chilled bowl beat the heavy cream with the confectioners' sugar until it just holds soft peaks, beat in the sour cream, and beat the mixture until it holds stiff peaks. Top the shortcakes with the cream mixture and the biscuit tops. **Serves 8.**

california

On this page,
Nacimiento-Fergusson
Road over the
coastal mountains,
Big Sur, California
and right,
a hammock on the
beach, Honululu, Hawaii

california and hawaii

Welcome to paradise. As powerful waves crash against the rugged cliffs of Big Sur, plump grapes ripen in the lush Napa Valley hills, and a coastal breeze whispers through the coconut palms on the island of Oahu. There is no other place on earth like these two Pacific Rim states, where glorious sunshine, magnificent beaches, and countless crops abound.

Californians enjoy a cuisine that is casual, light, and centered on fresh food. Hundreds of years ago natives were already enjoying wild strawberries, grapes, walnuts, garlic, sweet anise, and oregano, along with abundant mussels, crabs, and octopuses. Then, during the eighteenth century, California's Eden exploded with olives, figs, almonds, dates, chilies, peaches, plums, and nectarines brought by the Spanish missionaries. The padres also raised cattle, hogs, and sheep and planted what would become the top wine-producing vineyards in the country. Later, Mexican ranchers contributed Southwestern spiciness to the cuisine. The Gold Rush attracted both Europeans and Asians, and along with dreams of opportunity they brought their native foods: Italian artichokes, eggplant, and broccoli, French prunes, and Chinese vegetables.

Hawaiian cuisine has also benefited from international influences. The Polynesians carried bananas, sweet potatoes, and coconuts to the islands, and years later Japanese, Chinese, and other Southeast Asian groups introduced their style of cooking (grilling on the hibachi, stir-frying, and steaming). Rich volcanic soil, reliable rainfall, and plentiful sunshine produce prolific sugar cane, macadamia nut, melon, and papaya crops.

Blood Orange Sorbet

A SEASIDE BRUNCH

RED PEPPER AND
GOAT CHEESE SPIRALS
WITH OLIVES AND
BASIL OIL

★

GRILLED CHICKEN SALAD
WITH PAPAYA, WALNUTS,
AND MESCLUN

★

BLOOD ORANGE
SORBET

★

CORNMEAL
PISTACHIO COOKIES

★

FETZER BARREL SELECT
PINOT NOIR 1992

Serves 4

california and hawaii
menu

In typical West Coast fashion, our refreshing Seaside Brunch was created with relaxation in mind — both the starter and desserts can be made in advance, and the simple chicken entrée is taken care of on the grill. Here you will find plenty of local specialties: goat cheese, red peppers, and olives are combined in our pretty roll-up starter; our chicken is flavored with a delicate marinade of olive oil, garlic, and rosemary and served on a bed of mixed baby greens and sunny papaya; our cookies are filled with pistachios and our sorbet features blood oranges. Keep in mind that blood oranges have a short-lived availability in markets outside of California. You may have to purchase them through mail order, but the raspberry-reminiscent taste of these fruits is well worth it.

RED PEPPER AND GOAT CHEESE SPIRALS WITH OLIVES AND BASIL OIL

- 1/2 cup (about 1/4 pound) soft mild goat cheese such as Montrachet, at room temperature
- 1/3 cup minced fresh chives
- 2 7-ounce jars roasted red peppers (not strips), rinsed and patted as dry as possible between paper towels
- soft-leafed lettuce leaves for lining the plates
- 4 tablespoons basil-flavored olive oil (available at specialty foods shops)
- 2 tablespoons minced brine-cured black olives

In a bowl combine well the goat cheese, the chives, and salt and pepper to taste. On a sheet of plastic wrap arrange enough of the red pepper pieces, smooth sides down, trimming the pieces where necessary, to form a 6-inch square and spread half the goat cheese mixture onto the peppers, leaving a ½-inch border on the side farthest from you. Using the plastic wrap as an aid, roll up the pepper layer jelly-roll fashion away from you to enclose the goat cheese mixture. Wrap the pepper roll tightly in the plastic wrap and make another roll in the same manner with the remaining red pepper pieces and goat cheese mixture. Chill the red pepper rolls for at least 3 hours. *The red pepper rolls may be made 1 day in advance and kept wrapped and chilled.*

Discard the plastic wrap, pat the pepper rolls dry with paper towels, and with a sharp knife cut each roll crosswise into 10 spirals. Line 4 plates with the lettuce and divide the spirals among them. Spoon the oil over the spirals and sprinkle them with the olives. Serves 4.

GRILLED CHICKEN SALAD WITH PAPAYA, WALNUTS, AND MESCLUN

- 2 whole skinless boneless chicken breasts, halved
- 5 tablespoons olive oil
- 1 small garlic clove, minced
- 1 teaspoon fresh rosemary leaves, minced
- 1 1/2 tablespoons balsamic vinegar
- 1 shallot, minced
- 6 cups *mesclun* (mixed baby greens, available seasonally at specialty produce markets and some supermarkets), rinsed and spun dry
- 2 cups peeled, seeded, and diced papaya
- 1/2 cup lightly toasted chopped walnuts

On a large plate drizzle the chicken with 1 tablespoon of the oil, sprinkle it with the garlic, the rosemary, and salt and pepper to taste, turning it to coat it well, and let it marinate, chilled, turning it once, for 30 minutes.

In a small bowl whisk together the vinegar, the shallot, and salt and pepper to taste, add the remaining 4 tablespoons oil in a stream, whisking, and whisk the vinaigrette until it is emulsified.

Grill the chicken on an oiled rack set 5 to 6 inches over glowing coals for 4 to 5 minutes on each side, or until it is cooked through. (Alternatively, the chicken may be grilled in a preheated well-seasoned ridged grill pan in the same manner.) In a large bowl toss the *mesclun* and the papaya with just enough of the vinaigrette to coat the salad well, transfer the salad to a platter, and top it with the chicken, sliced, and the walnuts. Drizzle the remaining vinaigrette over the chicken. **Serves 4.**

CORNMEAL PISTACHIO COOKIES

- 1 cup plus 2 tablespoons all-purpose flour
- 1/3 cup yellow cornmeal
- 1/3 cup shelled pistachios, chopped fine
- 1/2 teaspoon finely grated lemon zest
- 1 stick (1/2 cup) unsalted butter, softened
- 1/2 cup sugar
- 1 large egg yolk
- 1/4 teaspoon vanilla
- 1/8 teaspoon almond extract

In a bowl whisk together the flour, the cornmeal, the pistachios, the zest, and a pinch of salt. In a large bowl with an electric mixer beat together the butter and the sugar until the mixture is light and fluffy, add the egg yolk, the vanilla, and the almond extract, and stir the mixture until it is combined well. Add the flour mixture and stir the dough until it is combined well. Form the dough into a 13- by 1½-inch log and chill the log, wrapped in wax paper, for 3 hours, or until it is firm.

Preheat the oven to 400° F. Lightly butter baking sheets.

Cut the dough log into ¼-inch-thick rounds (reshape the rounds if necessary), arrange the rounds 1 inch apart on the prepared baking sheets, and bake them in batches in the middle of the oven for 10 minutes, or until the edges are golden. Transfer the cookies to racks and let them cool. **Makes about 48 cookies.**

BLOOD ORANGE SORBET

- 2 ounces sugar cubes (about thirty 1/2-inch cubes)
- 2 1/4 pounds blood oranges (available from Frieda's, Inc. By Mail, tel. 800-241-1771)
- 1 tablespoon fresh lemon juice

For the zest garnish
- strips of blood orange zest, removed with a channel knife
- 1 large egg white, beaten lightly
- granulated sugar for coating the zest

fresh mint sprigs for garnish

Rub the sugar cubes over the surface of all but 2 of the oranges until each cube is slightly orange-colored and, using the fine side of a grater, grate the zest from the remaining 2 oranges, being careful not to grate the pith. Halve and squeeze enough of the oranges to yield 2 cups juice. In a saucepan heat 1 cup of the orange juice with the sugar cubes over moderately low heat, stirring, until the sugar is just dissolved. Transfer the mixture to a bowl, stir in the remaining 1 cup orange juice, the lemon juice, and the grated zest, and chill the mixture, covered loosely, until it is cold. Freeze the mixture in an ice-cream freezer according to the manufacturer's instructions.

Preheat the oven to 400° F.

Make the zest garnish: Roll up the zest strips into tight spirals and bake them on a baking sheet in the oven for 5 minutes. Brush the spirals lightly with the egg white, dip them lightly in the granulated sugar, and bake them for 5 minutes. Let the spirals cool and form them into decorative shapes.

Scoop the *sorbet* into bowls with a small ice-cream scoop and garnish it with the zest and the mint. **Makes about 2 cups, serving 4.**

Photo on page 165

Clockwise from top left:
Grilled Eggplant Antipasto;
Eggplant Curry (page 180);
Creamy Eggplant Salad

california and hawaii starters

GRILLED EGGPLANT ANTIPASTO

For the garlic and herb oil
- 2 garlic cloves, minced
- 2 tablespoons minced fresh parsley leaves
- 2 tablespoons coarsely chopped fresh basil leaves
- 2 tablespoons minced fresh mint leaves
- 6 tablespoons extra-virgin olive oil

- 1 eggplant (about 1 pound), unpeeled
- 1 1/2 teaspoons salt
- about 1/4 cup olive oil for brushing the eggplant
- fresh mint sprigs for garnish
- Italian or French bread, sliced and toasted, as an accompaniment

Make the garlic and herb oil: In a small bowl combine the garlic, the parsley, the basil, and the mint, stir in the olive oil, and let the oil mixture stand for 1 hour.

While the oil mixture is standing, cut the eggplant crosswise into ⅜-inch-thick slices, arrange the slices in one layer on a large rack set over a tray, and sprinkle them evenly with ¾ teaspoon of the salt. Turn the slices, sprinkle them with the remaining ¾ teaspoon salt, and let them drain, turning them after 30 minutes, for 1 hour.

Pat the slices dry very thoroughly with several changes of paper towels. Brush one side of as many slices as will fit on an oiled grill rack with some of the olive oil and grill the slices, oiled sides down, on the rack set 3 to 4 inches over glowing coals for 3 minutes. Brush the slices with some of the remaining olive oil, turn them, and grill them for 3 to 4 minutes more, or until they are tender. Grill the remaining slices in the same manner. (Alternatively, the eggplant may be grilled in a ridged grill pan over moderately high heat in the same manner.)

Transfer one third of the eggplant slices to a shallow dish just large enough to hold all of them in three layers. Stir the garlic and herb oil, drizzle about 2 tablespoons of it over the slices in the dish, and sprinkle the slices with pepper to taste. Layer the remaining slices in the same manner with the remaining garlic and herb oil and pepper to taste and chill the mixture, covered, turning the slices once, for at least 4 hours or overnight. Arrange the eggplant slices on a platter, garnish them with the mint sprigs, and serve them cold or at room temperature with the bread. Serves 4.

CREAMY EGGPLANT SALAD

- 4 eggplants (each about 1 pound), unpeeled
- 2 garlic cloves, minced, or to taste
- 2 tablespoons minced onion
- 3/4 cup mayonnaise
- 1 tablespoon fresh lemon juice, or to taste
- whole black olives for garnish
- fresh parsley sprigs for garnish
- *pita* triangles, toasted lightly, or sliced French bread as an accompaniment

Preheat the oven to 400° F. Line a large baking sheet with foil.

Prick the eggplants a few times each with a fork and bake them on the prepared baking sheet in the middle of the oven for 30 minutes. Turn the eggplants and bake them for 30 to 40 minutes more, or until they are very tender. Let the eggplants cool until they can be handled, peel them, and let them drain in a colander for 1 hour.

Discard the stem ends from the eggplants, chop the eggplant pulp until it is a chunky purée, and in a large bowl combine it with the garlic, the onion, the mayonnaise, the lemon juice, and salt and pepper to taste. Stir the salad until it is combined well and chill it, covered, for at least 2 hours and up to 48 hours. Spoon the salad onto a platter or into a shallow bowl, garnish it with the olives and the parsley, and serve it with the *pita* triangles or the bread slices. Serves 8 to 10.

Asparagus Napoleons with
Oriental Black Bean Sauce

ASPARAGUS NAPOLEONS WITH ORIENTAL BLACK BEAN SAUCE

For the pastry rectangles
- 1/2 pound frozen puff pastry, thawed
- an egg wash made by beating 1 large egg yolk with 2 teaspoons water

For the sauce
- 1 tablespoon cornstarch
- 2/3 cup chicken broth
- 1 1/2 tablespoons soy sauce
- 1 1/2 tablespoons Scotch or medium-dry Sherry
- 2 teaspoons sugar
- 1 tablespoon vegetable oil
- 1 tablespoon fermented black beans (available at Asian markets and some specialty foods shops), rinsed well and drained
- 2 tablespoons fine julienne strips of orange zest
- 1 1/2 tablespoons minced peeled fresh gingerroot
- 1 tablespoon minced garlic

1 1/2 pounds asparagus, trimmed and peeled

Preheat the oven to 400° F.
    Make the pastry rectangles: Roll out the pastry ⅛ inch thick on a lightly floured surface, cut out six 5- by 2-inch rectangles, and transfer them to a dampened baking sheet. Brush the tops of the rectangles with the some of the egg wash, being careful not to let the egg wash drip down the sides, score them in

a crosshatch pattern with the back of a paring knife, and brush them again with some of the remaining egg wash. Bake the rectangles in the upper third of the oven for 12 to 15 minutes, or until they are puffed and golden, transfer them with a spatula to racks, and let them cool. *The pastry rectangles may be made 1 day in advance, kept in an airtight container at room temperature, and reheated.* Halve the rectangles horizontally with a serrated knife and with a fork pull out carefully any uncooked dough.

Make the sauce: In a small bowl dissolve the cornstarch in 1/3 cup water and stir in the broth, the soy sauce, the Scotch or the Sherry, and the sugar. In a heavy saucepan heat the oil over moderately high heat until it is hot but not smoking and in it stir-fry the beans, the zest, the gingerroot, and the garlic for 1 minute, or until the mixture is very fragrant. Stir the broth mixture and add it to the bean mixture. Bring the sauce to a boil, stirring, simmer it for 2 minutes, and keep it warm. *The sauce may be made 1 day in advance, kept covered and chilled, and reheated.*

In a large deep skillet of boiling salted water cook the asparagus for 3 to 5 minutes, or until the stalks are just tender but not limp, and drain it well. Arrange the bottom half of each pastry rectangle on a plate and divide the asparagus among the pastries. Spoon the sauce over the asparagus and around the pastries on each plate and top the asparagus with the top halves of the pastries. **Serves 6.**

ONION, TOMATO, AND ANCHOVY TART

- 2 recipes pastry dough (page 15)
- 2 pounds onions, sliced thin (about 6 cups)
- 1/4 cup plus 2 tablespoons olive oil
- 1 28- to 32-ounce can whole plum tomatoes, drained and chopped coarse
- 2 large garlic cloves, minced
- 1 teaspoon dried thyme, crumbled
- 1 teaspoon dried rosemary leaves, crumbled
- 1 bay leaf
- 3 tablespoons dry bread crumbs
- 1/4 cup freshly grated Parmesan
- 2 2-ounce cans flat anchovy fillets, drained pitted Niçoise or Kalamata olives

On a floured surface roll out the dough into an 18- by 13-inch rectangle. Fit the dough into a jelly-roll pan, 15½ by 10½ by 1 inch, and crimp the edge decoratively. Prick the bottom of the shell with a fork and chill the shell.

In a large heavy stainless-steel or enameled skillet cook the onions in 1/4 cup of the oil, covered with a buttered round of wax paper and the lid, over low heat, stirring occasionally, for 30 minutes. Add the tomatoes, the garlic, the thyme, the rosemary, the bay leaf, and salt and pepper to taste and cook the mixture, covered, over low heat for 10 minutes. Cook the mixture, uncovered, over moderately high heat, stirring, for 10 minutes more, or until most of the liquid is evaporated, and let it cool.

Preheat the oven to 425° F.

Sprinkle the bread crumbs in the bottom of the shell, spread the onion mixture evenly in the shell, and sprinkle it with the Parmesan. Arrange the anchovy fillets in a diamond pattern on the onion mixture and arrange an olive in the center of each diamond. Drizzle the tart with the remaining 2 tablespoons oil, bake it in the lower third of the oven for 30 to 40 minutes, or until the crust is golden brown, and cut it into squares. **Serves 15 as an hors d'oeuvre.**

Tofu and Vegetable Tempura

TOFU AND VEGETABLE TEMPURA

- 6 tablespoons soy sauce
- 4 tablespoons *mirin* (syrupy rice wine, available at Asian markets and some specialty foods shops) or 2 teaspoons Scotch
- 4 teaspoons minced scallion greens plus 1/3 cup thinly sliced for garnish
- 1 pound firm tofu, rinsed, drained, and cut crosswise into 1/3-inch-thick slices (about 12 slices)
- 1 large egg yolk
- 1 cup plus 2 teaspoons all-purpose flour
- 1/2 teaspoon salt
- vegetable oil for deep-frying the tempura
- 3/4 cup julienne strips of radish
- 3/4 cup julienne strips of green bell pepper
- lemon wedges as an accompaniment

Preheat the oven to 200° F.

In a small saucepan combine well the soy sauce, the *mirin* or the Scotch, the minced scallion greens, and ½ cup water, bring the mixture to a simmer, and divide the dipping sauce among 6 small ramekins.

Pat the tofu pieces between several thicknesses and changes of paper towels until the paper towels remain dry. In a large bowl whisk together the egg yolk and 1 cup ice water, sift 1 cup of the flour and the salt into the mixture, and whisk the batter until it is combined but still slightly lumpy. In a deep fryer heat 2 inches of the oil until a deep-fat thermometer registers 375° F. Dip the tofu pieces into the batter, letting the excess batter drip off, fry them in batches in the oil, turning them, for 2 minutes, and transfer them with a slotted spoon as they are fried to a rack set over paper towels to drain. (Return the oil to 375° F. before adding each new batch.) Keep the tofu tempura warm on the rack in the oven.

While the tofu is frying, in a small bowl combine the radish and the bell pepper, sprinkle them with the remaining 2 teaspoons flour, and toss the mixture well. Add the vegetable mixture to the remaining batter and stir the mixture to coat the vegetables. To the 375° F. oil add the vegetable mixture carefully by heaping tablespoons in batches, using a fork and letting the excess batter drip back into the bowl, fry the vegetable tempura for 1 minute, or until they are pale golden, and transfer them with the slotted spoon to paper towels to drain.

Arrange the tofu tempura on 6 plates, top each piece with a vegetable tempura, and mound the sliced scallion greens decoratively on the plates. Serve the tempura with the dipping sauce and the lemon wedges. **Serves 6.**

SQUID, JERUSALEM ARTICHOKE, AND AVOCADO SALAD

- 2 1/2 pounds squid, cleaned (procedure follows) and the body sacs cut lengthwise to form flat pieces
- 1 cup thinly sliced peeled Jerusalem artichokes
- 3 tablespoons fresh lemon juice
- 2 avocados (preferably California), halved and pitted
- 3 4-inch hot green chilies, seeds and ribs discarded, minced (wear rubber gloves)
- 1/3 cup minced fresh coriander, or to taste
  French dressing (recipe follows)

Arrange the squid pieces skinned sides down on a cutting surface. Holding a cleaver or a very sharp knife at a 45-degree angle to the cutting surface score the squid in a crosshatch pattern at 1/8-inch intervals and cut it into 1-inch pieces following the scoring lines. In a saucepan of simmering salted water poach the squid for 1 minute, or until it is just white and opaque. Drain the squid in a colander, refresh it under cold water, and drain it well. (The squid will have curled into "flowers.")

Cut the artichoke slices into thin strips and in a ceramic or glass bowl toss the strips with the lemon juice. Scoop out balls from the avocados with a 1-inch melon-ball cutter, add them to the bowl, and toss them to coat them with the lemon juice. In a salad bowl combine the squid, the artichoke and avocado mixture, the chilies, and the coriander and toss the salad with the French dressing. **Serves 4.**

to *clean squid*

Pull the head and body of the squid apart, cut off the tentacles just below the eyes, and reserve the tentacles for another use. Discard the transparent quill from inside the body sac, rinse the body sac well, and peel off the purple membrane covering it. Pull off the flaps from the body sac gently to avoid tearing it and reserve them for another use.

FRENCH DRESSING

- 2 tablespoons fresh lemon juice
  Dijon-style mustard or dry mustard to taste if desired
- 1/3 to 1/2 cup olive oil, or to taste

In a bowl whisk together the lemon juice, salt and pepper to taste, and the mustard (for a sharper dressing), add the oil in a stream, whisking, and whisk the dressing until it is emulsified. **Makes about 1/2 cup.**

ARTICHOKES AND CLAMS WITH HERBED GARLIC BUTTER

- 3/4 stick (6 tablespoons) unsalted butter, plus additional to top the clams
- 2 garlic cloves, mashed to a paste
- 1 1/2 teaspoons minced fresh parsley leaves
- 1 teaspoon minced shallot
- 1 teaspoon salt
- 24 baby artichokes* (each the size of a small egg)
- 1/2 lemon for rubbing the artichokes, plus the juice of 1 1/2 lemons
- 24 littleneck clams or other small hard-shelled clams, shucked (procedure follows)

*available at specialty produce markets, some supermarkets, and by mail order from The Giant Artichoke, Castroville, CA, tel. (408) 633-2778

Preheat the oven to 400° F.

In a bowl cream ¾ stick of the butter and blend in thoroughly the garlic paste, the parsley, the shallot, the salt, and pepper to taste.

Cut off and discard the stems of the artichokes, cut the top off ½ inch above the base, and with scissors trim the tips of the remaining leaves. Rub the cut surfaces of the artichokes with the half lemon, dropping the artichokes into a bowl of cold water acidulated with the juice of half a lemon. In a stainless-steel or enameled saucepan of simmering salted water acidulated with the juice of the remaining 1 lemon simmer the artichokes, drained, for 15 to 20 minutes, or until they are tender. Drain the artichokes and scrape out the chokes with a small spoon.

Pat the artichokes dry and arrange them in the hollows of 4 *escargot* dishes (available at specialty kitchenware stores) or in 4 individual gratin dishes. Spread each artichoke with some of the garlic butter, top it with a clam, and put a dab of the additional butter on each clam. Bake the artichokes in the oven for 2 to 3 minutes, or until the butter begins to bubble. **Serves 4.**

to shuck hard-shelled clams

Scrub the clams thoroughly with a stiff brush under cold water, discarding any that have cracked shells or that are not shut tightly.

Wearing an oven mitt and working over a bowl to reserve the liquor, hold each clam in the palm of the hand with the hinge against the heel of the palm. Force a clam knife between the shells, cut around the inside edges to sever the connecting muscles, and twist the knife slightly to open the shells.

california and hawaii entrées

PORK KEBABS WITH PEANUT SAUCE

For the marinade
- 1/4 cup vegetable oil
- 1/4 cup medium-dry Sherry
- 1/4 cup soy sauce
- 3 tablespoons fresh lemon juice
- 2 tablespoons honey
- 2 tablespoons firmly packed brown sugar
- 1 tablespoon Asian sesame oil*
- 1 tablespoon minced peeled fresh gingerroot
- 2 garlic cloves, minced

- 3 pounds boneless fresh pork butt, cut into 2-inch cubes and patted dry

For the peanut sauce
- 1/3 cup smooth peanut butter
- 1/2 cup heavy cream
- 2 tablespoons soy sauce
- 2 tablespoons Asian sesame oil*
- hot chili oil* to taste
- fresh lemon juice to taste

*available at Asian markets and some specialty foods shops and supermarkets

Make the marinade: In a shallow dish stir together the vegetable oil, the Sherry, the soy sauce, the lemon juice, the honey, the sugar, the sesame oil, the gingerroot, the garlic, and salt to taste.

Add the pork and let it marinate, covered and chilled, tossing it occasionally, for at least 3 hours or overnight.

Drain the pork, reserving the marinade, thread it onto six 10-inch metal skewers, and brush the kebabs with some of the reserved marinade. Grill the kebabs on a rack set about 6 inches over glowing coals or broil them under a preheated broiler about

4 inches from the heat, turning them frequently, for 20 to 25 minutes, or until the juices run clear when the pork is pierced. Keep the kebabs warm on a platter, covered loosely.

Make the peanut sauce: In a saucepan bring ⅓ cup of the reserved marinade to a boil, discarding the rest, add the peanut butter, and cook the mixture over low heat, whisking, until it is smooth. Stir in the cream, the soy sauce, the sesame oil, the chili oil, and the lemon juice and heat the peanut sauce, stirring, until it is smooth.

Serve the kebabs with the sauce. **Serves 6.**

CALIFORNIA BURGERS

- 1 avocado, (preferably California)
- 2 tablespoons mayonnaise
- 2 teaspoons fresh lime juice
- 1 1/2 pounds ground chuck
- 2 teaspoons coarse salt
- 4 whole-grain hard rolls, halved and toasted lightly
- 1 vine-ripened tomato, cut into 4 thick slices
- 1/2 cup alfalfa sprouts

Halve and pit the avocado and in a small bowl mash it with the mayonnaise, the lime juice, and salt to taste.

Handling the ground chuck as little as possible, shape it gently into four 1-inch-thick patties and season the patties with pepper to taste. Heat a well-seasoned large cast-iron skillet over moderately high heat until it is hot, sprinkle it evenly with the coarse salt, and in it cook the patties, covered, for 3 minutes on each side for medium-rare meat.

Put the hamburgers on the bottom halves of the rolls and top them with the avocado mixture, the tomato, and the sprouts. Top the burgers with the top halves of the rolls. **Serves 4.**

CHARDONNAY-BRAISED CHICKEN WITH FENNEL AND LEMONGRASS

- 1 3 1/2- to 4-pound chicken, cut into serving pieces
- all-purpose flour seasoned with salt and pepper for dredging the chicken
- 2 tablespoons unsalted butter
- 2 tablespoons vegetable oil
- 3 cups sliced leeks, washed well and drained
- 1 1/2 pounds fennel bulb (sometimes called anise), sliced crosswise
- 8 garlic cloves, peeled
- 2 stalks of lemongrass (available at Asian markets and some specialty produce markets), the bottom 6 inches sliced very thin
- 2 cups Chardonnay
- 2 cups chicken broth
- 1 tablespoon fennel seeds
- 1 teaspoon cornstarch dissolved in 1 tablespoon cold water

Preheat the oven to 325° F.

Pat the chicken dry and dredge it in the seasoned flour, shaking off the excess. In an ovenproof kettle heat the butter and the oil over moderately high heat until the fat is hot but not smoking and in the fat brown the chicken, in batches, transferring it with tongs as it is browned to a plate. Add the leeks to the kettle and cook them over moderate heat, stirring, until they are softened. Add the sliced fennel, the garlic, the lemongrass, the Chardonnay, the broth, and the fennel seeds, bring the liquid to a boil, and return the chicken to the kettle. Braise the chicken, covered, in the oven, transferring the breast pieces after about 25 minutes to a platter for 45 minutes, or until it is tender when pierced with a fork. Transfer the remaining chicken pieces with tongs to the platter and season the braising mixture with salt and pepper to taste. Stir the cornstarch mixture and stir it into the braising mixture. Bring the sauce to a boil, stirring, boil it for 1 minute, and spoon it over the chicken. **Serves 4 to 6.**

BROILED SWORDFISH TERIYAKI

For the marinade
- 1/3 cup soy sauce
- 2 slices of fresh gingerroot, each the size of a quarter, flattened with the side of a cleaver
- 2 tablespoons medium-dry Sherry
- 1 tablespoon sugar
- 1 garlic clove, minced

- 4 1/2-pound swordfish steaks, each about 1 inch thick
  watercress sprigs for garnish

Make the marinade: In a small saucepan combine the soy sauce, the gingerroot, the Sherry, the sugar, and the garlic, bring the liquid to a boil over moderate heat, stirring until the sugar is dissolved, and let the marinade cool.

In a heavy plastic bag or large flat dish arrange the swordfish in one layer, add the marinade, and let the swordfish marinate, chilled, turning it, for 2 hours. Drain the swordfish, reserving the marinade, let it come to room temperature, and arrange it on the oiled rack of a broiler pan. Discard the gingerroot and in a saucepan boil the reserved marinade until it is reduced by half. Brush the swordfish with some of the marinade and broil it under a preheated broiler about 4 inches from the heat for 3 to 4 minutes. Turn the swordfish carefully, brush it with the remaining marinade, and broil it for 3 to 4 minutes more, or until it just flakes when tested with a fork. (Alternatively, the swordfish may be grilled on an oiled rack set 6 inches over glowing coals in the same manner.) Transfer the swordfish to a heated platter and garnish it with the watercress. **Serves 4.**

THAI BEEF SALAD WITH BARLEY

- 3 tablespoons rice
- 1 cup pearl barley
- 7 tablespoons fresh lemon juice, or to taste
- 1/4 cup soy sauce
- 3 tablespoons vegetable oil
- 1 pound ground round, crumbled
- 4 scallions, minced
- 1 teaspoon minced garlic
- 1 tablespoon minced fresh mint leaves or 1 teaspoon dried, crumbled
- 1/4 teaspoon cayenne
- 1 cup mung bean sprouts (available at Asian markets and some specialty produce markets and supermarkets), rinsed and patted dry
- 1 head of romaine, separated into leaves

In a dry small heavy skillet cook the rice over moderately high heat, stirring, for 3 to 4 minutes, or until it is golden, let it cool for 5 minutes, and in a blender or in a food processor grind it to a coarse powder.

Into a large saucepan of boiling salted water sprinkle the barley, stirring, and boil it, covered partially, for 40 minutes. Drain the barley in a colander and rinse it under cold water. Set the colander in a kettle over 1 inch boiling water and steam the barley, covered with a kitchen towel and the lid, for 15 minutes. Transfer the barley to a large bowl and while it is still warm toss it with 3 tablespoons of the lemon juice, 1 tablespoon of the soy sauce, and 1 tablespoon of the oil.

Heat a wok or a deep heavy skillet over high heat until it is hot, add the remaining 2 tablespoons oil, and heat it until it is smoking. In the oil stir-fry the beef, breaking up the lumps, for 15 to 30 seconds, or until it is browned lightly but still rare, and transfer it to a bowl. Add to the beef the rice powder, the remaining 4 tablespoons lemon juice, the remaining 3 tablespoons soy sauce, the scallions, the garlic, the mint, the cayenne, and salt and pepper to taste and combine the mixture well.

Add the beef mixture to the barley with the bean sprouts and toss the salad. Line a large shallow salad bowl with the romaine and mound the salad in the center. To serve, spoon the salad into the romaine leaves and wrap up the leaves, enclosing the filling. Serves 4 to 6.

FUSILLI WITH SUN-DRIED TOMATOES, BELL PEPPERS, AND GOAT CHEESE

- 2 garlic cloves, minced
- 1 cup chopped onion
- 1/4 cup olive oil
- 2 yellow bell peppers, chopped (about 2 1/2 cups)
- 3/4 cup dry white wine or dry vermouth
- 1/3 cup sun-dried tomatoes (packed in oil), drained and sliced thin
- 2 tablespoons drained bottled capers
- 1 cup shredded fresh basil leaves
- 1 pound *fusilli* or *rotelle* pasta
- 6 ounces mild goat cheese such as Montrachet, crumbled (about 1 1/2 cups)

In a large skillet cook the garlic and the onion in the oil over moderately low heat, stirring, until they are softened, add the bell peppers, and cook the vegetables, stirring, for 5 minutes. Add the wine or the vermouth, the sun-dried tomatoes, and the capers and boil the mixture until the liquid is reduced by half. Stir in the basil and salt and pepper to taste.

In a kettle of boiling salted water cook the pasta until it is *al dente*, transfer 2/3 cup of the cooking water to a large serving bowl, and drain the pasta. Whisk half of the goat cheese into the hot pasta water, add the vegetable mixture, the pasta, and the remaining goat cheese, and toss the mixture well. Serves 4 to 6.

GRILLED TUNA CAESAR SANDWICHES

- 3/4 teaspoon anchovy paste
- 1 tablespoon fresh lemon juice
- 2 tablespoons olive oil
- 1 garlic clove, chopped fine
- 1/3 cup mayonnaise
- 1 teaspoon Worcestershire sauce
- 3/4 teaspoon Dijon-style mustard
- 4 4-inch lengths of Italian bread, halved horizontally and toasted lightly
- 1 1/2 pounds tuna steak, 3/4 inch thick
- 8 romaine leaves
- 1/4 cup freshly grated Parmesan

In a bowl whisk together the anchovy paste, the lemon juice, the oil, the garlic, the mayonnaise, the Worcestershire sauce, the mustard, and salt and pepper to taste until the mixture is smooth. Spread the cut sides of the bread with some of the mayonnaise mixture and brush the remaining mayonnaise mixture on the tuna. Season the tuna with salt and pepper, cut it into 4 equal pieces, about the same size as the bread, and on an oiled rack set 6 inches over glowing coals grill it for 5 minutes on each side, or until it is just cooked through. Arrange 1 romaine leaf on each bottom half of the bread, top it with 1 piece of the tuna, and sprinkle the tuna with the Parmesan. Cover the tuna with the remaining romaine and the top halves of the bread, pressing them firmly. Makes 4 sandwiches.

california and hawaii
side dishes

EGGPLANT CURRY

- 1 cup finely chopped onion
- 1 tablespoon minced peeled fresh gingerroot
- 3 tablespoons vegetable oil
- 5 garlic cloves, minced
- 2 teaspoons ground coriander
- 2 teaspoons ground cumin
- 1/2 teaspoon turmeric
- 1/8 teaspoon cayenne
- 2 tablespoons chopped fresh coriander
- 1 eggplant (about 1 pound), unpeeled, cut into 1-inch pieces
- 1 14-ounce can plum tomatoes, drained and chopped, reserving the juice
- 1 tablespoon tomato paste

In a heavy kettle cook the onion and the gingerroot in the oil over moderately low heat, stirring, until the onion is very soft. Add the garlic, the ground coriander, the cumin, the turmeric, the cayenne, and 1 tablespoon of the fresh coriander and cook the mixture, stirring, for 1 minute. Stir in the eggplant and salt to taste, stirring to coat the eggplant with the spices, add the tomatoes with the reserved juice, and bring the mixture to a boil, stirring. In a small bowl stir together the tomato paste and ⅓ cup water, add the mixture to the eggplant mixture, and simmer the stew, covered, over low heat, stirring frequently, for 35 to 40 minutes, or until the eggplant is very tender and the liquid is thickened. Season the stew with salt and pepper. *The stew may be made 3 days in advance and kept covered and chilled.* Serve the stew hot or cold, sprinkled with the remaining 1 tablespoon fresh coriander. Serves 4.

Photo on page 168

Papaya Salad

MIXED FRUIT SALAD WITH ROSEMARY YOGURT DRESSING

For the dressing
- 1/2 cup plain yogurt
- 1/2 teaspoon finely chopped fresh rosemary leaves
- 2 teaspoons honey
- 1 tablespoon fresh lemon juice

- 2 navel oranges, the peel and pith cut away and the flesh cut into sections
- 3 kiwis, peeled, quartered lengthwise, and sliced thick crosswise
- 2 cups red seedless grapes, halved
- 10 dates, chopped fine

Make the dressing: In a bowl whisk together the yogurt, the rosemary, the honey, and the lemon juice and chill the dressing, covered, for 30 minutes.

In a large bowl toss the orange sections, the kiwis, the grapes, and the dates with the dressing until the fruit is coated. Serves 4 to 6.

PAPAYA SALAD

- 1 1/2 teaspoons distilled white vinegar
- 1 2-inch fresh red chili, seeded and minced (wear rubber gloves)
- 1/4 teaspoon sugar
- 1 papaya, peeled, seeded, and sliced thin lengthwise
- 1 large shallot, sliced thin

In a small bowl stir together the vinegar, the chili, the sugar, and salt to taste until the sugar is dissolved. On a platter arrange the papaya decoratively, sprinkle it with the shallot, and spoon the vinegar mixture over it. Serves 4.

CURRIED FRIED RICE WITH PINEAPPLE AND CASHEWS

- 1/4 cup vegetable oil
- 1 large onion, chopped (about 2 cups)
- 1 1/2 tablespoons curry powder
- 1 cup chopped fresh pineapple
- 1/2 cup coarsely chopped roasted cashews
- 1/4 cup minced fresh coriander
- 6 cups cold cooked long- or medium-grain white rice
- 1 teaspoon salt
- 1/2 teaspoon black pepper

In a large skillet (measuring at least 12 inches across) heat the oil over moderately high heat until it is hot but not smoking and in it sauté the onion, stirring, until it is golden. Add the curry powder and cook the mixture, stirring, for 5 seconds. Add the pineapple, the cashews, the coriander, and the rice and sauté the mixture, stirring and breaking up the rice, until it is combined well. Stir in 3 tablespoons water, the salt, and the pepper and cook the rice mixture for 1 minute. Serves 6.

SWEET ONION RINGS

- 1 cup all-purpose flour
- 1 cup beer
- 1 teaspoon salt
- 1 pound (about 2) large sweet onions, such as Maui, cut into 1/4-inch slices
- vegetable shortening for deep-frying the onion rings

In a bowl beat together the flour, the beer, and the salt until the batter is smooth and let the batter stand, covered, at room temperature for 3 hours. Separate the onion slices into rings and in a large bowl let the rings soak in ice water in the refrigerator for 2 hours. Drain the rings and pat them dry.

In a large deep skillet heat enough of the shortening to measure 2 inches when melted and continue to heat the fat until a deep-fat thermometer registers 375° F. Dip the onion rings into the batter, coating them well and letting the excess drip off, and fry them in batches, turning them, for 3 minutes, or until they are golden brown. (Make sure the oil returns to 375° F. before adding each new batch.) Drain the onion rings on paper towels and sprinkle them with salt. **Serves 4.**

TOMATO SALAD WITH CHICK-PEA DRESSING

- 2 1/4 cups drained cooked chick-peas
- 1/4 cup fresh lemon juice
- 2 garlic cloves, mashed to a paste
- 3/4 teaspoon salt
- 1/2 cup vegetable oil
- 4 large tomatoes, cored and cut into 1/2-inch slices
- minced fresh parsley leaves, paprika, and toasted pine nuts for garnish

In a food processor or in a blender purée the chick-peas, in batches, with the lemon juice, 2 tablespoons water, the garlic paste, and the salt until the mixture is smooth. With the motor running add the oil in a stream and blend the mixture until it is combined. Transfer the dressing to a bowl and let it stand, covered, for 1 hour.

Spread 1/4 cup of the dressing on each of 4 salad plates. Arrange the tomato slices on the plates, pressing them into the dressing slightly, spoon the remaining dressing over the tomatoes, and garnish each serving with some of the parsley, the paprika, and the pine nuts. Serve the salad at room temperature. **Serves 4.**

BASIL SUN-DRIED TOMATO BREAD

- 1 1/4-ounce package active dry yeast
- 1/4 teaspoon sugar
- 3/4 cup milk
- 1 cup grated jack cheese
- 1 tablespoon salt
- 2 tablespoons extra-virgin olive oil
- 1/2 cup sun-dried tomatoes (packed in oil), chopped fine
- 2 teaspoons minced garlic
- 4 cups packed fresh basil leaves, chopped
- 1 tablespoon chopped bottled *jalapeño* chilies (wear rubber gloves)
- 2 large eggs, beaten lightly
- 3 1/2 to 4 cups all-purpose flour

In a large bowl proof the yeast in 1/4 cup warm water with the sugar for 15 minutes, or until it is foamy. Stir in the milk, the jack cheese, the salt, the oil, the sun-dried tomatoes, the garlic, the basil, the *jalapeños*, the eggs, and enough of the flour to make a soft but not sticky dough. Knead the dough on a floured surface for 8 to 10 minutes, or until it is smooth and elastic, and form it into a ball. Transfer the dough to a lightly buttered bowl, turning it to coat it with the butter, and let it rise, covered with plastic wrap, in a warm place for 2 1/2 to 3 hours, or until it is double in bulk.

    Punch down the dough and form it into a loaf, tucking the seam under. Transfer the loaf to a buttered loaf pan, 9 by 5 by 3 inches, turning it to coat it with the butter, and let it rise, seam side down, covered loosely with a kitchen towel, in a warm place for 1 hour, or until it is double in bulk.

    Preheat the oven to 350° F.

    Bake the loaf in the middle of the oven for 50 minutes to 1 hour, or until it sounds hollow when tapped. Remove the bread from the pan and let it cool on a rack. **Makes 1 loaf.**

FENNEL, ORANGE, AND ONION SALAD WITH GINGER DRESSING

- 1 teaspoon coarsely grated peeled fresh gingerroot
- 2 tablespoons white-wine vinegar
- 1 teaspoon sugar
- 1 teaspoon soy sauce
- 3 tablespoons olive oil
- 2 navel oranges, the peel and pith cut away and the oranges sliced crosswise
- 1/2 fennel bulb, sliced paper-thin (about 1 1/2 cups)
- 1/2 cup paper-thin slices red onion
- 2 tablespoons chopped fresh coriander

In a small bowl whisk together the gingerroot, the vinegar, the sugar, and the soy sauce until the sugar is dissolved and whisk in the oil, whisking until the dressing is emulsified. On a large plate arrange the orange slices, the fennel slices, and the onion slices and drizzle the dressing over the salad. Sprinkle the salad with the coriander and salt and pepper to taste. **Serves 4.**

california and hawaii
desserts

FROZEN PINEAPPLE COCONUT MERINGUE CAKE

For the meringue layers
- 4 large egg whites
- 1 cup sugar

- 3 cups pineapple cream (recipe follows)

For the icing
- 1 1/2 cups heavy cream
- 1 tablespoon coconut-flavored liqueur

- 1 cup sweetened flaked coconut

Preheat the oven to 275° F. Line a buttered baking sheet with parchment paper or foil and on it trace 2 squares, using the top and bottom of a 9-inch-square pan as a guide (one square will be slightly larger than the other).

Make the meringue layers: In a large bowl with an electric mixer beat the whites with a pinch of salt until they hold soft peaks, add the sugar, 1 tablespoon at a time, beating, and beat the whites until they hold stiff, glossy peaks. Transfer the meringue to a pastry bag fitted with a ½-inch plain tip, pipe it to fill in the squares, and smooth the tops. Bake the meringues in the middle of the oven for 1 hour, or until they are firm when touched lightly and very pale golden. Remove the meringues with the parchment from the baking sheets, let them cool, and peel off the parchment carefully. With a serrated knife trim the meringue layers so that the smaller one will just fit inside the bottom of the pan and the larger will just fit inside the top of the pan. Reserve the trimmings.

Oil the pan with vegetable oil and line it with plastic wrap, leaving about a 5-inch overhang all around. Put the smaller meringue layer, smooth side down, in the lined pan. Stir the reserved meringue trimmings, crumbled, into the pineapple cream, pour the filling into the pan, smoothing it, and top it with the remaining meringue layer, smooth side up, pressing gently. Fold the plastic-wrap overhang over the top to enclose the cake and freeze the cake, wrapped well, overnight, or until it is frozen solid.

Make the icing: In a bowl beat the heavy cream until it just holds soft peaks, beat in the liqueur, and beat the icing until it holds stiff peaks.

Unwrap the cake and unmold it onto a plate, discarding the plastic wrap. Spread the top and sides of the cake with the icing and press the coconut onto the icing. Chill the cake for no more than 1½ hours and cut it into squares with a serrated knife.

PINEAPPLE CREAM

- 1 cup finely chopped fresh pineapple
- 2/3 cup sugar
- 1/4 cup amber rum
- 1 stick (1/2 cup) unsalted butter
- 1 whole large egg, plus 6 large egg yolks
- 1 cup plain yogurt

In a food processor or blender purée the pineapple. In a heavy saucepan simmer the pineapple purée, the sugar, and the rum for 5 minutes, stirring, add the butter, and stir the mixture until the butter is melted. In a bowl whisk together lightly the whole egg and the egg yolks and add the pineapple mixture in a stream, whisking. Transfer the mixture to the pan and cook it over moderately low heat, whisking constantly, for 5 to 8 minutes, or until the curd is thick enough to hold the mark of the whisk, but do not let it boil. Transfer the curd immediately to a bowl, cover its surface with plastic wrap, and let the curd cool. Chill the curd, covered with the plastic wrap, for 1 hour, or until it is cold. Whisk the yogurt into the curd. **Makes about 3 cups.**

BANANA CHEESECAKE WITH CHOCOLATE MACADAMIA CRUST

For the shell
- 1 cup chocolate wafer crumbs (about 20 wafers)
- 1/2 cup macadamia nuts, toasted lightly, cooled, and chopped fine
- 1/4 cup sugar
- 5 tablespoons unsalted butter, melted

For the filling
- 1 pound cream cheese, softened
- 1/2 cup sugar
- 1 1/2 cups mashed ripe banana (about 2 large bananas)
- 1 teaspoon vanilla
- 4 large eggs

For the topping
- 1 1/2 cups sour cream
- 1 tablespoon sugar
- 1 teaspoon vanilla

For the garnish
- 1/4 cup macadamia nuts, toasted lightly, and shaved (use the coarse side of a grater)
- 2 tablespoons shaved bittersweet chocolate

Preheat the oven to 350° F. Butter lightly a 9-inch springform pan.

Make the shell: In a bowl combine the chocolate wafer crumbs, the nuts, and the sugar, stir in the butter, and press the mixture onto the bottom and partially up the side of the prepared pan.

Make the filling: In a food processor or in a bowl with an electric mixer blend the cream cheese, the sugar, the banana, and the vanilla, add the eggs, 1 at a time, blending well after each addition, and blend the mixture until it is combined well.

Pour the filling into the shell, bake the cake in the middle of the oven for 45 minutes, and transfer it in the pan to a rack.

Make the topping: In a bowl combine the sour cream, the sugar, and the vanilla.

Spread the topping evenly over the cake and bake the cake in the middle of the 350° F. oven for 5 minutes more. Transfer the cake to the rack, let it cool, and chill it, covered loosely, overnight. Remove the side of the pan, transfer the cake to a serving plate, and garnish it with the nuts and the chocolate.

**Blood Orange Sorbet
(page 167)**

STRAWBERRY MOUSSE CAKE

For the cake
génoise batter (recipe follows)
1/3 cup rum syrup (recipe follows)
9 or 10 fresh strawberries, trimmed and halved lengthwise
strawberry mousse filling (recipe follows)

about 1/2 pint fresh strawberries
1/4 cup red currant jelly
1 fresh mint sprig

Preheat the oven to 350° F. Line the bottom of a buttered 8-inch springform pan with wax paper, butter the paper, and dust the pan with flour, knocking out the excess.

Make the cake: Pour the *génoise* batter into the pan, smoothing the top, and bake it in the middle of the oven for 20 to 25 minutes, or until the top is golden and a tester comes out clean. Let the cake cool in the pan on a rack for 5 minutes, remove the side of the pan, and invert the cake onto the rack. Remove the wax paper carefully and let the cake cool completely. *The génoise may be made 1 day in advance and kept wrapped in plastic wrap at room temperature.* Halve the cake horizontally with a serrated knife, arrange one half cut side up on a 7-inch cardboard round covered tightly with foil, and brush some of the rum syrup over the cake. Set the cake on the cardboard round on the bottom of the springform pan, wrap a 3-inch-wide doubled sheet of foil tightly around the layer to form a cylindrical collar, and secure the foil with tape. Replace the side of the pan around the foil and arrange the strawberries around the edge of the cake layer, cut sides flush with the foil collar and pointed ends up. Pour the strawberry mousse filling over the cake layer and strawberries, smoothing the top, cover it with the remaining cake layer, cut side down, and brush the cake with the remaining rum syrup to taste. Chill the cake, covered, for at least 4 hours or overnight.

Remove the side of the pan and the foil collar carefully. Arrange some of the strawberries, trimmed and sliced thin, in a decorative pattern on the cake. In a small saucepan melt the jelly with 1 tablespoon water over low heat, stirring, and brush the glaze over the strawberries, the cake layers, and the mousse. *The cake may be prepared up to this point 3 hours in advance and kept covered loosely and chilled.* Just before serving transfer the cake from the cardboard to a cake plate, arrange a strawberry, cut almost but not completely through into thin slices, leaving the stem end intact, and fanned open, in the center, and garnish it with the mint sprig. Arrange the remaining strawberries, trimmed and sliced thin, around the edge of the cake plate.

GÉNOISE BATTER

- 2 large eggs
- 1/3 cup sugar
- 1/3 cup all-purpose flour
- 1/4 teaspoon salt
- 1/2 teaspoon vanilla
- 2 tablespoons clarified butter (procedure follows), melted and cooled to lukewarm

In a metal bowl whisk together the eggs and the sugar, set the bowl over a pan of simmering water, and stir the mixture until it is warm and the sugar is dissolved. Remove the bowl from the pan and with an electric mixer beat the mixture at moderate speed for 10 to 15 minutes, or until it is triple in volume and cooled to room temperature. While the eggs are being beaten sift the flour with the salt onto a sheet of wax paper and in a bowl combine the vanilla and the clarified butter. Sift and fold the flour mixture in batches into the egg mixture until the mixture is just combined, stir one fourth of the mixture into the butter mixture, and fold the butter mixture quickly into the batter.

  to clarify butter

unsalted butter, cut into 1-inch pieces

In a heavy saucepan melt the butter over low heat. Remove the pan from the heat, let the butter stand for 3 minutes, and skim the froth. Strain the butter through a sieve lined with a double thickness of rinsed and squeezed cheesecloth into a bowl, leaving the milky solids in the bottom of the pan. Pour the clarified butter into a jar or crock and store it, covered, in the refrigerator. *The butter keeps, covered and chilled, indefinitely.* When clarified, butter loses about one fourth of its original volume.

RUM SYRUP

- 4 tablespoons sugar
- 4 tablespoons dark rum

In a small saucepan combine the sugar, 3 tablespoons water, and the rum, bring the mixture to a boil, stirring until the sugar is dissolved, and let the syrup cool to room temperature. *The syrup keeps, covered and chilled, indefinitely.* **Makes about 1/3 cup.**

STRAWBERRY MOUSSE FILLING

- 1 10-ounce package frozen strawberries in syrup, thawed and drained, reserving the syrup
- 1 envelope unflavored gelatin
- 2 tablespoons dark rum, or to taste
- 3/4 cup heavy cream

In a food processor purée the strawberries coarse. In a small saucepan sprinkle the gelatin over the reserved syrup combined with the rum, let it soften for 5 minutes, and heat the mixture over moderately low heat, stirring, until the gelatin is dissolved. With the motor running add the gelatin mixture in a stream to the strawberry purée and blend the mixture until it is combined. Transfer the strawberry mixture to a metal bowl set in a larger bowl of ice and cold water and stir the mixture until it is cold and thickened slightly, but do not let it begin to set. In a chilled bowl beat the cream until it holds soft peaks and fold it into the strawberry mixture. *Do not make the filling in advance.*

ALMOND TART

pastry dough (page 15)
raw rice for weighting the shell
1 stick (1/2 cup) unsalted butter, softened
1 cup firmly packed light brown sugar
5 tablespoons all-purpose flour
1/4 cup heavy cream
1/8 teaspoon almond extract
1 1/2 cups blanched sliced almonds, lightly toasted
whipped cream as an accompaniment

On a lightly floured surface roll out the dough into a 12-inch round. Fit the dough into a 10½-inch tart pan with a removable fluted rim and trim the edge. Prick the bottom of the tart shell with a fork and chill the shell for 1 hour.

Preheat the oven to 425° F.

Line the shell with foil and fill the foil with the rice. Bake the shell for 10 minutes and remove the foil and the rice carefully. Bake the shell for 5 to 8 minutes more, or until it is pale golden. Cool the shell in the pan on a rack.

Increase the oven temperature to 450° F.

In a bowl with an electric mixer beat the butter, the sugar, and the flour until the mixture is light and fluffy. Beat in the cream and the extract and fold in the almonds. Spread the almond mixture in the cooled tart shell and bake the tart for 10 to 15 minutes, or until the filling is golden brown but not set. Cool the tart completely in the pan on the rack. Serve the tart with the whipped cream.

BRANDIED FIG AND MASCARPONE CREAM PUFF RINGS

cream puff pastry (recipe follows)
an egg wash made by beating 1 egg yolk with 1 tablespoon water
1/3 cup sliced blanched almonds

For the filling
1/3 cup brandy
3 tablespoons sugar
2 cups dried Mission figs, stemmed (about 10 ounces)
1 cup *mascarpone* (available at cheese shops, specialty foods shops, and some supermarkets)
2 tablespoons honey

lightly sweetened whipped cream as an accompaniment

Preheat the oven to 450° F. Butter a baking sheet.

Spoon the cream puff pastry into a large pastry bag fitted with a ½-inch plain tip and pipe two 6-inch circles 3 inches apart onto the prepared baking sheet. Pipe another circle just inside each of the first 2 circles and pipe a third circle on top of each pair of circles. Brush the rings lightly with the egg wash and sprinkle them with the almonds. Bake the rings in the lower third of the oven for 15 minutes, reduce the oven temperature to 400° F., and using a sharp knife poke 4 holes into the sides of each ring to help release steam. Bake the rings for 10 to 15 minutes more, or until the almonds are golden brown, transfer the rings to racks, and let them cool until they are cool enough to handle. Halve the rings horizontally, scoop out carefully any uncooked dough, and arrange the bottom halves on serving plates.

Make the filling: In a saucepan combine ⅓ cup water, the brandy, the sugar, and the figs and simmer the mixture, covered, stirring occasionally, until the figs are softened, about 30 minutes. Strain the figs, reserving the liquid, and let them cool. In a food processor purée the figs, 3 tablespoons of the reserved liquid, the *mascarpone*, and the honey.

Transfer the filling to a pastry bag fitted with a ½-inch star tip and pipe the filling onto the bottom halves of the rings. Arrange the ring tops over the filling and garnish the rings with the whipped cream. **Serves 8 to 12.**

CREAM PUFF PASTRY

- 1 stick (1/2 cup) unsalted butter, cut into pieces
- 1/4 teaspoon salt
- 1 cup all-purpose flour
- 3 to 5 large eggs

In a heavy saucepan bring to a boil 1 cup water with the butter and the salt over high heat. Reduce the heat to moderate, add the flour all at once, and beat the mixture with a wooden spoon until it leaves the side of the pan and forms a ball. Transfer the mixture to a bowl and with an electric mixer at high speed beat in 3 of the eggs, 1 at a time, beating well after each addition. The batter should be stiff enough to just hold soft peaks. If it is too stiff break 1 or 2 more of the eggs into a bowl, beat the egg lightly, and add enough of it to the batter to thin it to the proper consistency.

BUTTERMILK DATE CREAM

- 3/4 cup sugar
- 2 tablespoons unflavored gelatin
- 1 cup buttermilk
- 2/3 cup fresh orange juice
- 1 cup heavy cream
- 1 1/2 cups chopped pitted dates

In a saucepan combine the sugar and ½ cup water and bring the mixture to a boil over moderate heat, stirring until the sugar is dissolved. In a small dish let the gelatin soften in ⅓ cup cold water for 10 minutes, stir the gelatin mixture into the syrup, and stir the mixture until it is dissolved. In a serving bowl combine the syrup mixture, the buttermilk, the orange juice, and a pinch of salt and chill the mixture for 1 hour, or until it is thickened, but do not let it set. In a chilled bowl beat the cream until it holds stiff peaks. Fold the dates and the whipped cream into the buttermilk mixture and chill the dessert for 3 hours, or until it is set. **Serves 8.**

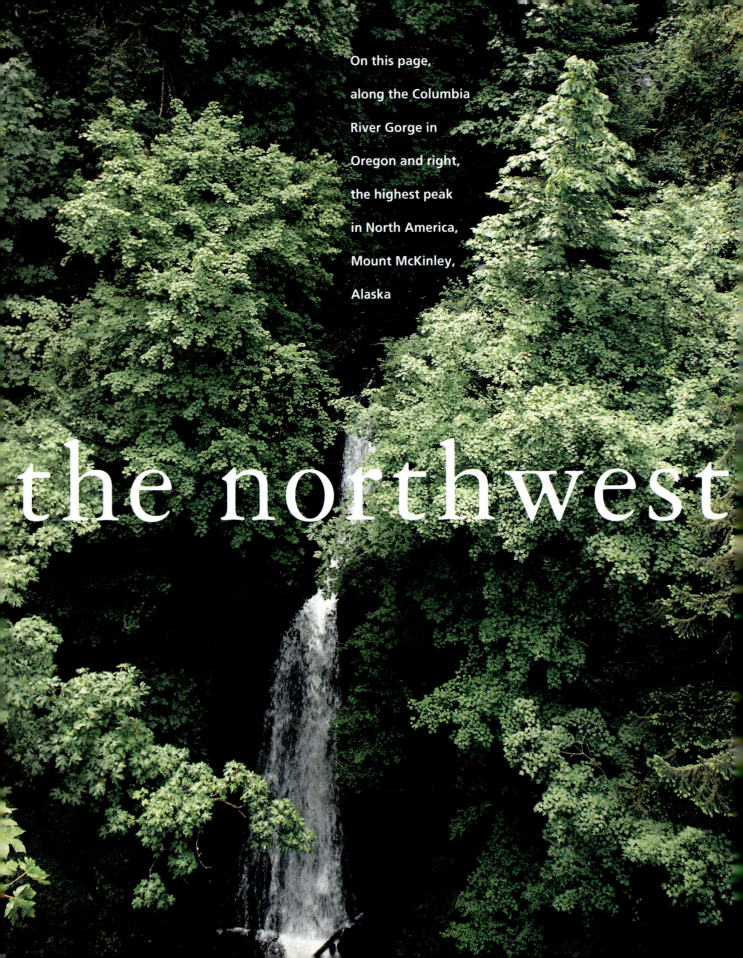

On this page, along the Columbia River Gorge in Oregon and right, the highest peak in North America, Mount McKinley, Alaska

the northwest

and alaska

Washington, Oregon, Alaska

the northwest and alaska

Here, the wilderness lives. Pink salmon leap through raging rivers, rain forests of cascading ferns and silken moss thrive, and, up north, polar bears strut across the unforgiving Arctic tundra. Like the hardy pioneers who first discovered this territory, today's inhabitants are committed to the land and enjoy a cuisine that is pure, fresh, and uncomplicated.

Mild temperatures, rich soil, and gentle rains combine to make the Pacific Northwest one of the most productive agricultural regions in the world. Native Chinook and Kwalhioqua lived well on the profusion of foods offered in the wild, including berries, fruit, salmon, halibut, crab, and clams. This native bounty has been supplemented today with abundant harvests of apples, pears, plums, peaches, cherries, broccoli, onions, lettuces, and hazelnuts.

French and British fur traders arrived in the late eighteenth century and paved the way for hundreds of Midwestern farmers (many of English, Scottish, Swedish, or Danish descent), who braved the 2,000-mile Oregon Trail across the Great Plains and over the Rocky Mountains. These determined settlers traveled by covered wagons carrying only food for the journey, saws and axes to clear the land, and fruit cuttings. When gold was discovered in Washington, prospectors came from England, Germany, and Scandinavia, all adapting their cuisine to regional ingredients. Soon after, Italians, Chinese, and Japanese came to build the railroads. As they settled into the area, they shared their farming knowledge.

The frozen Alaskan frontier was nearly impossible to inhabit. In the late nineteenth century, hardy, independent settlers from throughout the United States arrived by dogsled in search of gold. Unprepared for the severe climate and meager food supply, many died. Even today, the diet of the native Eskimos and Aleuts along the coast is composed primarily of salmon, halibut, and berries; inland, however, caribou, moose, and reindeer are plentiful. Other immigrants include Russians, who settled Sitka in the 1780s and introduced kasha (buckwheat groats) to the area, and, more recently, Japanese, Koreans, and Scandinavians. Some farming is possible in the more temperate Yukon River Basin, where potatoes, cabbage, radishes, rutabagas, and rhubarb are grown in the short, cool summers.

Baked Pears;
Walnut Cigarette Cookies

AN ELEGANT DINNER PARTY

ASPARAGUS
AND MUSHROOM
SALAD WITH
SHERRIED DRESSING

★

BAKED SALMON
STEAKS WITH SPINACH
AND HAZELNUTS

★

RICE, SWEET ONION,
AND PEA TIMBALES
WITH CORIANDER

★

BAKED PEARS

★

WALNUT CIGARETTE
COOKIES

★

COLUMBIA CREST
COLUMBIA VALLEY
CHARDONNAY 1992

Serves 8

the northwest and alaska menu

Northwestern fish, vegetables, and fruits are all highlighted in our Elegant Dinner Party. To honor the region's Asian population, we begin with a salad of steamed asparagus and *shiitake* mushrooms tossed in a Sherry vinegar, soy sauce, and ginger dressing. The simple salmon entrée that follows is baked to preserve its full flavor and sprinkled with hazelnuts, the pride of Oregon's Willamette Valley. As an accompaniment, local Washington Walla Walla onions sweeten our dainty rice timbales. And for dessert, baked pears and walnut cigarette cookies offer a refreshing finale. Bosc pears are best for baking, since they hold their long, tapered shape well. Buy firm pears and allow them to ripen at room temperature.

ASPARAGUS AND MUSHROOM SALAD WITH SHERRIED DRESSING

- 1/4 cup minced shallot
- 2 tablespoons olive oil
- 1 pound *shiitake* mushrooms, stems discarded and caps sliced
- 1/4 cup medium-dry Sherry

For the dressing
- 3 tablespoons Sherry vinegar (available at specialty foods shops and some supermarkets)
- 1 tablespoon soy sauce
- 2 teaspoons minced peeled fresh gingerroot
- 3/4 teaspoon sugar
- 4 tablespoons olive oil

- 2 pounds asparagus, cut diagonally into 1-inch pieces
- 8 large whole Boston lettuce leaves

In large skillet cook the shallot in the oil over moderately low heat until it is softened. Add the mushrooms and sauté them over moderately high heat, stirring, until they are tender and the liquid they give off is evaporated. Add the Sherry, ignite it carefully, and cook the mushrooms, shaking the skillet, until the flames subside. Stir in salt and pepper to taste.

Make the dressing: In a bowl whisk together the vinegar, the soy sauce, the gingerroot, the sugar, and salt and pepper to taste, add the oil in a stream, whisking, and whisk the dressing until it is emulsified.

In a large vegetable steamer set over simmering water steam the asparagus for 7 minutes, or until it is just crisp-tender, add the asparagus to the dressing, tossing it to coat it well, and stir in the mushroom mixture. Line 8 salad plates with the lettuce leaves, forming lettuce cups, and divide the salad among the lettuce. Serve the salad warm. **Serves 8.**

◯ BAKED SALMON STEAKS WITH SPINACH AND HAZELNUTS

- 8 3/4-inch-thick salmon steaks (about 1/2 pound each)
- 2 pounds spinach, coarse stems discarded and the leaves washed well
- 2 garlic cloves, minced
- 3 tablespoons olive oil
- 1/2 cup chopped hazelnuts
- 1 tablespoon fresh lemon juice

Preheat the oven to 450° F. Lightly oil a baking dish large enough to hold the salmon steaks in one layer.

In a large skillet cook the spinach in the water clinging to the leaves, covered, over moderate heat for 1 minute, or until it is wilted, and drain it well. Squeeze the spinach to remove most of the water and chop it coarse. In the skillet cook the garlic in the oil over moderately low heat, stirring occasionally, until it is softened, stir in the hazelnuts, and cook the mixture, stirring, for 1 minute. Stir in the spinach, the lemon juice, and salt and pepper to taste and combine the mixture well. Arrange the salmon steaks in one layer in the prepared baking dish, season them with salt and pepper to taste, and top them with the spinach mixture. Bake the salmon steaks in the middle of the oven for 8 to 10 minutes, or until they just flake. **Serves 8.**

◯ RICE, SWEET ONION, AND PEA TIMBALES WITH CORIANDER

- 2 cups Walla Walla onion (available seasonally at specialty produce markets) or other sweet onion, chopped
- 1 large garlic clove, chopped
- 1/4 cup vegetable oil
- 1 cup chicken broth
- 1 1/4 cups long-grain white rice
- 1/4 cup chopped fresh coriander, plus sprigs for garnish
- 1 cup thawed frozen peas

In a large deep skillet cook the onion and the garlic in 2 tablespoons of the oil over moderate heat, stirring, until the onion is golden. In a blender purée the mixture with the broth, pour the purée into a saucepan, and stir in 1 cup plus 2 tablespoons water. Bring the mixture to a simmer and keep it warm. In the skillet heat the remaining 2 tablespoons oil over moderate heat until it is hot but not smoking and in it cook the rice, stirring, for 5 to 7 minutes, or until it is golden. Remove the skillet from the heat, stir in the broth mixture slowly, and cook the rice, covered, over moderately low heat for 15 minutes. Remove the skillet from the heat, sprinkle the chopped coriander and the peas over the rice, and let the mixture stand, covered, for 5 minutes. Fluff the rice with a fork, distributing the peas evenly. Using a 2/3-cup timbale mold or custard cup and forming 1 timbale at a time, pack the rice mixture into the mold or cup and invert it onto plates. Garnish the timbales with the coriander sprigs. **Makes 8 timbales.**

Deception Pass, off Whidbey Island, Washington

BAKED PEARS

- 8 Bosc pears with stems intact
- 1 lemon, halved
- 1 1/2 cups dry white wine or dry vermouth
- 1 1/4 cups sugar
-     the zest of 2 navel oranges removed with a vegetable peeler
- 2 3-inch cinnamon sticks
- 1/3 cup orange-flavored liqueur

Preheat the oven to 375° F.

Peel the pears, leaving the stems intact and dropping the pears as they are peeled into a bowl of cold water acidulated with the juice of the lemon. In a saucepan combine the wine or the vermouth, 2 cups water, the sugar, the zest, the cinnamon sticks, and the liqueur, bring the liquid to a boil, stirring until the sugar is dissolved, and simmer the syrup for 5 minutes.

Arrange the pears, drained, on their sides in a baking dish just large enough to hold them in one layer and pour the syrup over them. Cover the dish tightly with foil and bake the pears in the middle of the oven for 30 minutes. Remove the foil, turn the pears over gently, and replace the foil. Bake the pears for 20 to 30 minutes more, or until they are tender. Let the pears cool, transfer them carefully to a deep serving dish, and ladle the cooking syrup with the zest over them. Chill the pears, covered, overnight and serve them with some of the syrup. **Serves 8.**

Photo on page 193

WALNUT CIGARETTE COOKIES

- 1/2 stick (1/4 cup) unsalted butter, softened
- 1/2 cup sugar
- 2 large egg whites
- 1/4 teaspoon salt
- 1/4 cup cake flour (not self-rising)
- 1/3 cup walnuts, toasted lightly and minced

Preheat the oven to 375° F. Butter baking sheets.

In a bowl with an electric mixer cream the butter with the sugar until the mixture is light and fluffy, add the egg whites and the salt, and beat the mixture for 10 seconds, or until it is combined well but not frothy. Sift the flour over the mixture and fold it in with the walnuts. Drop level teaspoons of the batter 4 inches apart onto the prepared baking sheets and spread the batter into 2-inch rounds.

Bake the cookies in batches in the middle of the oven for 6 to 8 minutes, or until they are just firm enough to remove from the baking sheet. Working quickly with 1 cookie at a time, loosen the cookies from the sheet with a metal spatula and roll them quickly, rough sides out, around the handle of a wooden spoon or around a chopstick to form a thin cylinder, transferring them as they are rolled to a rack to cool. (If the cookies become too brittle, return them to the oven for 30 seconds to soften them.) *The cookies keep in an airtight container for 3 days.* **Makes about 28 cookies.**

Photo on page 193

the northwest and alaska starters

Curried Crab and Mushroom Salad

CURRIED CRAB AND MUSHROOM SALAD

- 3/4 cup mayonnaise
- 4 teaspoons curry powder, or to taste
- 2 teaspoons minced fresh tarragon, or to taste, plus sprigs for garnish
- 1 1/2 pounds king crab meat, picked over
- 1/2 pound small white mushrooms, sliced thin
- 1/4 cup fresh lemon juice
- 6 ribs of celery, cut into matchsticks and soaked in a bowl of ice and cold water for about 20 minutes

In a bowl whisk together the mayonnaise, the curry powder, the minced tarragon, and 1 to 2 tablespoons water, or enough to thin the sauce to the desired consistency. Stir in the crab meat, the mushrooms, and the lemon juice and on 8 salad plates mound the mixture on the celery, drained. Garnish the salads with the tarragon sprigs. **Serves 8.**

MELTED BRIE, PEAR, AND HAM TOASTS

- 1/4 pound baked ham, minced
- 2 teaspoons Dijon-style mustard
- 10 1/2-inch-thick diagonal slices of French or Italian bread, toasted lightly
- 1 1/2 pears, peeled and cut into 20 wedges
- 1/2 pound Brie or Saga Blue, rind discarded and the cheese cut into 10 wedges and softened
- 20 small sprigs of watercress for garnish

Preheat the oven to 400° F.

In a bowl combine the ham and the mustard. Arrange the bread in a jelly-roll pan, top each slice with some of the ham mixture and 2 of the pear wedges, and top each toast with 1 wedge of the cheese. Bake the toasts in the oven for 6 to 8 minutes, or until the cheese is melted, garnish them with the watercress, and sprinkle them with pepper. **Makes 10 hors d'oeuvres.**

HERBED POACHED OYSTERS

- 3/4 cup dry white wine or dry vermouth
- 2/3 cup finely chopped shallots
- 1/4 teaspoon dried tarragon, crumbled
- 1 tablespoon all-purpose flour
- 36 oysters, shucked, reserving 2/3 cup strained liquor
- 3 tablespoons heavy cream
- 2 tablespoons unsalted butter
- 1/4 cup minced fresh parsley leaves
- thick slices of crusty bread, toasted and buttered, as an accompaniment

In a large saucepan simmer the wine or the vermouth with the shallots and the tarragon until it is reduced to ¼ cup. In a small bowl whisk together the flour and the reserved oyster liquor until the flour is dissolved and whisk the mixture into the shallot mixture. Add the cream and simmer the mixture, whisking, for 2 minutes. Add the oysters and the butter, simmer the oysters until their edges curl, and stir in the parsley and salt and pepper to taste. Serve the oysters in small bowls with the toasted bread. **Serves 6.**

CHICKEN LIVER AND GRANNY SMITH APPLE PÂTÉ

- 1 1/2 Granny Smith apples, peeled, cored, and chopped
- 1 1/4 cups chopped shallot or onion
- 1/4 teaspoon ground allspice
- 9 tablespoons unsalted butter
- 1 1/2 pounds chicken livers, trimmed
- 1/2 cup sparkling apple cider
- 2 tablespoons brandy
- 1/3 cup heavy cream
- freshly grated nutmeg to taste
- toast points or crackers as an accompaniment

In a large skillet cook the apples and the shallot or the onion with the allspice in 6 tablespoons of the butter over moderately low heat, stirring occasionally, until the mixture is soft and transfer the mixture to a food processor. To the skillet add the remaining 3 tablespoons butter and heat it over moderately high heat until it is hot. Add the chicken livers, sauté them until they are browned on the outside but still pink within, and transfer them to the food processor. Deglaze the skillet with the cider and the brandy, scraping up the brown bits, reduce the liquid over moderately high heat, stirring, to about 3 tablespoons, and transfer it to the food processor. Purée the liver mixture, blend in the cream, and season the pâté with the nutmeg and salt and pepper. If a smoother consistency is desired, force the pâté through a fine sieve into a bowl. Transfer the pâté to a serving bowl and chill it, covered with plastic wrap, for 4 hours, or until it is firm. Serve the pâté at room temperature with the toast points or the crackers. **Makes about 3 cups.**

LINGUINE WITH ASPARAGUS LEMON CREAM SAUCE

- 3/4 pound *linguine*
- 1 pound asparagus, chopped coarse
- 1/2 cup minced scallion
- 2 garlic cloves, minced
- 2 tablespoons unsalted butter
- 1 cup heavy cream
- 1/3 cup finely chopped fresh basil leaves
- 1/2 cup freshly grated Parmesan
- 1/2 teaspoon freshly grated lemon zest
- 1/3 cup finely chopped walnuts, toasted lightly

In a kettle of boiling salted water cook the *linguine* for 8 to 10 minutes, or until it is *al dente*, and drain it. While the *linguine* is cooking, in a skillet cook the asparagus, the scallion, and the garlic in the butter over moderate heat, stirring, until the asparagus is just tender, add the cream and the basil, and bring the liquid to a simmer, stirring. Add the Parmesan, the zest, and salt and pepper to taste and stir the sauce until it is combined well. Serve the sauce over the *linguine* and sprinkle it with the walnuts. **Serves 6.**

NEW POTATOES WITH DILLED VODKA CREAM AND SALMON ROE

- 20 1- to 2-inch small red (new) potatoes (about 1 1/4 pounds), scrubbed
- 1/2 cup well-chilled heavy cream
- 2 tablespoons sour cream
- 2 tablespoons minced fresh dill
- 1 1/2 tablespoons vodka
- 4 ounces salmon roe

In a steamer rack set over boiling water steam the potatoes, covered, for 12 to 15 minutes, or until they are tender, let them cool, and halve them. With a small melon-ball cutter scoop some potato out of each half to form a cup, arrange the potato cups on a platter, and chill them, covered, for 30 minutes.

In a bowl beat the heavy cream until it holds soft peaks, beat in the sour cream, the dill, the vodka, and salt and pepper to taste, and beat the mixture until it holds stiff peaks. Divide the cream mixture among the potato cups and top it with the salmon roe. *The hors d'oeuvres may be made 3 hours in advance and kept covered loosely and chilled.* **Makes 40 hors d'oeuvres.**

CARROT BLINI

- 1 cup all-purpose flour
- 1 teaspoon baking powder
- 1 teaspoon salt, or to taste
- 1 cup milk
- 1 large egg
- 1/2 stick (1/4 cup) unsalted butter, melted, plus additional melted butter for brushing the griddle and the *blini*
- 1 cup carrot purée (procedure follows) sour cream and caviar as accompaniments

Preheat the oven to 200° F.

Into a bowl sift together the flour, the baking powder, and the salt. In another bowl beat together the milk, the egg, and ½ stick of the butter until the mixture is just combined and stir in the flour mixture. Add the carrot purée and combine the mixture well. Heat a heavy griddle over moderately high heat until it is hot and brush it generously with some of the additional melted butter. Spoon tablespoons of the batter onto the griddle, spreading the batter with the back of a spoon to form 3-inch rounds, and cook the *blini* for 1 to 2 minutes, or until the undersides are golden brown. Turn the *blini* and cook them for 1 minute more, or until the undersides are golden brown. Transfer the *blini* as they are cooked to an ovenproof platter, brush them with some of the additional melted butter, and keep them warm, covered, in the oven. Serve the *blini* with the sour cream and the caviar. **Serves 6.**

 *to* purée carrots

1 pound carrots, sliced thick

In a steamer set over boiling water steam the carrots, covered, for 10 to 12 minutes, or until they are tender. In a food processor or blender purée the carrots, scraping down the sides of the bowl frequently with a rubber spatula, until the purée is smooth. Transfer the purée to a bowl and chill it, covered. **Makes about 1 1/3 cups.**

the northwest and alaska entrées

Poached Salmon with Green Peppercorn, Ginger, and Orange Sauce; Braised Onion Ribbons with Celery (page 209); Sliced Baked Potatoes with Parsley Butter (page 210)

POACHED SALMON WITH GREEN PEPPERCORN, GINGER, AND ORANGE SAUCE

- 1 cup dry white wine or dry vermouth
- 4 slices of fresh gingerroot, flattened with the side of a knife
- 1 tablespoon black peppercorns, bruised
- 1 bay leaf
- 1 2 1/2-pound piece of salmon fillet

For the sauce
- 1/2 cup sour cream
- 1/4 cup mayonnaise
- 2 teaspoons Dijon-style mustard
- 1 1/2 tablespoons grated peeled fresh gingerroot
- 1 teaspoon freshly grated orange zest
- 2 tablespoons fresh orange juice
- 1 1/2 tablespoons drained green peppercorns
- 1/2 teaspoon sugar
- 1 tablespoon white-wine vinegar

braised onion ribbons with celery (page 209) and sliced baked potatoes with parsley butter (page 210) as accompaniments

Preheat the oven to 400° F. Butter a large baking dish.
In a small saucepan bring 2 cups water and the wine or the vermouth to a boil with the gingerroot, the black peppercorns, and the bay leaf and let the mixture stand, off the heat, for 5 minutes. In the prepared baking dish arrange the salmon, skin side down, and sprinkle it with salt to taste. Add the wine mixture and poach the salmon, covered tightly with foil, in the middle of the oven for 20 to 25 minutes, or until it just flakes and is cooked through.
Make the sauce while the salmon is poaching: In a bowl whisk together the sour cream, the mayonnaise, the mustard, the gingerroot, the zest, the orange juice, the green peppercorns, the sugar, the vinegar, and salt to taste and let the sauce stand at room temperature for 20 minutes for the flavor to develop.
Serve the salmon with the sauce, the onion ribbons, and the potatoes. Serves 6.

GRILLED LAMB CHOPS IN ORANGE MARINADE

- 6 1/2-pound shoulder lamb chops, each 1/2 inch thick
- 1 cup fresh orange juice
- 1 tablespoon dried hot red pepper flakes
- 3 tablespoons soy sauce
- 1 teaspoon sugar
- 1 teaspoon dried rosemary, crumbled
- 1/2 cup vegetable oil

In a shallow ceramic or glass dish large enough to hold the lamb chops in one layer combine the orange juice, the red pepper flakes, the soy sauce, the sugar, the rosemary, and the oil, add the lamb chops, coating them with the marinade, and let them marinate, covered and chilled, turning them occasionally, for at least 6 hours or overnight.

Drain the chops and grill them 6 inches over glowing coals for about 10 minutes on each side for medium-rare meat. (Alternatively, the chops may be grilled in a ridged grill pan over moderately high heat in the same manner.) Arrange the chops on a heated platter and let them stand for 5 minutes before serving. **Serves 6.**

CORNISH GAME HENS STUFFED WITH SAUSAGE AND FENNEL

- 1 pound pork sausage meat, crumbled
- 1 1/2 sticks (3/4 cup) unsalted butter
- 2/3 cup minced fennel bulb (sometimes called anise, available at most supermarkets)
- 1 onion, minced
- 2 garlic cloves, minced
- 1/2 cup coarse dry bread crumbs, toasted
- 1 teaspoon crushed fennel seeds
- 1 teaspoon dried sage, crumbled
- 4 1 1/4-pound Cornish game hens

Preheat the oven to 400° F.

In a skillet cook the sausage in 2 tablespoons of the butter over moderate heat, stirring, until it is no longer pink and transfer it to a large bowl. In the skillet cook the fennel bulb, the onion, and the garlic in ½ stick of the remaining butter over moderately low heat, tossing the mixture, for 1 minute, and add the mixture to the sausage with the bread crumbs, the fennel seeds, the sage, and salt and pepper to taste. Combine the stuffing well and let it cool.

Rinse the hens, pat them dry, and sprinkle them inside and out with salt and pepper. Pack the cavities loosely with the stuffing. Truss the hens, arrange them on a rack in a roasting pan, and spread them with the remaining 6 tablespoons butter. Roast the hens in the oven, basting them with the pan juices twice, for 20 minutes, reduce the oven temperature to 350° F., and roast the hens, basting them twice, for 25 minutes more, or until the juices run clear when the fleshy part of a thigh is pricked with a skewer. Transfer the hens to a cutting board and discard the trussing strings. Split the hens in half lengthwise, keeping the stuffing inside each half, remove and discard the backbones, and arrange the hens on a heated platter. **Serves 8.**

CHICKEN WITH EGGPLANT

- 1 1-pound eggplant, peeled if desired and cut crosswise into 1/2-inch-thick slices
- 1 teaspoon salt
- 3/4 cup vegetable oil, plus additional if necessary
- 1 1/2 tablespoons fresh lemon juice, plus additional to taste
- 1 tablespoon minced fresh sage or 1 teaspoon dried, crumbled
- 1 garlic clove, minced
- 2 3/4-pound whole chicken breasts, skinned, boned, and halved
- all-purpose flour seasoned with salt and pepper for dusting the chicken
- 1/2 cup dry white wine or dry vermouth
- 3/4 cup chicken broth
- 1/2 stick (1/4 cup) unsalted butter, cut into bits
- 2 tablespoons minced fresh parsley leaves
- thin lemon slices for garnish

Waterfront near Fisherman's Quay, Sitka, Alaska

Sprinkle the eggplant slices with the salt and let them drain in a colander, turning them once, for 1 hour. Rinse the slices and pat them dry. In a large dish combine ½ cup of the oil, 1½ tablespoons of the lemon juice, the sage, the garlic, and pepper to taste, in it arrange the eggplant slices in one layer, and let them marinate, turning them once, for 30 minutes. Transfer the slices with tongs to the rack of a broiler pan, brush them with the remaining marinade or, if necessary, some of the additional oil, and broil them under a preheated broiler about 4 inches from the heat for 3 minutes. Turn the slices, brush them with the remaining marinade or more of the additional oil, and broil them for 3 minutes more, or until they are tender and browned lightly.

With a sharp knife cut each chicken breast half horizontally into 2 slices, flatten the slices between sheets of wax paper, and dust them with the seasoned flour. In a large stainless-steel or enameled skillet sauté the chicken slices in the remaining ¼ cup oil over moderately high heat for 30 seconds on each side, or until they are golden, and transfer them with tongs to a plate. To the skillet add the wine or the vermouth and deglaze the skillet, scraping up the brown bits. Boil the liquid until it is reduced to about 2 tablespoons, add the broth, and reduce the liquid to about ½ cup.

Remove the skillet from the heat and in it arrange the chicken slices alternately with the eggplant slices. Add the butter, heat the mixture over moderate heat, swirling the skillet, until the butter is melted, and sprinkle it with the parsley, the additional lemon juice, and salt and pepper to taste. Heat the chicken and eggplant, basting them with the sauce, until they are heated through, transfer them with a slotted spatula to a heated platter, and pour the sauce over them. Garnish the dish with the lemon slices. Serves 4.

PUMPKIN WAFFLES WITH HONEYED APPLE CIDER SAUCE

- 2 1/4 cups all-purpose flour
- 1/2 cup firmly packed light brown sugar
- 4 teaspoons baking powder
- 1 teaspoon salt
- 4 large eggs
- 1 1/2 cups canned pumpkin purée
- 3/4 stick (6 tablespoons) unsalted butter, melted and cooled
- 2 teaspoons freshly grated orange zest
  honeyed apple cider sauce (recipe follows) as an accompaniment

Preheat the oven to 350° F.

Into a bowl sift together the flour, the sugar, the baking powder, and the salt. In another bowl beat the eggs until they are very light and beat in gradually the pumpkin purée and the butter. Sift the flour mixture over the pumpkin mixture, add the zest, and fold the dry ingredients into the pumpkin mixture gently but thoroughly until the batter is just combined.

Pour 1 cup of the batter into the center of a preheated oiled 8-inch-square electric waffle iron, cook the waffle according to the manufacturer's instructions, and transfer it with a fork to an ungreased baking sheet. Make more waffles with the remaining batter in the same manner. "Crisp" the waffles in one layer on baking sheets in the oven for 5 minutes and transfer them to a heated platter. Serve the waffles with the honeyed apple cider sauce. **Makes about 6 waffles.**

HONEYED APPLE CIDER SAUCE

- 1 1/2 cups apple cider
- 1/3 cup honey
- 1/3 cup sugar
- 1 large Granny Smith apple, peeled, cored, and cut into 1/4-inch dice
- 2 tablespoons cornstarch
- 1/8 teaspoon cinnamon
- 1/8 teaspoon freshly grated nutmeg
- 2 tablespoons fresh lemon juice
- 1 1/2 tablespoons unsalted butter

In a small heavy saucepan combine the cider, the honey, and the sugar and simmer the mixture, uncovered, stirring, until the sugar is dissolved. Add the apple and simmer the mixture, covered, for 5 minutes, or until the apple is tender. In a small bowl whisk together the cornstarch, the cinnamon, the nutmeg, the lemon juice, and a pinch of salt until the mixture is smooth, whisk the mixture into the cider mixture, and simmer the sauce, whisking, for 1 minute, or until it is thickened. Remove the pan from the heat and whisk in the butter. Serve the sauce warm. *The sauce may be made 1 week in advance and kept covered and chilled.* **Makes about 2 1/2 cups.**

BEEF SOUP WITH POTATOES AND BEETS

- 2 tablespoons vegetable oil
- 1 1/2 pounds boneless beef chuck, cut into 1/2-inch cubes
- 2 tablespoons all-purpose flour
- 1 tablespoon sweet paprika (preferably Hungarian)
- 4 cups beef broth
- 1 teaspoon dill seeds
- 2 large carrots, chopped coarse
- 3/4 pound fresh beets, peeled and cut into 1/4-inch-thick strips (about 2 cups)
- 1 1/2 pounds boiling potatoes
- 1 tablespoon red-wine vinegar, or to taste
- sour cream as an accompaniment

In a large heavy kettle heat the oil over moderately high heat until it is hot but not smoking and in it brown the beef. Sprinkle the beef with the flour and the paprika and cook it over moderately low heat, stirring, for 3 minutes. Add the broth, 4 cups water, and the dill seeds, bring the liquid to a boil, and simmer the mixture, covered partially, for 2 hours, or until the beef is just tender. Add the carrots, the beets, and the potatoes, peeled and cut into ¼-inch-thick slices, simmer the soup for 20 minutes, or until the vegetables are tender, and stir in the vinegar and salt and pepper to taste. Serve the soup with the sour cream. **Makes about 6 cups, serving 4 to 6.**

ROAST GOOSE WITH MUSHROOM, HAZELNUT, AND CURRANT STUFFING AND PORT GRAVY

For the stuffing
- 1 1/2 cups chopped onion
- 1 1/2 cups chopped celery
- 1 stick (1/2 cup) unsalted butter
- 1 1/2 pounds mushrooms, chopped (about 8 cups)
- 3/4 cup currants
- 1 teaspoon dried sage, crumbled
- 1 teaspoon dried thyme, crumbled
- 3/4 cup hazelnuts, toasted and skinned (procedure follows), chopped
- 10 slices of homemade-type white bread, cut into 1/2-inch cubes, toasted, and cooled (about 6 cups)
- 1/4 cup minced fresh parsley leaves

- 1 12-pound goose, the loose fat removed, the neck and liver reserved for another use, and the remaining giblets chopped coarse
- 1 carrot, chopped
- 1 rib of celery, chopped
- 1 onion, chopped
- 2 1/2 cups chicken broth
- 1 cup dry white wine or dry vermouth
- 1/4 cup Tawny Port
- 1/3 cup all-purpose flour

Make the stuffing: In a large skillet cook the onion and the celery in the butter over moderately low heat, stirring occasionally, until the vegetables are softened, add the mushrooms, and cook the mixture over moderate heat, stirring occasionally, until the mushrooms are tender and all but about ⅓ cup of the liquid is evaporated. Stir in the currants, the sage, the thyme, and salt and pepper to taste and cook the mixture, stirring, for 1 minute. Transfer the mixture to a large bowl, add the hazelnuts, the toasted bread cubes, the parsley, and salt and pepper to taste, and combine the stuffing gently but thoroughly. *The stuffing may be made 1 day in advance and kept covered and chilled. (Do not stuff the goose in advance.)*

    Preheat the oven to 425° F. Butter a 2-quart baking dish.

    Rinse the goose, pat it dry, and season it inside and out with salt and pepper. Pack the neck cavity loosely with some of the stuffing, fold the neck skin under the body, and fasten it with a skewer. Pack the body cavity loosely with some of the remaining stuffing and truss the goose. Transfer the remaining stuffing to the prepared baking dish and reserve it, covered and chilled. Put the goose, breast side up, on a rack in a roasting pan, scatter the carrot, the celery, the onion, and the chopped giblets in the bottom of the pan, and roast the goose in the middle of the oven for 30 minutes. Reduce the oven temperature to 325° F., pour 1 cup boiling water over the goose, and roast the goose, basting it occasionally with the pan juices and skimming off the fat, for 2 to 2½ hours more, or until the juices run clear when the fleshy part of a thigh is pricked with a skewer and a meat thermometer inserted in the fleshy part of a thigh registers 175° F. During the last hour of roasting bake the reserved stuffing, drizzled with ½ cup of the broth and covered, in the 325° F. oven. Transfer the goose to a heated platter, remove the skewer and the trussing strings, and keep the goose warm, covered loosely with foil.

    Pour off the fat from the pan juices and reserve it. Add the wine or the vermouth and the Port to the pan, deglaze the pan over moderately high heat, scraping up the brown bits, and boil the mixture until it is reduced by half. In a saucepan whisk together ¼ cup of the reserved fat and the flour and cook the *roux* over moderately low heat, whisking, for 3 minutes. Add the remaining 2 cups broth in a stream, whisking, and bring the mixture to a boil. Strain the wine mixture through a fine sieve into the saucepan, pressing hard on the solids, and simmer the gravy, whisking occasionally, for 3 minutes, or until it is thickened. Stir in salt and pepper to taste, simmer the gravy for 2 minutes, and transfer it to a heated sauceboat. Serve the goose with the reserved stuffing and the gravy. **Serves 8.**

  *toast and skin hazelnuts*

Preheat the oven to 350° F.

    Toast the hazelnuts in one layer in a baking pan in the oven for 10 to 15 minutes, or until they are colored lightly and the skins blister. Wrap the nuts in a kitchen towel and let them steam for 1 minute. Rub the nuts in the towel to remove as much of the skin as possible and let them cool.

Totem pole, Sitka National Historical Park, Alaska

the northwest and alaska
side dishes

BEETS AND BEANS WITH MUSTARD HORSERADISH SAUCE

- 1 1/2 pounds beets, scrubbed and trimmed, leaving 1 inch of the stem ends intact
- 1 pound green or wax beans, trimmed and cut into 1-inch pieces
- 3 tablespoons vegetable oil
- 1 teaspoon all-purpose flour
- 1 teaspoon sugar
- 2 tablespoons cider vinegar, or to taste
- 1/2 cup chopped red onion
- 2 teaspoons drained bottled horseradish
- 1 1/2 tablespoons Dijon-style mustard

In a kettle cover the beets with 2 inches water, bring the water to a boil, and simmer beets for 25 to 30 minutes, or until they are tender. In a colander refresh the beets under cold water, slipping off the skins and stems, quarter the beets, and slice them crosswise. In a large saucepan of boiling salted water cook the beans for 2 to 3 minutes, or until they are crisp-tender, and drain them well.

In a large skillet heat the oil over moderate heat until it is hot, add the flour and the sugar, and cook the mixture, whisking, for 30 seconds. Whisk in the vinegar, the onion, the horseradish, and ¼ cup water, bring the mixture to a boil, and remove the skillet from the heat. Whisk in the mustard, add the beets and the beans, and toss the mixture until it is combined well. **Serves 6.**

BRAISED ONION RIBBONS WITH CELERY

- 3 1/2 pounds onions, halved lengthwise and cut crosswise into 1/2-inch-thick slices
- 1/4 cup olive oil
- 7 ribs of celery, cut diagonally into 1/2-inch-thick slices

In a large heavy skillet cook the onions in the oil, covered, over moderately low heat, stirring occasionally, for 45 minutes, season them with salt and pepper, and cook them, uncovered, over moderately high heat, stirring occasionally, for 30 minutes, or until they are tender and beginning to turn golden. Add the celery and cook the vegetables, stirring, for 5 minutes, or until the celery is crisp-tender. **Serves 6**.

Photo on page 202

CREAMED SPINACH AND PEARS

- 2 pounds fresh spinach, washed well and the coarse stems discarded
- 2 pears, peeled, quartered, and sliced thin crosswise
- 1/2 stick (1/4 cup) unsalted butter, softened
- 1/4 cup heavy cream
- 1/8 teaspoon freshly grated nutmeg, or to taste

In a kettle cook the spinach in the water clinging to its leaves, covered, over moderate heat, stirring occasionally for 3 minutes, or until it is wilted. Drain the spinach in a colander, refresh it under cold water, and squeeze it dry by handfuls. In a skillet cook the pears in 1 tablespoon of the butter over moderate heat, stirring occasionally, until they are very tender. In a food processor or blender purée the pears with the spinach, in batches add the remaining 3 tablespoons butter, the cream, the nutmeg, and salt and pepper to taste, and purée the mixture until it is smooth. In a saucepan heat the purée over moderately low heat, stirring, until it is heated through and transfer it to a heated serving dish. **Serves 6 to 8**.

APPLE, CRANBERRY, AND RADISH SALAD

- 1 cup chopped celery
- 2 unpeeled tart green apples, cored, chopped, and tossed with 1 tablespoon fresh lemon juice
- 1/2 cup dried cranberries (available at specialty foods shops)
- 2 cups chopped radishes
- 3/4 cup hazelnuts, chopped if desired
- 1/4 cup thinly sliced scallion
- 3/4 teaspoon finely chopped fresh sage leaves
- 2 tablespoons minced fresh parsley leaves
- 1/2 cup mayonnaise
- watercress for lining the bowl

In a bowl combine well the celery, the apples and lemon juice, the cranberries, and the radishes, add the hazelnuts, the scallion, the sage, the parsley, the mayonnaise, and salt and pepper to taste, and stir the salad until it is combined well. Spoon the salad into a bowl lined with the watercress. **Serves 6**.

the northwest and alaska side dishes

SCALLOPED RUTABAGAS

- 2 pounds rutabagas, peeled and cut into 1-inch cubes
- 2 tablespoons unsalted butter
- 2 tablespoons all-purpose flour
- 2 cups milk
- freshly grated nutmeg to taste
- 3/4 cup coarsely grated Gruyère (about 4 ounces)

In a steamer set over boiling water steam the rutabagas, covered, for 10 to 12 minutes, or until they are just tender, let them cool, and pat them dry. Transfer the rutabagas to a buttered 1½-quart shallow gratin dish.

Preheat the oven to 375° F.

In a heavy saucepan melt the butter over moderately low heat, stir in the flour, and cook the *roux,* whisking, for 3 minutes. Add the milk in a stream, whisking, and simmer the mixture, whisking occasionally, for 10 minutes. Stir in the nutmeg and salt and pepper to taste. Pour the sauce over the rutabagas, sprinkle the top with the Gruyère, and bake the mixture in the oven for 25 minutes, or until the sauce is bubbling and the top is golden. **Serves 6.**

SLICED BAKED POTATOES WITH PARSLEY BUTTER

- 6 russet (baking) potatoes
- 3/4 stick (6 tablespoons) unsalted butter
- 2 tablespoons minced fresh parsley leaves

Preheat the oven to 400° F.

Prick the potatoes a few times with a fork and bake them in the middle of the oven for 1 hour. In a small saucepan melt the butter and stir in the parsley and salt and pepper to taste. Cut the warm baked potatoes crosswise into ¼-inch-thick slices, arrange the slices, overlapping them, on plates, and drizzle each serving with some of the parsley butter. **Serves 6.**

Photo on page 202

KASHA WITH BROCCOLI AND ROASTED BELL PEPPER

- 3 cups chicken broth (preferably low-salt)
- 5 tablespoons olive oil
- 1 1/2 cups whole kasha
- 1 large egg, beaten lightly
- 1 large onion, chopped
- 2 garlic cloves, minced
- 1 1/2 pounds broccoli, cut into small flowerets
- 2 roasted red bell peppers (procedure on page 147), chopped
- 2 tablespoons fresh lemon juice, or to taste

In a saucepan combine the broth and 2 tablespoons of the oil and bring the liquid to a boil. In a bowl combine the kasha and the egg, stirring to coat the kasha with the egg, transfer the mixture to a large deep skillet with a lid, and cook the kasha, uncovered, over moderately high heat, stirring and breaking up the lumps, for 2 to 4 minutes, or until the grains are separated and toasted lightly. Remove the skillet from the heat, stir in the broth mixture, and simmer the kasha, covered, for 15 to 20 minutes, or until the liquid is absorbed.

While the kasha is cooking, in a skillet cook the onion and the garlic in the remaining 3 tablespoons oil over moderately low heat, stirring, until the onion is softened. Add the broccoli, 2 tablespoons water, and salt and black pepper to taste, increase the heat to moderate, and cook the mixture, covered, for 3 to 5 minutes, or until the broccoli is just tender. Stir the vegetables and the roasted bell peppers into the kasha and add the lemon juice and salt and pepper to taste. **Serves 6 to 8.**

the northwest and alaska
desserts

FRUIT SALAD WITH HONEY HAZELNUT BRITTLE

- 1/2 cup coarsely chopped hazelnuts
- 1/4 cup honey
- 1/8 teaspoon salt
- 1 1/2 teaspoons sugar
- 2 tablespoons fresh lemon juice
- 2 tablespoons sweet vermouth
- 2 cups pitted cherries
- 3 cups mixed berries, such as blackberries, boysenberries, fresh currants, or raspberries
- 2 cups seedless green or red grapes
- 2 cups sliced peaches

In a small heavy saucepan cook the hazelnuts with the honey and the salt over moderate heat, stirring, for 5 minutes, or until the nuts are golden and the honey is a deep caramel color. Pour the mixture onto a piece of foil, let it cool completely, and break the brittle into small pieces.

In a large bowl whisk together the sugar, the lemon juice, and the vermouth until the sugar is dissolved, add the fruit, and toss the salad until it is just combined. Serve the salad in bowls sprinkled with the brittle. **Serves 6 to 8.**

Blackberry Cobbler

BLACKBERRY COBBLER

- 2 tablespoons cornstarch
- 1 1/2 cups sugar
- 1 tablespoon fresh lemon juice
- 4 cups blackberries, picked over, rinsed, and drained well
- 1 cup all-purpose flour
- 1 teaspoon baking powder
- 1/2 teaspoon salt
- 3/4 stick (6 tablespoons) cold unsalted butter, cut into bits
- vanilla ice cream as an accompaniment

Preheat the oven to 400° F.

In a bowl stir together the cornstarch and ¼ cup cold water until the cornstarch is dissolved, add 1 cup of the sugar, the lemon juice, and the blackberries, and combine the mixture gently but thoroughly. Transfer the mixture to an 8-inch cast-iron skillet or 8-inch-square baking pan 2 inches deep.

In a bowl combine well the flour, the remaining ½ cup sugar, the baking powder, and the salt and blend in the butter until the mixture resembles coarse meal. Add ¼ cup boiling water and stir the mixture until it just forms a dough. Bring the blackberry mixture to a boil on top of the stove, drop spoonfuls of the dough carefully on the boiling mixture, and bake the cobbler in the middle of the oven for 20 to 25 minutes, or until the topping is golden. (If using a cast-iron skillet, bake the cobbler on a foil-lined baking sheet to catch any overflow.) Serve the cobbler warm with the ice cream.

BAKED NECTARINE PUDDING

- 5 nectarines, quartered
- 1 tablespoon fresh lemon juice
- 2/3 cup milk
- 1/3 cup heavy cream
- 1/3 cup plus 2 tablespoons sugar
- 1/3 cup all-purpose flour
- 2 large eggs
- 1 teaspoon vanilla
- 1 teaspoon cinnamon
- 1 tablespoon unsalted butter
- hot maple syrup as an accompaniment

Preheat the oven to 425° F. Butter a 1½-quart casserole.

In a bowl toss the nectarines with the lemon juice. In the prepared casserole arrange the nectarines decoratively. In a blender or food processor blend the milk, the cream, ⅓ cup of the sugar, the flour, the eggs, and the vanilla until the batter is just combined and pour the batter over the nectarines. In a small bowl combine the remaining 2 tablespoons sugar with the cinnamon, sprinkle the mixture on top of the batter, and dot it with the butter. Bake the pudding in the upper third of the oven for 40 to 45 minutes, or until the top is golden and the pudding is set, and serve it warm or at room temperature with the maple syrup. **Serves 4 to 6.**

Hazelnut orchard, Oregon

COTTAGE CHEESE CAKE WITH GLAZED APRICOTS

- 1 1/2 cups graham cracker crumbs
- 3/4 stick (6 tablespoons) unsalted butter, melted
- 1 teaspoon cinnamon
- 4 large eggs
- 1 cup sugar
- 4 cups small-curd cottage cheese, blended until smooth in a food processor
- 1 cup sour cream
- 1/4 cup all-purpose flour
- 2 tablespoons fresh lemon juice
- 1 teaspoon freshly grated lemon zest
- 1 tablespoon vanilla
- 1/2 teaspoon salt

For the topping
- 1/4 cup apricot jam
- 2 teaspoons Frangelico
- 5 fresh apricots, halved and pitted

Preheat the oven to 350° F. Butter a 9-inch springform pan.

In a bowl combine the crumbs, the butter, and the cinnamon, press the mixture onto the bottom and halfway up the side of the prepared pan, and bake the shell in the oven for 5 minutes. Let the shell cool on a rack.

In a bowl with an electric mixer beat the eggs with the sugar until the mixture ribbons when the beaters are lifted, add the cottage cheese, the sour cream, the flour, the lemon juice, the zest, the vanilla, and the salt, and beat the mixture until it is combined well. Pour the mixture into the shell and bake the cheesecake in the pan on a baking sheet in the lower third of the oven for 1 hour and 15 minutes. Turn off the heat but do not open the oven door and let the cake stand in the oven for 2 hours. Let the cake cool completely on a rack and chill it, covered, overnight. Run a knife around the cake, remove the side of the pan, and transfer the cake to a stand or plate.

Make the topping: In a small saucepan melt the jam over moderate heat, stirring, strain it through a fine sieve into a bowl, and stir in the Frangelico. Arrange the apricot halves, cut sides down, on top of the cake and brush them with the glaze.

GLAZED APPLE CAKE

- 3 large McIntosh apples (about 1 1/2 pounds), cored and quartered
- 1 2-inch strip of lemon zest
- 1 stick (1/2 cup) unsalted butter, softened
- 1 cup sugar
- 1 large egg
- 2 1/4 cups all-purpose flour
- 2 teaspoons baking soda
- 1 teaspoon cinnamon
- 1/2 teaspoon freshly grated nutmeg
- 1/4 teaspoon ground cloves
- 1/4 teaspoon salt
- 1/2 cup finely chopped pecans, toasted
- 2 Granny Smith apples, peeled, cored, halved lengthwise, and sliced thin crosswise
- 1/4 cup apricot jam, strained
- whipped cream as an accompaniment

In a stainless-steel or enameled saucepan combine the McIntosh apples with ¼ cup water and the zest, bring the water to a boil, and simmer the mixture, covered, for 20 minutes, or until the apples are tender. Cook the mixture, uncovered, over moderately high heat, stirring, until most of the water is evaporated, force it through the fine disk of a food mill into a bowl, and let the purée cool.

Preheat the oven to 350° F. Butter generously a 9-inch springform pan.

In a large bowl cream the butter, beat in the sugar, and beat the mixture until it is light and fluffy. Beat in the egg and the purée. Into a bowl sift together the flour, the baking soda, the cinnamon, the nutmeg, the cloves, and the salt. Stir the flour mixture gently into the apple mixture with the pecans and transfer the batter to the prepared pan. Arrange the Granny Smith apple slices decoratively in bunches on the batter, pressing them slightly into the batter, and bake the cake in the oven for 1 hour and 15 minutes, or until a tester inserted in the center comes out clean.

In a small saucepan melt the jam over low heat, brush it over the top of the cake, and let the cake cool in the pan on a rack for 20 minutes. Run a sharp knife around the edge of the cake and remove the side of the pan. Serve the cake warm or at room temperature with the whipped cream.

Page numbers in *italics* indicate color photographs

◉ entries can be prepared in 45 minutes or less

◉+ entries can be prepared in 45 minutes but require additional unattended time

index

a

ACORN SQUASH, Baked Candied, 29
ALLSPICE, Cornish Hens with Molasses and, Broiled, 27
ALMOND(S)
   Rice, Baked with Peas, Celery and, 79
   Tart, 188
AMBROSIA PUNCH, 39
ANCHOVY(IES)
   Deviled Eggs with Olives and, 21
   Onion, and Tomato Tart, 171
ANTIPASTO, Eggplant, *168*, 169
APPLE(S). *See also* Cider
   Brown Betty, 31
   Cake, Glazed, 215
   Cheese Quick Bread, *104*, 105
   Cranberry, and Radish Salad, 209
   Granny Smith, and Chicken Liver Pâté, 199
   Pie, 108
   and Spinach Salad, 52
   Squash, and Onion Tart with Sage, 13, 15
APPLESAUCE, Chunky Lemon, *104*, 105
APRICOTS, Glazed, with Cottage Cheese Cake, 214
ARTICHOKES and Clams with Herbed Garlic Butter, 175
ASPARAGUS
   in Ambush, 27
   Lemon Cream Sauce, with Linguine, 200
   and Mushroom Salad with Sherried Dressing, 194
   Napoleons with Oriental Black Bean Sauce, *170*, 170
ASPIC, Tomato, with Horseradish, 65
AVOCADO
   and Chicken Salad, with Bacon Dressing, 75
   and Grapefruit Salad with Pine Nut Dressing, 145
   Guacamole, *154*, 155
   Squid, and Jerusalem Artichoke Salad, 174

b

BACON
   Dressing, with Chicken and Avocado Salad, 75
   with Escarole Salad, Wilted, 17
   Rye Bread Stuffing with Sauerkraut, Raisins and, 107
   Twists and Gorgonzola Croutons, with Spinach Salad, *115*, 116
BANANA(S)
   Cheesecake with Chocolate Macadamia Crust, 185
   Foster, 84
BARBECUE(D)
   Oxtails and Red Beans, 73
   Pork Spareribs, Chili-Marinated, 153
   Sauce, Lentils Baked in, 131
BARLEY, with Thai Beef Salad, 178
BASIL
   Oil, and Olives, with Red Pepper and Goat Cheese Spirals, 166
   Sun-Dried Tomato Bread, 183
   Tomato Soup, Chilled, *42*, 43
BEAN(S). *See also* Green Beans
   Black, Oriental Sauce, with Asparagus Napoleons, *170*, 170
   Chicken in Succotash, *89*, 91
   Honey Baked, *28*, 28
   quick-soaking, 73
   Red, and Oxtails, Barbecue, 73
   White, and Fish Salad with Fried Onions, 121
BEEF
   Brisket with Root Vegetables, Beer-Braised, *98*, 99
   Burgers, California, 177
   Cabbage Rolls, Stuffed, 100
   Chili "Five Way", Cincinnati-Style, 103
   Meat Loaf, 23
   Onions Stuffed with Ground Meat, Tomatoes, and
      Peppers (Picadillo), 150
   Pot Roast with Vegetables, *124*, 124
   Salad, Thai, with Barley, 178
   Skirt Steak and Peppers, Marinated, 117
   Skirt Steak, Grilled Marinated, with Bell Peppers,
      Onions, and Flour Tortillas (Fajitas), *148*, 148
   Soup with Potatoes and Beets, 206
   Stew with Turnips, Spiced, 49
BEER
   Braised Brisket with Root Vegetables, 98, 99
   Marinated Leg of Lamb, Grilled Butterflied, with Onions, 125

BEET(S)
 and Beans with Mustard Horseradish Sauce, 208
 Beef Soup with Potatoes and, 206
 Cranberry Soup, with Orange, 14
 Harvard, 29
 and Onion Salad, Roasted, 130
 Sweet-and-Sour, with Caraway, 53
BELL PEPPER(S). *See* Pepper(s)
BEVERAGES.
 Ambrosia Punch, 38
 Ice-Cream Sodas, Strawberry, 55
 Limeade, *63, 67, 82*
BISCUITS
 Cream, *89,* 91, *106*
 Shortcakes, Mango Strawberry, 161
BLACK BEAN SAUCE,
 Oriental, with Asparagus Napoleons, *170,* 170
BLACKBERRY
 Cobbler, *212,* 213
 Jam Cake with Penuche Frosting, 93
BLACK-EYED PEAS, Hoppin' John, 79
BLINI, Carrot, 201
BLUEBERRY
 Cream Cheese Pie, 56
 Gingerbread, 119
 Tart, 109
BLUE CHEESE, Radishes Stuffed-, 96
BLUEFISH, Grilled Marinated, 48
BOSTON BROWN BREAD, *30,* 30
BOURBON Marinade, with Spareribs, 75
BRANDY ALEXANDER Mousses, 59
BREAD(S), QUICK
 Apple Cheese, *104,* 105
 Biscuits, Cream, *89,* 91
 Boston Brown Bread, *30,* 30
 Corn Bread, Buttermilk, 65
 Muffins, Yam Cornmeal, 157
BREAD(S), YEAST
 Basil Sun-Dried Tomato, 183
 Cottage Cheese, Herbed, 119
 Cream Kuchen, Celery and Kielbasa, 96
 Focaccia, Potato Rosemary, *128,* 129
 Swedish Rye (Limpa), 106
BREAD-AND-BUTTER PICKLES, 52

BREAD PUDDING
 and Butter, with Longhorn Cheese and Raisins,
  New Mexican (Capirotada), 159
 Rhubarb, 32
BRIE, Melted, Pear, and Ham Toasts, 198
BRISKET with Root Vegetables, Beer-Braised, *98,* 99
BRITTLE, Hazelnut, with Fruit Salad, 211
BROCCOLI
 Cream Sauce, with Scrod, *22,* 23
 and Roasted Bell Pepper, with Kasha, 210
BROWNIE(S)
 Chocolate Peanut Butter Swirl, 111
 Pudding Cake, 109
BROWN SUGAR
 and Nectarine Ice Cream, 110
 Pecan Cookies, 143
 Walnut Fudge, 40
BRUSSELS SPROUTS,
 Shredded, with Chestnuts and Brown Butter, 52
BULGUR
 Indian Pudding with, 135
 Jambalaya with Ham, Clams, and Vegetables, 74
 Lettuce Rolls with Vegetables and, 123
 Wild Rice, and Herb Salad (Tabbouleh), 107
BURGERS, California, 177
BUTTER
 Brown, and Chestnuts, with Brussels Sprouts, Shredded, 52
 Brown, Fettuccine with Pine Nuts, Prosciutto and, *152,* 153
 clarifying, 187
 Herbed Garlic, with Artichokes and Clams, 175
 Lemon Garlic, with Green Beans, 29
 Parsley, with Sliced Baked Potatoes, 210
 Sage, Lemon, and Garlic, 25
 Tomato, 25
BUTTERMILK
 Corn Bread, 65
 Date Cream, 189
 Dressing, with Coleslaw, 78
 Dressing, with Cucumber and Tomato Salad, 92
 Layer Cake with Chocolate Sour Cream Frosting, 135
 Lemon Chess Tartlets, *37,* 39
BUTTERNUT SQUASH
 to steam and purée, 95
 Tartlets with Cheese Lattice and Sunflower Seed Crust, *94,* 95
BUTTERSCOTCH Pudding, 134

C

CABBAGE. *See also* Sauerkraut
Coleslaw with Buttermilk Dressing, 78
Corn, and Pepper Slaw, 30
Rolls, Stuffed, 100

CAKE(S)
Apple, Glazed, 215
Blackberry Jam, with Penuche Frosting, 93
Brownie Pudding, 109
Buttermilk Layer, with Chocolate Sour
    Cream Frosting, 135
Cheesecake, Banana, with Chocolate
    Macadamia Crust, 185
Chocolate Roll, Mocha Cream, with Mocha Sauce, 58
Coffeecake, Moravian Sugar, 57
Cottage Cheese, with Glazed Apricots, 214
Cranberry Walnut Crumb, 33
Cupcakes, Wellesley Fudge, 31
Genoise Batter, 187
Gingerbread, Blueberry, 119
Lady Baltimore, 37, 38
Molasses, with Maple Frosting, 17
Pineapple Coconut Meringue, Frozen, 184
Pound Cake, Pecan Lemon, 85
Shortcakes, Mango Strawberry, 161
Strawberry Mousse, 186
Upside-Down, Pineapple, 41
Zucchini Raisin Whiskey, 132

CALIFORNIA Burgers, 177
CANDIED, Acorn Squash, Baked, 29
CANTALOUPE Sherbet, 143
CAPIROTADA, New Mexican Bread-and-Butter Pudding
    with Longhorn Cheese and Raisins, 159
CARAMEL Cranberry Sauce, with Cranberry Mousse, Frozen, 40
CARAWAY with Beets, Sweet-and-Sour, 53

CARROT(S)
Blini, 201
and Potato Soup, Chilled Curried, 70
Pudding, Sweet, 132
purée, 201

CASHEWS, Curried Fried Rice with Pineapple and, 181
CATFISH, Po' Boys 74

CELERY
Ham, and Cheddar Salad, 21
and Kielbasa Cream Kuchen, 96
Onion Ribbons Braised with, 208
Pine Nut Slaw, 131
Rice, Baked with Peas, Almonds and, 79
CHARDONNAY-Braised Chicken with Fennel and
    Lemongrass, 177

CHEDDAR
Ham, and Celery Salad, 21
Ham, and Mushroom Phyllo Triangles, Herbed, 45
Tomato Sauce on Toast (Rinktum Ditty), 26

CHEESE. *See also* Cheddar; Cottage Cheese; Goat Cheese
Apple Quick Bread, *104*, 105
Blue-Cheese-Stuffed Radishes, 96
Brie, Melted, Pear, and Ham Toasts, 198
and Chorizo-Stuffed Peppers with Tomatillo Sauce, *144*, 144
Cream Cheese Blueberry Pie, 56
Gorgonzola Croutons and Bacon Twists, with Spinach
    Salad, *115*, 116
Lattice and Sunflower Seed Crust, with Butternut
    Squash Tartlets, *94*, 95
Longhorn, and Raisins, with New Mexican Bread-and-
    Butter Pudding (Capirotada), 159
Macaroni and, with Peppers, 155
Mascarpone and Fig Cream Puff Rings, Brandied, 188
Potato Pie with Chilies, Olives and, 157
Pudding with Zucchini and Leek, 105
Quesadillas, Smoked Turkey and, 147
Spread, Port and Black-Walnut, 97

CHEESECAKE
Banana, with Chocolate Macadamia Crust, 185
Cottage Cheese, with Glazed Apricots, 214
CHERRIES, with Pork Shoulder, Cider-Braised, 99
CHESTNUTS, and Brown Butter, with Brussels
    Sprouts, Shredded, 52

CHICKEN
Chardonnay-Braised, with Fennel and Lemongrass, 177
with Eggplant, 204
Potpie, Pennsylvania Dutch-Style, 51
Salad, Avocado and, with Bacon Dressing, 75
Salad, Grilled, with Papaya, Walnuts, and Mesclun, 166
Spiced Roast, with Rice, Chorizo, and Pepper Stuffing, 154
in Succotash, *89*, 91
Wings, Spicy Fried, 64

○+ **CHICKEN LIVER** and Granny Smith Apple Pâté, 199
CHICK-PEA
  Dressing, with Tomato Salad, 182
  Nibbles, 12
CHILES RELLENOS, *144,* 144
CHILI, CHILIES
  Cheese-and-Chorizo-Stuffed Peppers
    with Tomatillo Sauce (Rellenos), *144,* 144
  Chipotle Shrimp, Grilled, 146
  Cincinnati-Style, "Five Way," 103
  Coriander Dressing, with Mexican Salad, Layered, 142
○ Crumbs, with Sautéed Green Beans, 130
  -Marinated Pork Spareribs, Barbecued, 153
  Onions Stuffed with Ground Meat,
    Tomatoes and (Picadillo), 150
  Pepper and Tomato Sauce, with Eggs, on
    Tortillas (Huevos Rancheros), 151
  Potato Pie with Cheese, Olives and, 157
  Yellow Squash Baked with Tomatoes and, 117
CHIPOTLE Shrimp, Grilled, 146
CHOCOLATE
  Kahlúa Cream Pie, 160
  Macadamia Crust, with Banana Cheesecake, 185
  Peanut Butter Swirl Brownies, 111
  Roll, Mocha Cream, with Mocha Sauce, 58
  Sour Cream Frosting, with Buttermilk Layer Cake, 135
CHORIZO and Cheese-Stuffed Peppers with Tomatillo
    Sauce, *144,* 144
  with Lentil Soup, 122
  Rice, and Pepper Stuffing, with Spiced
    Roast Chicken, 154
CHOWDER, Clam, Manhattan-Style, 44
○ **CIDER** Apple, Honeyed Sauce, 205
  Pork Shoulder, Braised-, with Cherries, 99
CINCINNATI-STYLE Chili "Five Way," 103
CLAM(S)
  and Artichokes, with Herbed Garlic Butter, 175
  Bulgur Jambalaya with Ham, Vegetables and, 74
  Chowder, Manhattan-Style, 44
  Clambake in a Pot, *24,* 25
  hard-shelled, shucking, 175
○ Marinière with Tomato and Onion, 18, 19
○ **COBBLER,** Blackberry, *212,* 213
COCONUT Pineapple Meringue Cake, Frozen, 184
COD, Salt, Fritters, Island-Style, 71

COFFEECAKE, Moravian Sugar, 57
COLESLAW, with Buttermilk Dressing, 78
COMPOTE, Onion, Peach, and Raisin, 96
CONFECTIONS
○ Brittle, Hazelnut, with Fruit Salad, 211
○ Fudge, Brown Sugar Walnut, 40
COOKIES
  Brown Sugar Pecan, 143
  Cornmeal Pistachio, 167
  Oatmeal Raisin, 111
  Sugar, Old-Fashioned, 41
  Trail Mix, 134
  Walnut Cigarette, *193,* 197
CORIANDER
  Chili Dressing, with Mexican Salad, Layered, 142
○ Garlic Dressing, with Romaine Salad, 158
○ with Rice, Sweet Onion, and Pea Timbales, 195
CORN
○+ Cabbage, and Pepper Slaw, 30
  Clambake in a Pot, *24,* 25
  Pudding, Three-, 158
  Succotash, Chicken in, *89,* 91
  Tortillas, 141
○ **CORN BREAD,** Buttermilk, 65
CORNISH HENS
○ with Molasses and Allspice, Broiled, 27
  Stuffed with Sausage and Fennel, 203
CORNMEAL
  Fritters, Spicy Deep-Fried, 69
  Muffins, Yam, 157
  Pistachio Cookies, 167
  Pudding, Three-Corn, 158
COTTAGE CHEESE
  Bread, Herbed, 119
  Cake with Glazed Apricots, 214
  Dome with Peach Sauce, 159
CRAB
○ and Mushroom Salad, Curried, *198,* 198
  Salad, *50,* 51
CRANBERRY
○ Apple, and Radish Salad, 209
  Beet Soup with Orange, 14
  Gravy, with Roast Turkey, 101
  Mousse, Frozen, with Cranberry Caramel Sauce, 40
  Walnut Crumb Cake, 33

d

CREAM(ED), CREAMY *See also* Sour Cream

- Asparagus Lemon Sauce, with Linguine, 200
- Biscuits, *89, 91, 106*
  Broccoli Sauce, with Scrod, *22,* 23
  Buttermilk Date, 189
  Chocolate Kahlúa Pie, 160
  Dilled Vodka and Salmon Roe, with New Potatoes, 200
  Eggplant Salad, *168,* 169
  Kuchen, Celery and Kielbasa, 96
  Mocha, Chocolate Roll with Mocha Sauce, 58
  Pineapple, 184
- Puff Pastry, 189
- Spinach and Pears, 209

CREAM CHEESE Blueberry Pie, 56

- **CROUTONS,** Gorgonzola, and Bacon Twists with Spinach Salad, *115,* 116

CRUST
Chocolate Macadamia, with Banana Cheesecake, 185
Pecan Crumb, with Key Lime Pie, 83
Sunflower Seed, and Cheese Lattice, with Butternut Squash Tartlets, *94, 95*
Walnut, with Maple Pumpkin Pie, 32

CUCUMBER
Cups with Horseradish Yogurt, 44
- Sauce, Dilled, Mussels and New Potatoes in, 19
- Sauce, Dilled, Shrimp in, 70
- and Tomato Salad with Buttermilk Dressing, 92
- **CUPCAKES,** Wellesley Fudge, 31
- +**CURD,** Lime, 41

CURRANT, Mushroom, and Hazelnut Stuffing and Port Gravy, with Roast Goose, 206

CURRY(IED)
Carrot and Potato Soup, Chilled, 70
- Crab and Mushroom Salad, *198,* 198
Eggplant, *168,* 180
- Fried Rice with Pineapple and Cashews, 181

CUSTARD
Farina Flan, 160
Rhubarb Pie, 110

DATE, Buttermilk, Cream, 189

DELTA DOGS, 69

DESSERTS. *See also* Cake(s); Cookies; Custard; Frozen Desserts; Fruit Desserts; Mousse(s); Pie(s); Pudding; Tart(s)
Brownies, Chocolate Peanut Swirl, 111
Cheese Dome with Peach Sauce, 159
Doughnuts, Spiced Potato, 133
Lemon Buttermilk Chess Tartlets, *37,* 39

DESSERT SAUCE(S)
Cranberry Caramel, with Cranberry Mousse, Frozen, 40
- Mocha, 59
- Peach, 159

DEVILED EGGS
with Anchovies and Olives, 21
Potato Skins, 123

DILL(ED)
- Cucumber Sauce, Mussels and New Potatoes in, 19
- Cucumber Sauce, Shrimp in, 70
Summer Squash Salad, 66
Vodka Cream and Salmon Roe, with New Potatoes, 200

- **DIPPING SAUCE,** Sour Cream, 123

DIP
- Red Pepper, Spiced, 147
Spinach, with Scallops, Crisp-Fried, 20

DOUGH. *See* Pastry

DOUGHNUTS, Spiced Potato, 133

DUCK, Crispy Braised, with Turnips and Olives, 127

e

EGG(S)
- Deviled, with Anchovies and Olives, 21
- Frittata, Ham and Vegetable, 146
- with Tomato and Pepper Sauce on Tortillas (Huevos Rancheros), 151

EGGPLANT
- Antipasto, Grilled, *168,* 169
- with Chicken, 204
- Curry, *168,* 180
- Salad, Creamy, *168,* 169

ESCAROLE
- Braised, in Tomato Sauce, 53
- Salad, Wilted, with Bacon, 17

f

FAJITAS, Beef, *148,* 148

FENNEL
- Chicken, Chardonnay-Braised, with Lemongrass and, 177
- Cornish Game Hens Stuffed with Sausage and, 203
- Orange, and Onion Salad with Ginger Dressing, 183

FETTUCCINE
- with Leek and Sour Cream Sauce, 45
- with Pine Nuts, Prosciutto, and Brown Butter, *152,* 153
- FIG and Mascarpone Cream Puff Rings, Brandied, 188
- **FILLING,** Strawberry Mousse, 187
- **FISH.** *See also* Shellfish
- Anchovies and Olives, with Deviled Eggs, 21
- Anchovy, Onion, and Tomato Tart, 171
- Bluefish, Grilled Marinated, 48
- Catfish Po' Boys, 74
- Cod, Salt, Fritters, Island-Style, 71
- Red Snapper with Tomatoes and Olives, Baked, 150
- Salmon, Poached with Green Peppercorn, Ginger, and Orange Sauce, *202,* 202
- Salmon Roe and Dilled Vodka Cream, with New Potatoes, 200
- Salmon Steaks, Baked, with Spinach and Hazelnuts, 195
- Scrod with Broccoli Cream Sauce, *22,* 23
- Swordfish Teriyaki, Broiled, 178
- Trout Spread, Smoked Herbed, 121
- Tuna Caesar Sandwiches, Grilled, 179
- and White Bean Salad with Fried Onions, 121

FLAN, Farina, 160
FOCACCIA, Potato Rosemary, *128,* 129
FRITTATA, Ham and Vegetable, 146
FRITTERS
- Cornmeal, Spicy Deep-Fried, 69
- Salt Cod, Island-Style, 71

FROSTING
- Chocolate Sour Cream, with Buttermilk Layer Cake, 135
- Maple, with Molasses Cake, 17
- Penuche, with Blackberry Jam Cake, 93
- Wellesley Fudge Cupcakes, 31

FROZEN DESSERTS. *See also* Ice Cream
- Cranberry Mousse, with Cranberry Caramel Sauce, 40
- Pineapple Coconut Meringue Cake, 184
- Sherbet, Cantaloupe, 143
- Sorbet, Blood Orange, *165,* 167, *185*

FRUIT(S). *See also* names of fruits
- Salad, Mixed, with Rosemary Yogurt Dressing, 181

FRUIT DESSERTS
- Apple Brown Betty, 31
- Apple Cake, Glazed, 215
- Apple Pie, 108
- Bananas Foster, 84
- Blackberry Cobbler, *212,* 213
- Blueberry Cream Cheese Pie, 56
- Blueberry Tart, 109
- Date Buttermilk Cream, 189
- Fig and Mascarpone Cream Puff Rings, Brandied, 188
- Key Lime Pie with Pecan Crumb Crust, 83
- Lime Curd, 41
- Nectarine Pudding, Baked, 213
- Peach Lattice-Crust Pie, *63,* 67, *82*
- Pears, Baked, *193,* 197
- Rhubarb Bread Pudding, 32
- Rhubarb Custard Pie, 110
- Salad with Hazelnut Brittle, 211

FUDGE
- Brown Sugar Walnut, 40
- Wellesley Cupcakes, 31
- **FUSILLI** with Sun-Dried Tomatoes, Bell Peppers, and Goat Cheese, 179

g

GARLIC
- Baguette Toasts, *42*, 43
- Coriander Dressing, with Romaine Salad, 158
- Herbed Butter, with Artichokes and Clams, 175
- Lemon Butter, with Green Beans, 29
- Sage, and Lemon Butter, 25

GENOISE Batter, 187

GINGER
- Dressing, with Fennel, Orange, and Onion Salad, 183
- Green Peppercorn, and Orange Sauce, with Poached Salmon, *202*, 202

GINGERBREAD, Blueberry, 119

GLAZED
Apple Cake, 215
Apricots, with Cottage Cheese Cake, 214

GOAT CHEESE
- Fusilli with Sun-Dried Tomatoes, Bell Peppers and, 179
- and Pea Tart, *46*, 47
- and Red Pepper Spirals with Olives and Basil Oil, 166

GOOSE, Roast, with Mushroom, Hazelnut, and Currant Stuffing and Port Gravy, 206

- **GORGONZOLA** Croutons and Bacon Twists, with Spinach Salad, *115*, 116
- **GRAPEFRUIT** and Avocado Salad with Pine Nut Dressing, 145

GRATIN, Potato and Onion, Country, 118

GRAVY
Cranberry, with Roast Turkey, 101
Port, and Mushroom, Hazelnut, and Currant Stuffing, with Roast Goose, 206

GREEN BEANS
and Beets with Mustard Horseradish Sauce, 208
- with Lemon Garlic Butter, 29
- Sautéed, with Chili Crumbs, 130

GREEN ONION(S). *See* Scallion(s)
GREENS. *See* Lettuce; names of greens
GRITS, Three-Corn Pudding, 158
- **GUACAMOLE,** *154*, 155

h

HAM
- Brie, Melted, and Pear Toasts, 198
- Bulgur Jambalaya with Clams, Vegetables and, 74
- Celery, and Cheddar Salad, 21
- Cheddar, and Mushroom Phyllo Triangles, Herbed, 45
- and Vegetable Frittata, 146

HAZELNUT(S)
- Brittle, with Fruit Salad, 211
- Mushroom, and Currant Stuffing, and Port Gravy, with Roast Goose, 206
- and Spinach, Salmon Steaks Baked with, 195
- toasting and skinning, 207

HERB(S), HERBED. *See also* names of herbs
Cottage Cheese Bread, 119
Garlic Butter, with Artichokes and Clams, 175
- Oysters, Poached, 199
Phyllo Triangles, Ham, Cheddar, and Mushroom, 45
Potato Salad, Two-, 66
- Smoked Trout Spread, 121
Wild Rice, and Bulgur Salad (Tabbouleh), 107

HONEY(ED)
- Apple Cider Sauce, 205
Baked Beans, *28*, 28

HOPPIN' JOHN, 79
HORS D'OEUVRES. *See* Starters
HORSERADISH
Mustard Sauce, with Beets and Beans, 208
with Tomato Aspic, 65
Yogurt, with Cucumber Cups, 44

HUEVOS RANCHEROS (Eggs with Tomato and Pepper Sauce on Tortillas), 151

i

ICE CREAM
Nectarine and Brown Sugar, 110
Sodas, Strawberry, 55
Strawberry, 55

INDIAN PUDDING with Bulgur, 135

j

JAMBALAYA, Bulgur, with Ham, Clams, and Vegetables, 74
JERUSALEM ARTICHOKE, Squid, and Avocado Salad, 174

k

KAHLÚA, Chocolate Cream Pie, 160
KAILKENNY (Kale and Mashed Potatoes), 53
KASHA with Broccoli and Roasted Bell Pepper, 210
KEBABS
Pork, with Peanut Sauce, 176
Venison and Zucchini, with Citrus Pepper Marinade, 126
KIELBASA and Celery Cream Kuchen, 96

l

LADY BALTIMORE CAKE, *37,* 38
LAMB
Chops, Grilled, in Orange Marinade, 203
Leg of, Grilled Beer-Marinated Butterflied, with Onions, 125
LEEK
Cheese Pudding with Zucchini and, 105
and Sour Cream Sauce, with Fettuccine, 45
LEMON
Applesauce, Chunky, *104,* 105
Asparagus Cream Sauce, with Linguine, 200
Buttermilk Chess Tartlets, *37,* 39
Garlic Butter, with Green Beans, 29
Pecan Pound Cake, 85
Sage, and Garlic Butter, 25
LEMONGRASS, Chicken, Chardonnay-Braised, with Fennel and, 177

LENTIL(S)
in Barbecue Sauce, Baked, 131
Soup with Chorizo, 122
LETTUCE. *See also* names of greens
Rolls with Bulgur and Vegetables, 123
LIMA BEANS, Chicken in Succotash, *89,* 91
LIME
Curd, 41
Key Lime Pie with Pecan Crumb Crust, 83
Limeade, *63, 67, 82*
Soup, *138,* 141
LIMPA (Swedish Rye Bread), 106
LINGUINE with Asparagus Lemon Cream Sauce, 200
LOBSTER, Clambake in a Pot, *24, 25*

m

MACADAMIA Chocolate Crust, with Banana Cheesecake, 185
MACARONI and Cheese with Peppers, 155
MANGO Strawberry Shortcakes, 161
MANHATTAN-STYLE Clam Chowder, 44
MAPLE
Frosting, with Molasses Cake, 17
Pumpkin Pie, with Walnut Crust, 32
MARINATED, MARINADE
Beer-, Leg of Lamb, Grilled Butterflied, with Onions, 125
Bluefish, Grilled, 48
Bourbon, with Spareribs, 75
Chili-, Pork Spareribs, Barbecued, 153
Citrus Pepper, with Venison and Zucchini Kebabs, 126
Orange, Grilled Lamb Chops in, 203
Pork Kebabs with Peanut Sauce, 176
Skirt Steak and Peppers, 116, 117
Skirt Steak, Grilled, with Bell Peppers, Onions, and Flour Tortillas (Fajitas), *148,* 148
Swordfish Teriyaki, Broiled, 178
MASCARPONE and Fig Cream Puff Rings, Brandied, 188
MEAT(S). *See* Beef; Lamb; Oxtails; Pork; Rabbit; Venison
MEAT LOAF, 23
MERINGUE
Pineapple Coconut Cake, Frozen, 184
Sweet Potato Pie, 82

MESCLUN, Chicken Salad, Grilled, with Papaya, Walnuts and, 166
MEXICALI Potato Pie, 157
MEXICAN Salad with Coriander Chili Dressing, Layered, 142
MOCHA
Cream Chocolate Roll, 58
Sauce, 59
MOLASSES
Cake with Maple Frosting, 17
Cornish Hens with Allspice and, Broiled, 27
MORAVIAN Sugar Coffeecake, 57
MORELS, with Rabbit and Sausage, 102
MOUSSE(S)
Brandy Alexander, 59
Cranberry, Frozen, with Cranberry Caramel Sauce, 40
Strawberry Cake, 186
Strawberry Filling, 187
MUSHROOM(S)
and Asparagus Salad with Sherried Dressing, 194
and Crab Salad, Curried, *198*, 198
Ham, and Cheddar Phyllo Triangles, Herbed, 45
Hazelnut, and Currant Stuffing and Port Gravy, with Roast Goose, 206
Morels, with Rabbit and Sausage, 102
Shiitake and Bell Peppers, Roasted, with Penne, 126
MUSSELS, and New Potatoes in Dilled Cucumber Sauce, 19
MUSTARD Horseradish Sauce, with Beets and Beans, 208

n

NAPOLEONS, Asparagus with Oriental Black Bean Sauce, *170*, 170
NECTARINE
and Brown Sugar Ice Cream, 110
Pudding, Baked, 213
NOODLE(S)
Peanut Sesame, *80*, 81
Soup, Scallion, 90
NUTS. *See* names of nuts

O

OATMEAL Raisin Cookies, 111
OIL, Basil, and Olives, with Red Pepper and Goat Cheese Spirals, 166
+OKRA, Onion, and Tomato Salad, 66
OLIVES
and Basil Oil, with Red Pepper and Goat Cheese Spirals, 166
+Deviled Eggs with Anchovies and, 21
Duck, Crispy Braised, with Turnips and, 127
Potato Pie with Cheese, Chilies and, 157
Red Snapper, Baked with Tomatoes and, 150
ONION(S) *See also* Scallion(s)
and Beet Salad, Roasted, 130
Clams Marinière with Tomato and, *18*, 19
Fennel, and Orange Salad with Ginger Dressing, 183
Fried, with Fish and White Bean Salad, 121
with Leg of Lamb, Grilled Beer-Marinated Butterflied, 125
+Okra, and Tomato Salad, 66
Peach, and Raisin Compote, 96
and Potato Gratin, Country, 118
Ribbons Braised with Celery, 209
Skirt Steak, Grilled Marinated, with Bell Peppers, Flour Tortillas and (Fajitas), *148*, 148
Squash, and Apple Tart with Sage, *13*, 15
Stuffed with Ground Meat, Tomatoes, and Peppers (Picadillo), 150
Sweet, Rice, and Pea Timbales with Coriander, 195
Sweet, Rings, 182
Tomato, and Anchovy Tart, 171
Vidalia "Flowers", with Pecans, Roasted, *76, 77*
White, Clambake in a Pot, *24, 25*
ORANGE
Blood, Sorbet, *165, 167, 185*
Cranberry Beet Soup with, 14
Fennel, and Onion Salad with Ginger Dressing, 183
Green Peppercorn, and Ginger Sauce, with Poached Salmon, *202*, 202
Marinade, Grilled Lamb Chops in, 203
Rice Pudding à l'Orange, 84
OXTAILS and Red Beans, Barbecue, 73
OYSTERS
Fried, with Tartar Sauce, 69
Herbed Poached, 199

P

PANCAKES
Carrot Blini, 201
Green Onion, 77
Two-Grain, 26
PAPAYA
Chicken Salad, Grilled, with Walnuts, Mesclun and, 166
Salad, *180*, 181
PARSLEY Butter, with Sliced Baked Potatoes, 210
PASTA
Fettuccine with Leek and Sour Cream Sauce, 45
Fettuccine with Pine Nuts, Prosciutto, and Brown Butter, *152*, 153
Fusilli with Sun-Dried Tomatoes, Bell Peppers, and Goat Cheese, 179
Linguine with Asparagus Lemon Cream Sauce, 200
Macaroni and Cheese with Peppers, 155
Noodle Soup, Scallion, 90
Noodles, Peanut Sesame, *80*, 81
Penne with Roasted Shiitake Mushrooms and Bell Peppers, 126
PASTRY. *See also* Pie(s); Tart(s); Tartlets
Cream Puff, 189
Dough, 15
Phyllo Triangles, Ham, Cheddar, and Mushroom, Herbed, 45
Sunflower Seed Dough, 95
Walnut Crust, with Maple Pumpkin Pie, 32
PÂTÉ, Chicken Liver and Granny Smith Apple, 199
PEA(S)
Black-Eyed, Hoppin' John, 79
fresh, cooking, 47
and Goat Cheese Tart, *46*, 47
Rice, Baked with Celery, Almonds and, 79
Rice, and Sweet Onion Timbales with Coriander, 195
PEACH
Onion, and Raisin Compote, 96
Pie, Lattice-Crust, *63*, *67*, *82*
Sauce, 159
PEANUT
Sauce, with Pork Kebabs, 176
Sesame Noodles, *80*, 81
PEANUT BUTTER Chocolate Swirl Brownies, 111

PEAR(S)
Baked, *193*, 197
Melted Brie, and Ham Toasts, 198
and Spinach, Creamed, 209
PECAN(S)
Brown Sugar Cookies, 143
Crumb Crust, with Key Lime Pie, 83
Lemon Pound Cake, 85
with Vidalia Onion "Flowers", Roasted, *76*, 77
PENNE with Roasted Shiitake Mushrooms and Bell Peppers, 126
PENNSYLVANIA DUTCH-STYLE Chicken Potpie, 51
PENUCHE FROSTING, with Blackberry Jam Cake, 93
PEPPER(S). *See also* Chili, Chilies
Cabbage, and Corn Slaw, 30
Fusilli with Sun-Dried Tomatoes, Goat Cheese and, 179
with Macaroni and Cheese, 155
Red, and Goat Cheese Spirals with Olives and Basil Oil, 166
Red, Dip Spiced, 147
Rice, and Chorizo Stuffing, with Spiced Roast Chicken, 154
Roasted, and Broccoli, with Kasha, 210
roasting, 147
and Shiitake Mushrooms, Roasted, with Penne, 126
Skirt Steak, Grilled Marinated, with Onions, Flour Tortillas and (Fajitas), *148*, 148
and Skirt Steak, Marinated, 116, 117
PEPPER, PEPPERCORN
Citrus Marinade, with Venison and Zucchini Kebabs, 126
Green, Ginger, and Orange Sauce, with Poached Salmon, 202, *202*
PHYLLO TRIANGLES, Ham, Cheddar, and Mushroom, Herbed, 45
PICADILLO-Stuffed Onions, 150
PICKLES, Bread-and-Butter, 52
PIE(S). *See also* Pastry; Tart(s); Tartlets
Apple, 108
Blueberry Cream Cheese, 56
Chicken Potpie, Pennsylvania Dutch-Style, 51
Chocolate Kahlúa Cream, 160
Key Lime with Pecan Crumb Crust, 83
Maple Pumpkin, with Walnut Crust, 32
Peach, Lattice-Crust, *63*, *67*, *82*
Rhubarb Custard, 110
Sweet Potato Meringue, 8

PINEAPPLE
Coconut Meringue Cake, Frozen, 184
Cream, 184
Curried Fried Rice with Cashews and, 181
Upside-Down Cake, 41
PINE NUT(S)
Celery Slaw, 131
Dressing, with Avocado and Grapefruit Salad, 145
Fettuccine with Prosciutto, Brown Butter and, *152*, 153
PISTACHIO Cornmeal Cookies, 167
PORK. *See also* Bacon; Ham; Sausage
Chops with Cracked Rye, Braised, 48
Kebabs with Peanut Sauce, 176
Onions Stuffed with Ground Meat, Tomatoes, and Peppers (Picadillo), 150
Rice, and Tomato Casserole, 72
Shoulder with Cherries, Cider-Braised, 99
Spareribs, Barbecued Chili-Marinated, 153
Spareribs with Bourbon Marinade, 75
PORT
and Black-Walnut Cheese Spread, 97
Gravy, and Roast Goose with Mushroom, Hazelnut, and Currant Stuffing, 206
POTATO(ES)
Beef Soup with Beets and, 206
Doughnuts, Spiced, 133
Gratin, Onion and, Country, 118
Mashed, Kale and, 53
New, Mussels and, in Dilled Cucumber Sauce, 19
New, with Dilled Vodka Cream and Salmon Roe, 200
Pie, with Cheese, Chilies, and Olives, 157
Red, Clambake in a Pot, *24, 25*
Rosemary Focaccia, *128*, 129
Salad, Herbed Two-, 66
Sautéed Provençale, *128*, 129
Skins, Deviled, 123
Sliced Baked, with Parsley Butter, 210
Soup, Carrot and, Chilled Curried, 70
POT ROAST with Vegetables, 124
POULTRY. *See* Chicken; Cornish Hens; Duck; Goose; Turkey
POUND CAKE, Pecan Lemon, 85

PROCEDURES
butternut squash, to steam and purée, 95
butter, to clarify, 187
carrots, to purée, 201
clams, hard-shelled, to shuck, 175
dried beans, to quick-soak, 73
hazelnuts, to toast and skin, 207
jars for pickling and preserving, to sterilize, 52
peas, fresh, to cook, 47
peppers, to roast, 147
tortillas, to warm, 149
PROSCIUTTO, Pine Nuts, and Brown Butter, with Fettuccine, *152*, 153
PUDDING
Bread-and-Butter, with Longhorn Cheese and Raisins, New Mexican (Capirotada), 159
Bread, Rhubarb, 32
Butterscotch, 134
Cake, Brownie, 109
Carrot, Sweet, 132
Cheese, with Zucchini and Leek, 105
Corn, Three-, 158
Indian, with Bulgur, 135
Nectarine, Baked, 213
Rice, à l'Orange, 84
PUFF PASTRY, Cream, 189
PUMPKIN Maple Pie, with Walnut Crust, 32
Waffles with Honeyed Apple Cider Sauce, 205
PUNCH, Ambrosia, 38

q

QUESADILLAS, Cheese and Smoked Turkey, 147

r

RABBIT and Sausage with Morels, 102
RADISH(ES)
- Apple, and Cranberry Salad, 209
- Blue-Cheese-Stuffed, 96

RAISIN(S)
and Longhorn Cheese, with New Mexican
  Bread-and-Butter Pudding (Capirotada), 159
Oatmeal Cookies, 111
Onion, and Peach Compote, 96
Rye Bread Stuffing with Sauerkraut, Bacon and, 107
Zucchini Whiskey Cake, 132
RED BEANS and Oxtails, Barbecue, 73
RED PEPPER(S). *See* Pepper(s)
- RED SNAPPER with Tomatoes and Olives, Baked, 150

RHUBARB
Bread Pudding, 32
Custard Pie, 110
RICE. *See also* Wild Rice
Baked, with Peas, Celery, and Almonds, 79
Chorizo, and Pepper Stuffing, with Spiced Roast Chicken, 154
- Curried Fried, with Pineapple and Cashews, 181
Pork, and Tomato Casserole, 72
Pudding à l'Orange, 84
Risotto with Zucchini and Scallops, 49
- Steamed, 71
- Timbales, Sweet Onion and Pea, with Coriander, 195
- RINKTUM DITTY (Tomato Cheddar Sauce on Toast), 26
RISOTTO, with Zucchini and Scallops, 49
- ROMAINE Salad with Coriander Garlic Dressing, 158
ROSEMARY
Potato Focaccia, *128*, 129
Yogurt Dressing, with Mixed Fruit Salad, 181
- RUM Syrup, 187
RUTABAGAS, Scalloped, 210
RYE, Cracked, with Pork Chops, Braised, 48
RYE BREAD
Stuffing with Sauerkraut, Bacon, and Raisins, 107
Swedish (Limpa), 106

s

SAGE
- Lemon, and Garlic Butter, 25
Squash, Apple, and Onion Tart with, *13*, 15
SALAD(S). *See also* Slaw(s)
- Apple and Spinach, 52
- Apple, Cranberry, and Radish, 209
- Asparagus and Mushroom, with Sherried Dressing, 194
- Avocado and Grapefruit, with Pine Nut Dressing, 145
Beef, Thai, with Barley, 178
Beet and Onion, Roasted, 130
Chicken and Avocado, with Bacon Dressing, 75
Chicken, Grilled, with Papaya, Walnuts, and Mesclun, 166
- Crab, *50*, 51
- Crab and Mushroom, Curried, *198*, 198
Cucumber and Tomato, with Buttermilk Dressing, 92
Eggplant, Creamy, *168*, 169
- Escarole, Wilted, with Bacon, 17
- Fennel, Orange, and Onion, with Ginger Dressing, 183
Fish and White Bean, with Fried Onions, 121
Fruit, Mixed, with Rosemary Yogurt Dressing, 181
Ham, Celery, and Cheddar, 21
Mexican Layered, with Coriander Chili Dressing, 142
- +Okra, Onion, and Tomato, 66
- Papaya, *180*, 181
- Potato, Herbed Two-, 66
- Romaine, with Coriander Garlic Dressing, 158
- Spinach, with Gorgonzola Croutons and Bacon Twists, *115*, 116
Squid, Jerusalem Artichoke, and Avocado, 174
Summer Squash, Dilled, 66
Tomato, with Chick-Pea Dressing, 182
Wild Rice, Bulgur and Herb (Tabbouleh), 107
SALAD DRESSING
Bacon, with Chicken and Avocado Salad, 75
Buttermilk, with Coleslaw, 78
- Buttermilk, with Cucumber and Tomato Salad, 92
Chick-Pea, with Tomato Salad, 182
Coriander Chili, with Layered Mexican Salad, 142
- Coriander Garlic, with Romaine Salad, 158
- French, 174
- Ginger, with Fennel, Orange, and Onion Salad, 183
- Pine Nut, with Avocado and Grapefruit Salad, 145
Rosemary Yogurt, with Mixed Fruit Salad, 181
- Sherried, with Asparagus and Mushroom Salad, 194

SALMON
- Poached with Green Peppercorn, Ginger, and Orange Sauce, *202*, 202
- Roe and Dilled Vodka Cream, with New Potatoes, 200
- Steaks, Baked, with Spinach and Hazelnuts, 195
- **SALSA**, Tomato, *154*, 155

SANDWICHES
- Catfish Po' Boys, 74
- Tuna Caesar, Grilled, 179

SAUCE(S). *See also* Butter; Dessert Sauce(s); Gravy
- Asparagus Lemon Cream, with Linguine, 200
- Barbecue, Lentils Baked in, 131
- Black Bean Oriental, with Asparagus Napoleons, *170*
- Broccoli Cream, with Scrod, *22*, 23
- Cheddar Tomato, on Toast (Rinktum Ditty), 26
- Dilled Cucumber, Mussels and New Potatoes in, 19
- Dilled Cucumber, Shrimp in, 70
- Dipping, Sour Cream, 123
- Green Peppercorn, Ginger, and Orange, with Poached Salmon, *202*, 202
- Honeyed Apple Cider, 205
- Leek and Sour Cream, with Fettuccine, 45
- Mustard Horseradish, with Beets and Beans, 208
- Peanut, with Pork Kebabs, 176
- Tartar, with Fried Oysters, 69
- Tomatillo, with Cheese-and-Chorizo Stuffed Peppers, *144*, 144
- Tomato and Pepper, with Eggs, on Tortillas, 151
- Tomato, Braised Escarole in, 53

SAUERKRAUT, Rye Bread Stuffing with Bacon, Raisins and, 107

SAUSAGE. *See also* Chorizo
- Cornish Game Hens Stuffed with Fennel and, 203
- Kielbasa and Celery Cream Kuchen, 96
- and Rabbit, with Morels, 102

SCALLION(S)
- Green Onion Pancakes, 77
- Noodle Soup, 90

SCALLOPED Rutabagas, 210

SCALLOPS
- Crisp-Fried, with Spinach Dip, 20
- and Zucchini, with Risotto, 49
- **SCROD** with Broccoli Cream Sauce, *22*, 23
- **SEAFOOD.** *See* Shellfish; Squid

SEED(S)
- Squash, Toasted Spiced, 20
- Sunflower, Pastry Dough, 95
- **SESAME** Peanut Noodles, *80*, 81

SHELLFISH. *See also* Clam(s)
- Clambake in a Pot, *24*, 25
- Crab and Mushroom Salad, Curried, *198*, 198
- Crab Salad, *50*, 51
- Mussels and New Potatoes in Dilled Cucumber Sauce, 19
- Oysters, Fried, with Tartar Sauce, 69
- Oysters, Herbed Poached, 199
- Scallops and Zucchini, with Risotto, 49
- Scallops, Crisp-Fried, with Spinach Dip, 20
- Shrimp, Grilled Chipotle, 146
- Shrimp in Dilled Cucumber Sauce, 70
- **SHERBET**, Cantaloupe, 143
- **SHERRIED** Dressing, with Asparagus and Mushroom Salad, 194
- **SHIITAKE MUSHROOMS**, and Bell Peppers, Roasted, with Penne, 126
- **SHORTCAKES**, Mango Strawberry, 161

SHRIMP
- in Dilled Cucumber Sauce, 70
- Grilled Chipotle, 146

SLAW(S)
- Cabbage, Corn, and Pepper, 30
- Celery Pine Nut, 131
- Coleslaw with Buttermilk Dressing, 78
- **SOPA DE LIMA** (Lime Soup), *138*, 141
- **SORBET**, Blood Orange, *165*, *167*, *185*

SOUP
- Carrot and Potato, Chilled Curried, 70
- Clam Chowder, Manhattan-Style, 44
- Cranberry Beet, with Orange, 14
- Lentil, with Chorizo, 122
- Lime, *138*, 141
- with Potatoes and Beets, 206
- Scallion Noodle, 90
- Tomato Basil, Chilled, *42*, 43

SOUR CREAM
Chocolate Frosting, with Buttermilk Layer Cake, 135
Dipping Sauce, 123
and Leek Sauce, with Fettuccine, 45

SPARERIBS
with Bourbon Marinade, 75
Pork, Barbecued Chili-Marinated, 153

SPICED, SPICY. See also names of spices
Beef Stew with Turnips, 49
Chicken Wings, Fried, 64
Cornmeal Fritters, Deep-Fried, 69
Doughnuts, Potato, 133
Red Pepper Dip, 147
Squash Seeds, Toasted, 20

SPINACH
and Apple Salad, 52
Dip, with Scallops, Crisp-Fried, 20
and Hazelnuts, Baked with Salmon Steaks, 195
and Pears, Creamed, 209
Salad with Gorgonzola Croutons and Bacon Twists, 115, 116

SPREAD
Port and Black-Walnut Cheese, 97
+ Smoked Trout, Herbed, 121

SQUASH
Acorn, Baked Candied, 29
Apple, and Onion Tart with Sage, 13, 15
Butternut, to steam and purée, 95
Butternut, Tartlets with Cheese Lattice and Sunflower Seed Crust, 94, 95
Seeds, Toasted Spiced, 20
Summer, Baked with Tomatoes and Chili, 117
Summer, Salad, Dilled, 66

SQUID
cleaning, 174
Jerusalem Artichoke, and Avocado Salad, 174

STARTERS. See also Soup
Antipasto, Grilled Eggplant, 168, 169
Artichokes and Clams with Herbed Garlic Butter, 175
Asparagus and Mushroom Salad with Sherried Dressing, 194
Asparagus Napoleons with Oriental Black Bean Sauce, 170, 170
Avocado and Grapefruit Salad with Pine Nut Dressing, 145
Blini, Carrot, 201
Blue-Cheese-Stuffed Radishes, 96
Celery and Kielbasa Cream Kuchen, 96
Cheese-and-Chorizo-Stuffed Peppers with Tomatillo Sauce, 144, 144
Chick-Pea Nibbles, 122
Clams Marinière with Tomato and Onion, 18, 19
Compote, Onion, Peach, and Raisin, 96
Crab and Mushroom Salad, Curried, 198, 198
Cucumber Cups with Horseradish Yogurt, 44
+ Deviled Eggs with Anchovies and Olives, 21
Dipping Sauce, Sour Cream, 123
Eggplant Salad, Creamy, 168, 169
Fettuccine with Leek and Sour Cream Sauce, 45
Fish and White Bean Salad with Fried Onions, 121
Frittata, Ham and Vegetable, 146
Fritters, Cod, Salt, Island-Style, 71
Fritters, Cornmeal, Spicy Deep-Fried, 69
Ham, Celery, and Cheddar Salad, 21
Lettuce Rolls with Bulgur and Vegetables, 123
Linguine with Asparagus Lemon Cream Sauce, 200
Mussels and New Potatoes in Dilled Cucumber Sauce, 19
Oysters, Fried, with Tartar Sauce, 69
Oysters, Herbed Poached, 199
+ Pâté, Chicken Liver and Granny Smith Apple, 199
Phyllo Triangles, Ham, Cheddar, and Mushroom, Herbed, 45
Potatoes, New, with Dilled Vodka Cream and Salmon Roe, 200
Potato Skins, Deviled, 123
Quesadillas, Cheese and Smoked Turkey, 147
Red Pepper and Goat Cheese Spirals with Olives and Basil Oil, 166
Red Pepper Dip, Spiced, 147
Scallops, Crisp-Fried, with Spinach Dip, 20
Shrimp, Grilled Chipotle, 146
Shrimp in Dilled Cucumber Sauce, 70
Spread, Cheese, Port and Black-Walnut, 97
+ Spread, Smoked Trout, Herbed, 121
Squash Seeds, Toasted Spiced, 20
Squid, Jerusalem Artichoke, and Avocado, 174
Tart, Onion, Tomato, and Anchovy, 171
Tartlets, Butternut Squash, with Cheese Lattice and Sunflower Seed Crust, 94, 95
Tempura, Tofu and Vegetable, 172, 173
Toasts, Garlic Baguette, 42, 43
Toasts, Melted Brie, Pear, and Ham, 198

t

STEAK
Skirt, and Peppers, Marinated, 116, 117
Skirt, Grilled Marinated, with Bell Pepper, Onions and Flour Tortillas (Fajitas), *148*, 148
STEW, Beef, with Turnips, Spiced, 49
STOCK, Turkey Giblet, 101
STRAWBERRY
Ice Cream, 55
Ice-Cream Sodas, 55
Mango Shortcakes, 161
◌ Mousse Filling, 187
Mousse Cake, 186
Syrup, 55
STUFFED
Cabbage Rolls, 100
Cornish Game Hens, with Sausage and Fennel, 203
Onions, with Ground Meat, Tomatoes, and Peppers (Picadillo), 150
Peppers, Cheese-and-Chorizo, with Tomatillo Sauce, *144*, 144
◌ Radishes, Blue Cheese-, 96
STUFFING
Mushroom, Hazelnut, and Currant, with Roast Goose and Port Gravy, 206
Rice, Chorizo, and Pepper, with Spiced Roast Chicken, 154
Rye Bread, with Sauerkraut, Bacon, and Raisins, 107
SUCCOTASH, Chicken in, *89*, 91
SUGAR. *See also* Brown Sugar
Coffeecake, Moravian, 57
Cookies, Old-Fashioned, 41
SUMMER SQUASH
Baked with Tomatoes and Chili, 117
Salad, Dilled, 66
SUN-DRIED TOMATO(ES)
Basil Bread, 183
◌ Fusilli with Bell Peppers, Goat Cheese and, 179
◌+ **SUNFLOWER SEED** Pastry Dough, 95
SWEDISH Rye Bread (Limpa), 106
SWEET-AND-SOUR Beets with Caraway, 53
SWEET POTATO Meringue Pie, 82
SWORDFISH Teriyaki, Broiled, 178
◌ **SYRUP** Rum, 187
Strawberry, 55

TABBOULEH, Wild Rice, 107
TART(S)
Almond, 188
Blueberry, 109
Onion, Tomato, and Anchovy, 171
Pea and Goat Cheese, *46*, 47
Squash, Apple, and Onion, with Sage, *13*, 15
TARTAR SAUCE with Fried Oysters, 69
TARTLETS
Butternut Squash, with Cheese Lattice and Sunflower Seed Crust, *94*, 95
Lemon Buttermilk Chess, *37*, 39
TEMPURA, Tofu and Vegetable, *172*, 173
TERIYAKI, Swordfish, Broiled, 178
THAI Beef Salad with Barley, 178
◌ **TIMBALES,** Rice, Sweet Onion, and Pea, with Coriander, 195
TOAST(S)
◌ Asparagus in Ambush, 27
◌ Brie, Melted, Pear, and Ham, 198
◌ Garlic Baguette, *42*, 43
◌ Tomato Cheddar Sauce on (Rinktum Ditty), 26
TOFU and Vegetable Tempura, *172*, 173
TOMATILLO Sauce, with Cheese-and-Chorizo-Stuffed Peppers, *144*, 144
TOMATO(ES). *See also* Sun-Dried Tomato(es)
Aspic with Horseradish, 65
◌ Butter, 25
◌ Cheddar Sauce on Toast (Rinktum Ditty), 26
◌ Clams Marinière with Onion and, *18*, 19
Fried Ripe and Green, 81
Onion, and Anchovy Tart, 171
Onions Stuffed with Ground Meat, Peppers and (Picadillo), 150
and Pepper Sauce, with Eggs, on Tortillas, 151
Pork, and Rice Casserole, 72
◌ Red Snapper, Baked with Olives and, 150
◌ Salad, Cucumber and, with Butttermilk Dressing, 92
Salad, with Chick-Pea Dressing, 182
◌+ Salad, Okra, Onion and, 66
◌ Salsa, *154*, 155
◌ Sauce, Escarole Braised in, 53
◌+ Soup, Basil, Chilled, *42*, 43
Yellow Squash Baked with Chili and, 117

TORTILLAS
Beef Fajitas, *148*
Corn, 141
Flour, 149
Huevos Rancheros, 151
Quesadillas, Cheese and Smoked Turkey, 147
warming, 149

TRAIL MIX Cookies, 134

TROUT Spread, Smoked Herbed, 121

TUNA, Caesar Sandwiches, Grilled, 179

TURKEY
Giblet Stock, 101
Roast, with Cranberry Gravy, 101
Smoked, and Cheese Quesadillas, 147

TURNIPS
with Beef Stew, Spiced, 49
Duck, Crispy Braised, with Olives and, 127

V

VEGETABLE(S). *See also* names of vegetables
Bulgur Jambalaya with Ham, Clams and, 74
and Ham Frittata, 146
Lettuce Rolls with Bulgur and, 123
with Pot Roast, 124
Root, with Brisket, Beer-Braised, *98, 99*
and Tofu Tempura, *172, 173*

VENISON and Zucchini Kebabs with Citrus Pepper Marinade, 126

VIDALIA ONION "Flowers", with Pecans, Roasted, *76, 77*

VODKA Cream and Salmon Roe, Dilled, with New Potatoes, 200

W

WAFFLES, Pumpkin, with Honeyed Apple Cider Sauce, 205

WALNUT(S)
Black-, and Port Cheese Spread, 97
Brown Sugar Fudge, 40
Chicken Salad, Grilled, with Papaya, Mesclun and, 166
Cigarette Cookies, *193*, 197
Cranberry Crumb Cake, 33
Crust, with Maple Pumpkin Pie, 32

WHISKEY Zucchini Raisin Cake, 132

WHITE BEAN and Fish Salad with Fried Onions, 121

WILD RICE, Bulgur, and Herb Salad (Tabbouleh), 107

Y

YAM Cornmeal Muffins, 157

YELLOW PEPPER(S). *See* Pepper(s)

YELLOW SQUASH. *See* Summer Squash

YOGURT
Horseradish, with Cucumber Cups, 44
Rosemary Dressing, with Mixed Fruit Salad, 181

Z

ZUCCHINI
Cake, Raisin Whiskey, 132
Cheese Pudding with Leek and, 105
and Scallops, with Risotto, 49
and Venison Kebabs with Citrus Pepper Marinade, 126

table setting
acknowledgments

Items in the photographs not credited are privately owned. All addresses, except where noted, are in New York City.

NEW ENGLAND

Squash, Apple, and Onion Tart with Sage (page 13): New Hampshire Sheraton-style drop-leaf table with original paint, circa 1830, from Judith and James Milne, Inc.—American Country Antiques, 506 East 74th Street.

Clams Marinière with Tomato and Onion (page 18): "Petro" handmade glass soup bowls by Annieglass—Annieglass Studio, tel.(408) 426-5086. Hand-painted ceramic dinner and service plates by Antheor; handmade glass candelabrum by Glassworks of London—Barneys New York, Seventh Avenue and 17th Street. "Integrale" stainless-steel flatware—Pavillon Christofle, 680 Madison Avenue. "Column" handmade goblets by Melanie Guernsey—The Elements, 14 Liberty Way, Greenwich, CT. Glasses (holding flowers)—The Pottery Barn, 117 East 59th Street. "Valencia" cotton fabric (tablecloth) and "Cordoba" cotton fabric (pillows), both available through decorator—Brunschwig & Fils, Inc., 979 Third Avenue.

Scrod with Broccoli Cream Sauce (page 22): Herend "Queen Victoria" porcelain platter—Cardel, Ltd., 621 Madison Avenue.

Clambake in a Pot (page 24): Stainless-steel stockpot—Bridge Kitchenware Corporation, 214 East 52nd Street.

Honey Baked Beans (page 28); Boston Brown Bread (page 30): Collection of nineteenth-century Americana—Gail Lettick's Pantry & Hearth Antiques, 121 East 35th Street. Cotton tablecloth by ANTA—Bergdorf Goodman, 754 Fifth Avenue.

THE MID-ATLANTIC

Lady Baltimore Cake; Lemon Buttermilk Chess Tartlets (page 37): Wedgwood china dessert plates, circa 1845; English silver-plate and ivory server, circa 1905—James II Galleries, Ltd., 15 East 57th Street. Reed & Barton sterling tray—F. Gorevic & Son, Inc., 635 Madison Avenue.

Chilled Tomato Basil Soup; Garlic Baguette Toasts (page 42): Schott-Zwiesel "Crystal Boutique" bowls—Cardel, Ltd., 621 Madison Avenue. "Chinon" silver-plate flatware—Pavillon Christofle, 680 Madison Avenue.

Crab Salad (page 50): "Sevilla" porcelain salad, luncheon, and dinner plates; "Pointus" stainless-steel flatware designed by Phillippe Starck—The L•S Collection, 765 Madison Avenue. Embroidered linen tablecloth and napkin—Léron, 750 Madison Avenue.

THE SOUTH

Lattice-Crust Peach Pie; Limeade; Watermelon (page 63): Porcelain "Fish" dessert plates by Pillivuyt—Barneys New York, 106 Seventh Avenue. Glass Pitcher—Conran's, 160 East 54th Street.

Spicy Fried Chicken Wings (page 64); Green Onion Pancakes (page 77); Delta Dogs (page 69): ANTA ceramic dinner plate and Patrick Frey napkin from Bergdorf Goodman, 754 Fifth Avenue.

Roasted Vidalia Onion "Flowers" with Pecans (page 76): Calphalon aluminum gratin pan—Bloomingdale's, 1000 Third Avenue.

THE HEARTLAND

Butternut Squash Tartlets with Cheese Lattice and Sunflower Seed Crust (page 94): New Hampshire Sheraton-style drop-leaf table with original paint, circa 1830, from Judith and James Milne, Inc.—American Country Antiques, 506 East 74th Street.

Beer-Braised Brisket with Root Vegetables (page 98): Mosse earthenware platter—Dean & DeLuca, 560 Broadway.

Table Setting (page 108): Enamelware dinner plates, Ojibwa-made bark canoe, handmade yellow birch table with cherry wood top and yellow birch chairs with woven splint backs and seats (from a set of eight chairs and the table)—Whispering Pines, 516 Main Street, Piermont, NY 10968. Blue glasses, cotton napkins, wood napkin rings, woven straw mats—Pottery Barn, 117 East 59th Street. Wineglasses—Williams-Sonoma, 20 East 60th Street.

THE MOUNTAIN STATES

Pot Roast with Vegetables (page 124); Roasted Beet and Onion Salad (page 130): "Famille Verte" porcelain platter and bowl by Mottahedeh—Scully & Scully, 506 Park Avenue. Cotton place mat—D. F. Sanders & Co., 952 Madison Avenue.

THE SOUTHWEST

Sopa de Lima (page 139): Hand-thrown ceramic soup bowls and plates by Gorky Gonzalez (from a sevice for 8), copper skillet, hand-thrown ceramic bowl, and hand-carved pine coffee table—Amigo Country, 19 Greenwich Avenue.

Chiles Rellenos (page 144): Handmade ceramic dinner plates by Sara Post—Zona, 97 Greene Street. Guatemalan cotton place mat by Jorge Santos—Distant Origin, 153 Mercer Street.

Beef Fajitas; Flour Tortillas (page 148); Tomato Salsa; Guacamole (page 154): Handmade ceramic plates and serving pieces, straw basket, cotton towel and fabric—Pan American Phoenix, The Market at Citicorp, 153 East 53rd Street.

Fettuccine with Pine Nuts, Prosciutto, and Brown Butter (page 152): Deruta "Bello" and "Circo" ceramic soup and dinner plates—Mayhew, 507 Park Avenue.

Assorted Southwestern Harvests (page 156): Mexican wineglasses—Pan American Phoenix, The Market at Citicorp Center, 153 East 53rd Street. Linen napkins—Frank McIntosh at Henri Bendel, 10 West 57th Street. Dough bowl; earthenware pitcher by Barbara Eigen; Ponderosa pine "Parson's" table—Zona, 97 Greene Street.

CALIFORNIA AND HAWAII

Table Setting (page 164): Haviland "Océane" Limoges dinner and salad plates—Baccarat, 625 Madison Avenue. *Pâte de verre* and silver-plate flatware; *pâte de verre* and crystal wineglasses, both from the Trapani Collection by Garouste & Bonetti—Daum Boutique, 694 Madison Avenue. Cotton napkins—Pottery Barn, 117 East 59th Street. "Sea Urchin" plaster napkin rings designed by Jane Krolik—Chateau X, tel.(212) 477-3123. "Tiki" glasses (with flowers)—Frank McIntosh Shop at Henri Bendel, 712 Fifth Avenue. Flowers—Maui North Shore Farms, Maui, HI, tel. (800) 301-7111. "Les Algues" cotton fabric (tablecloth), available through decorator—Brunschwig & Fils, 979 Third Avenue.

Grilled Eggplant Antipasto; Eggplant Curry; Creamy Eggplant Salad (page 168): Hand-painted ceramic platters by Susan Eslick—Bergdorf Goodman, 754 Fifth Avenue.

Asparagus Napoleons with Oriental Black Bean Sauce (page 170): Coalport porcelain plate, circa 1810—Bardith Ltd., 901 Madison Avenue.

Tofu and Vegetable Tempura (page 172): Porcelain plates designed by Janna Josephson—Janna: Original Art Plates, Suite 501, 19 Hudson Street.

Papaya Salad (page 180): Handmade earthenware dishes with crackle glaze by Patricia Glave—Contemporary Porcelain, 105 Sullivan Street.

THE NORTHWEST AND ALASKA

Baked Pears; Walnut Cigarette Cookies (page 193): Anneglass plates and bowl—Bergdorf Goodman, 754 Fifth Avenue. Hand-painted coconut-shell bowl by Chateau X—Barneys New York, Seventh Avenue and 17th Street.

Curried Crab and Mushroom Salad (page 198): "Parrots of Paradise" porcelain dinner plates by Lynn Chase Designs Inc.—The Naked Zebra, 279 Greenwich Avenue, Greenwich, CT.

Blackberries (page 211); Blackberry Cobbler (page 212): Nineteenth-century spongeware bowls, tin flour sifter and sugar caster, handmade nutmeg grater, and milk bottle; apron and tea towel, circa 1920; pine country table, circa 1900—Gail Lettick's Pantry & Hearth Antiques, 121 East 35th Street.

The following photographers have generously given their permission to reprint the photographs below. Many have previously appeared in *Gourmet* Magazine.

Cotten Alston: "Virginia's Hunt Country" (page 72); "A Fresh Snowfall at Bridger Bowl, Montana" (jacket and page 112). Copyright © 1992. "The corn is high in rural Illinois" (page 87); "Carl Sandburg's Birthplace, Galesburg, Illinois" (page 92); "Ristras of dried chilies, New Mexico" (page 138); "Taos Pueblo, New Mexico" (page 140); "Nacimiento-Fergusson Road over the coastal mountains, Big Sur, California" (jacket and page 162). Copyright © 1993. Reprinted by permission of the photographer.

Ken Bates: "Dutch Belted Cows, California" (jacket and page 181). Copyright © 1989. Lobster buoys on Cape Cod, Massachusetts (page 16). Copyright © 1993. Reprinted by permission of the photographer.

Richard Bowditch: "The Farmers' Museum and Village Crossroads in Cooperstown, New York" (page 34). Copyright © 1989. "The Flatiron Building, New York City (page 54); "A shady spot for a lazy afternoon on Key West, Florida" (page 60). Copyright © 1992. "The vegetable garden at Mount Vernon, Virginia" (page 8); "Along the Columbia River Gorge in Oregon" (page 190). Copyright © 1993. Reprinted by permission of the photographer.

Sonja Bullaty: "Autumn in the White Mountains in New Hampshire" (page 11). Copyright © 1993. Reprinted by permission of the photographer.

Kay Chernush: "Fly fishing the Yellowstone River, Montana" (page 113); "Paradise Valley in the Montana Rockies" (page 133). Copyright © 1994. Reprinted by permission of the photographer.

Lans Christensen: "Boathouses on the Mississippi in Red Wing, Minnesota" (page 86). Copyright © 1985. Hazelnut orchard, Oregon (page 214); "Deception Pass off Whidbey Island, Washington" (jacket and page 196). Copyright © 1988. "Sunrise at Mount Moran, Snake River, Idaho" (page 118). Copyright © 1994. Reprinted by permission of the photographer.

Mark Ferri: "Little Italy, New York City" (jacket and page 56). Copyright © 1991. Reprinted by permission of the photographer.

Steve Firebaugh: "The Highest Peak in North America, Mount McKinley, Alaska" (page 191); "Kachemak Bay Wilderness Lodge on Kenai Peninsula" (page 192). Copyright © 1994. Reprinted by permission of the photographer.

Karen Halverson: "Red Rock Country, Arizona" (pages 142 and 158). Copyright © 1993. Reprinted by permission of the photographer.

Ronny Jaques: "Local color from a jacaranda tree in Fort Lauderdale, Florida" (jacket and page 61). Copyright © 1986. Reprinted by permission of the photographer.

Mathias Oppersdorff: "Waterfront near Fisherman's Quay, Sitka, Alaska" (page 204); "Totem Pole, Sitka National Historical Park, Alaska" (page 208). Copyright © 1986. "First Congregational Church, Williamstown, Massachusetts" (page 10). Copyright © 1987. "Jim Moore's Place at Campbell's Ferry, Idaho" (page 120). Copyright © 1988. "Sabino Canyon, Tucson, Arizona" (jacket and page 136). Copyright © 1990. "A flock of Adirondack chairs patiently lines Blue Mountain Lake in the Adirondacks, New York" (page 35). Copyright © 1993. Reprinted by permission of the photographer.

Nik Wheeler: "A hammock on the beach, Honolulu, Hawaii" (page 163). Copyright © 1993. "California's first commercial banana grove" (page 164). Copyright © 1994. Reprinted by permission of the photographer.

Romulo A. Yanes: "Wild Phlox" (jacket and page 62). Copyright © 1986. "Cranberries in Nantucket, Massachusetts" (page 5). Copyright © 1987. "Museum of International Folk Art in Santa Fe, New Mexico" (page 137). Copyright © 1989. "A picnic in Maine" (frontispiece). Copyright © 1993. Reprinted by permission of the photographer.

Grateful acknowledgment is made to the following contributors for permission to reprint recipes previously published in *Gourmet* Magazine:

Georgia Chan Downard: "Blood Orange Sorbet" (page 167). Copyright © 1988. Reprinted by permission of the author.

Fred Feretti: "Papaya Salad" (page 181). Copyright © 1990. Reprinted by permission of the author.

Faye Levy: "Grilled Eggplant Antipasto" (page 169); "Eggplant Curry" (page 180); "Creamy Eggplant Salad" (page 169). Copyright © 1990. Reprinted by permission of the author.

Bill Neal: "Delta Dogs" (page 69); "Green Onion Pancakes" (page 77). Copyright © 1990. Reprinted by permission of Darhansoff & Verrill.

Elizabeth Lambert Ortiz: "Sopa de Lima (Lime Soup)" (page 41). Copyright © 1985. Reprinted by permission of the author.

Dorian Leigh Parker: "Honey Baked Beans" (page 28); "Boston Brown Bread" (page 30). Copyright © 1990. Reprinted by permission of the author.

Barbara Hanson Pierce: "Roasted Vidalia Onion 'Flowers' with Pecans" (page 77). Copyright © 1991. Reprinted by permission of the author.

Elisabeth Rozin: "Peanut Sesame Noodles" (page 81). Copyright © 1992. Reprinted by permission of Alfred A. Knopf, Inc.

Shirley Sarvis: "Fettuccine with Pine Nuts, Prosciutto, and Brown Butter" (page 153). Copyright © 1989. Reprinted by permission of the author.

Irene Sax: "Capirotada (New Mexican Bread-and-Butter Pudding with Longhorn Cheese and Raisins)" (page 159). Copyright © 1983. Reprinted by permission of the author.

Richard Sax: "Chicken in Succotash" (page 91). Copyright © 1985. Reprinted by permission of the author.

Kathryn Stewart: "Blackberry Cobbler" (page 213). Copyright © 1989. Reprinted by permission of Susan Stewart.

Zanne Early Zakroff: "Crab Salad" (page 51). Copyright © 1992. Reprinted by permission of the author.